RELATIONSHIFT

Jacinth Ivie Baublitz, ACSW

Cover by

Carlos Murphy Trademark used with permission of Foodmakers, Inc.

FIRST EDITION

© 1983 by Jacinth Ivie Baublitz

First Printing 1983
Second Printing March, 1986
Third Printing, October, 1986

All rights reserved, including the right to reproduce this book or portions thereof in any form whatsoever. Inquiries and requests for permission to reprint or for additional copies of this and other books by Jacinth Ivie Baublitz, ACSW should be addressed to J.I. Baublitz, P.O. Box 2227, Midland, MI, 48641-2227.

Library of Congress Catalog Card Number: 82-90925   ISBN 0-9610316-0-3

Printed in the United States of America

For

Carol, Jan, Judy, and Lynne

the first Relationshippers

and for

Richard

my best critic and my best friend

ACKNOWLEDGMENTS

Sincere appreciation is expressed to the following people for their aid, time, and support in the creation of this book:

Karen Barnes, Karen Wurtzel, and Janet Ross for providing equipment and encouragement.

Glenn White for providing a quiet and organized place to work.

Mrs. Christine Seago for inculcating the rules of writing (1962, in the classroom of good old Lufkin High School).

Richard Pendell Jr., of Pendell Printing for technical advice.

Patients and students who lent their experiences and their contracts to this work.

Richard Jentsch for his expertise and tireless efforts in editing.

Jessica and Stefanie Baublitz who had a preoccupied Mommy for a while but who were always patient, encouraging, and understanding.

Family and friends who tolerated me as a one topic person for the entire course of this work.

Table of Contents

Acknowledgments	....	v
Forward	....	ix
Preface	....	xi
Chapter I	**Relationshit**............................	1
	The Story of Allen & Judy	1
Chapter II	"... And Then the Handsome Young Penguin..."....................	11
Chapter III	The Facts of Life about Relationshipping..	15
Chapter IV	Separating the Penguins from the Platypuses	21
Chapter V	The Interaction Stage	27
	Fall-outs and Fall-ins..............	27
	One Night Stands.	29
	The Incredible Carlos Murphy........	32
	The Demon (Instant) Sex...........	33
	Primary Feelings	34
	Primary Characteristics.............	36
	Primary Risks.....................	37
	Developmental Tasks...............	42
	Interaction Stage Questions	47
	Interaction Stage Summary..........	48
Chapter VI	**Contract Communication: Interaction Stage**................	51
	Simple Initial Contracts	52
Chapter VII	The Testing Stage	69
	The Testing Stage Time Factor	71
	Primary Feelings	71
	Primary Characteristics.............	72
	Primary Risks.....................	74
	Developmental Tasks...............	93
	Testing Stage Questions	93
	Testing Stage Summary	94

Chapter VIII	Contract Communication: Testing Stage	95
Chapter IX	The Negotiation Stage	107
	Primary Feelings	110
	Primary Characteristics	111
	Primary Risks	113
	Developmental Tasks	118
	Negotiation Stage Questions	126
	Negotiation Stage Summary	127
Chapter X	Contract Communication: Negotiation Stage	129
Chapter XI	The Termination Stage	143
	Primary Feelings	146
	Primary Characteristics	150
	Primary Risks	154
	Developmental Tasks	158
	Termination Stage Questions	162
	Termination Stage Summary	163
Chapter XII	Contract Communication: Termination Stage	165
Chapter XIII	Complicated Relationshipping	175
Chapter XIV	Contract Communication: Complicated Relationshipping	187
Chapter XV	On Becoming a Platyypus	197
Continuum Chart		200
Footnotes		202
Bibliography		203

FOREWORD

Contemporary society consists of some of the most successful self-actualized lonely people in the world. With the earth's bounty available, people of developed nations no longer must worry about the fulfillment of basic food and safety needs. They are free to seek personal enrichment and satisfaction. Counseling and psychotherapy reinforce individual rights to happiness while self-help books, in continual demand, also aid the individual growth process. Individuals are blossoming in their abilities to deal with stress, to develop talents, and to be successful at work. Society, at the peak of individual achievement, is learning something about itself; regardless of the level of personal accomplishment, success may be meaningless and empty without a loving partner with whom to share it. When work is done, when one's potential is touched, when one has made the world a better place, there is no ultimate fulfillment without a continuing and loving interaction with another person. Current society consists of many upward moving, self-actualizing lonely people.

Nowadays people expect more of each other. It is no longer enough to love and provide for one another. Partners are expected *to understand, to communicate,* and *to fill each other's emotional needs*. Even in cases of financial hardship, people do not expect less of their partners. They instead expect their companions to give more as a compensation for the outside deficits.

Society has learned a great deal about what individuals can do and what they want. Methods to achieve the wide variety of goals are available from many sources. However, until *Relationshift,* people have learned very little about achieving the most elusive of contemporary human goals: the ability to establish and maintain long term successful couplehood. Although the literature is rich regarding what individuals can accomplish both separately and together, there is virtually no information concerning the relationship itself. There is much emphasis regarding what individuals require of each other and what they require of a relationship, but very little awareness of what the Relationshipping process itself requires of individuals.

This book is not *about* relationships. It demonstrates the process of Relationshipping as experienced by people who applied the theory of Relationshift. Aware that predictable difficulties arise and also aware that performance of certain developmental tasks is required, the participants grapple with the *process* rather than with each other. They discover a mutually beneficial system of communication and teamwork which surpasses any prior experiences.

Relationshift requires a major change in mental attitude as partners approach one another. Certain prerequisites exist for any couple to have the potential of success. With those prerequisites met, two people enter onto a Relationshipping continuum consisting of four stages. Each stage contains certain typical feelings, characteristics, risks, and developmental tasks. As a child must first learn to crawl before becoming strong enough to be able to stand, so must a relationship be strengthened through successful accomplishment of its own developmental tasks in order to negotiate the predictable difficulties ahead.

Relationshift is the result of seven years applied theory in my clinical practice and four years application with students in Relationshipping classes and workshops. The people are real and the contracts, though disguised, are genuine. All names and physical characteristics have been changed, and in many cases the pseudonyms were chosen by the real life counterparts. Each situation represents many similar adventures in communication and closeness.

People who apply these concepts have an advantage in pursuing healthy long term successful partnerships. *Relationshift* offers pertinent information regarding the life cycle of caring. Easily applicable theory, concrete life situations, and actual working agreements combine to make *Relationshift* a handbook for anyone who desires to be involved in intimate relationships. People who follow its precepts discover there is no reason why anyone should be lonely anymore.

Preface

Relationshift, first discovered and tested in the clinical model, was originally envisioned as a new therapeutic approach for couples with problems. As the conceptualization became complete, there was the realization that Relationshift is much more than only a therapeutic technique. The ramifications of the theory encompass all in-depth personal relationships; it is a breakthrough which patently affects human happiness. By explaining the dynamic process by which successful long term associations are developed and maintained, it has application to every individual who wants to become closely involved with another person.

In writing *Relationshift*, I have therefore addressed several populations and several purposes. Although of tremendous impact for therapeutic professionals, I have limited the use of psychological jargon and utilized the format of the self help book. Within that framework, I have included topics and sub-topics as well as a flow of information conducive to use both as a manual and as a supplementary textbook. It is also a reference book. Each chapter is complete in itself, resulting in some repetition but allowing for quick research as people encounter the predictable difficulties inherent in relating intimately over time.

Relationshift is a self help book, an adjunct for people in counseling and therapy, a manual for relationships, a supplementary textbook, and a quick and easy reference book. Uniquely fitting into everyday life, it is meant to provide people with information, guidelines, and skills to promote success and happiness in their most meaningful life experiences.

CHAPTER I

Relationshit

There really are some people in our society who are capable of establishing open direct communication in close relationships without the use of outside tools. I met one in 1972 and another in '76. These people are rare because they are a cultural oddity — duck-billed platypuses in a world of penguins. Instead of playing a game of emotional hide-and-seek, they tend to be fairly self confident, somewhat aware of their own needs, and — most importantly — know risk-taking for what it really is: simply taking a risk rather than tempting disaster. Odd as they are, I have rarely seen a platypus professionally. My practice is made up almost entirely of penguins who, in one way or another, would like to be platypuses.

One does not have to be crazy to be a penguin. In fact, many penguins are alert, attractive people who are intelligent, verbal, and successful in their vocations. They are, however, generally unhappy in their significant romantic relationships. They proceed along culturally accepted and expected guidelines to achieve the also expected "happily ever after" relationship. Instead, they usually arrive at a complicated and constipated communication system that can only appropriately be called Relationshit.

Courtship customs today are based on Relationshit. Unless two people know each other fairly well prior to initiating courtship, they immediately begin an indirect system of feeling each other out and guessing. This is called "The Six Hour Chance To Impress Him (or Her) That Absolutely Everything Depends On".

The Story of Allen and Judy

Allen is a 36 year old architect, two years divorced. Judy is 33, also divorced, and an interior designer. After dinner and a play, they are sitting in a cozy bar, putting their respective best feet forward while wondering what to do next. As the hour gets later, their nerves get tighter. Both would like to know each other better. Both have had a series of negative experiences. Both feel pressure to perform sexually. It is the perfect time to define some guidelines and establish an environment between them in which a relationship with real communication can grow and flourish. Instead, since they like each other too much to risk openly, they begin to guess what the other wants and expects.

Without realizing it, they thus increase their risk factor incredibly. While many people's expectations are similar, the chance that they will have the same expectations at the same point in time is significantly low. Neither penguins nor platypuses can read minds. Penguins, however, try desperately hard to do so, leaving themselves vulnerable to misunderstandings, cross-communication, and rejection by default.

But back to Allen and Judy who, by this time, are finishing a very enjoyable evening. They are pleased and comfortable with each other. Allen says that he will call, but they do not make any concrete plans. They are soon to discover the difference between intention and follow-through.

Driving home, Allen recalls the pleasant evening. He does not feel wildly in love as he used to feel driving home as a teenager. No lightning bolts of romantic love or passion were evoked by Judy, but it was still a very enjoyable time. He intends to call her.

Allen becomes involved in business, and the week passes; then another week. He has thought of Judy several times, but he has not called. He finds it more difficult to ask her out the second time than it was the first time. The immediate pleasure of the evening has receded and what he recalls mostly is that something was missing – the lightning bolts, the special feeling of being touched personally and directly by another person. Also, too much time has now elapsed, and she just might say no (and reject him!) if he calls now.

Judy is going through quite another process. At first, she eagerly awaits Allen's call. Then she begins to wonder what she has done wrong. She has obviously flunked the "Six Hour Chance". Adding this to previous pleasant evenings that had no follow-through, Judy concludes erroneously that she is not a lovable person and that men do not enjoy being with her. If sex was involved, she further concludes that sex was all Allen was after, anyway.

Seeing Judy's misery, a mutual friend approaches Allen and Allen says, "She's really a nice girl. I don't know why I'm not interested in her. I really think there's something wrong with me".

Allen and Judy are victims of relationshit, a system so subtle and so much a part of social custom that neither Allen nor Judy realize its impact. Any platypus could recognize the symptoms, but being penguins, both Allen and Judy conclude something is wrong with the person rather than something possibly being wrong with the system.

Penguins are unsuccessful in their relationships for three basic reasons. First is an over-emphasis on sex. Second is a basic ignorance of facts about relationships and a substitution of folklore and magical expectations in the place of those facts. Third is an exaggeration of the idea of personal risk. The relationshit system encourages inappropriate sex, simple ignorance, and exaggerated ideas of risk (rejection!) which lead penguins down the primrose path to confusion and failure.

Carol, age 35 and divorced six years, said to me: "Times have really changed. Used to be, my dates were thrilled if I had an orgasm at all. Now they want to know if it's vaginal or clitoral. And if it's not multiple, then I'm not a truly sensuous woman."

Men also complain of the pressure toward sexual performance. As a result of performance anxiety, a large majority suffer from temporary impotence.

Mark, age 37, who tried to respond to the macho myth that he could have sex any time, any place, with any reasonably attractive woman, says, "I want to find a woman I can fall in love with, not go to bed with. At least not right away like it's the most important thing. I've been to bed with enough women that it's just part of the evening now. It's not special anymore and sometimes the sex thing works for me and sometimes it doesn't."

Mark, like any other product, tried to market himself by sex. However, he found that instant erections, like instant coffees, are simply not as good as those that have been brewed and simmered.

These sexual attitudes typify the age: the era of the Instant and the Throwaway. There are instant potatoes, instant soup, and instant erections. There are throwaway diapers, throwaway cutlery, and throwaway partners.

Contrary to old custom and conventional thought, current courtships seek instant relationships founded on instant sex with an expectation that it will provide a quicker route to emotional intimacy. Unfortunately, there is no shortcut. In spite of today's emphasis and preoccupation with sex, emotional intimacy requires more than a physical act.

Unlike Allen and Judy, Marty and Carol felt an immediate and strong attraction to each other upon meeting. They were just short of bells ringing and rosy clouds. Saying goodnight and parting were so difficult that it seemed better not to say goodnight at all. Their six week long love affair was characterized by constant contact: long telephone calls when they weren't together and constant thoughts focused on each other as well as anxiety about the next encounter. Both worked at their respective jobs, but neither was very productive. They did not see their friends and all regular routine was suspended. Then it was gone as suddenly as it began. Carol still doesn't know why Marty disappeared. When his calls became less frequent, she would call him.

When he begged off an evening to do his wash, she offered to do it for him. She was sure something was wrong and confronted him with it. He reassured her that he had recently been very busy and there was nothing wrong with their relationship. Nevertheless, that was their last evening together. Carol has since decided that the ending was due to one of two things: either she somehow screwed it up or all men are bastards anyway.

Perhaps the two of them simply burned themselves out. The level of that intensity is difficult to maintain, and sooner or later harsh reality has to intrude. Work must be produced, apartments have to be cleaned, the emotions have to rest.

Perhaps Marty met someone else who lit his fire more brightly. Perhaps he felt pressured or maybe became frightened by such intensity. Since Marty would not respond to Carol's questions, she will never know why it didn't work out between them. All the "perhaps" and "maybes" become unanswerable questions which leave her anxious and insecure about herself, men, and future potential relationships. Relationshit.

The hidden truth is that Marty and Carol failed because of simple ignorance. They did not know how to build a foundation together correctly, resulting in having no foundation in spite of their expended energy and constant contact.

For platypuses who know the stages of Relationshipping and the pitfalls of those stages, what happened to Marty and Carol is no mystery. To the initiated it is a classic case of "Too Much Too Soon" in which each becomes the other's world, draining each other of vital energy which supports the tie between them but disconnects them from the world at large.

Too Much Too Soon is a deceptive emotional parasite which thrives on simulated intimacy. Most people are not aware of the dangers involved because cultural myths depict euphoric preoccupation with each other. After all, isn't this what being in love is supposed to be? It is true that these feelings can lead to a true love bonding. However, it is also true that more than half of these extraordinary chemical reactions explode rather than continue to mix well. It is impossible to love someone we do not know. Loving involves a knowledge and acceptance of a wide range of behaviors and personality characteristics that occur over time. Such intensity at an early level only reflects one's desires and hopes. In Too Much Too Soon there is a disproportionate and inappropriate amount of emotional attachment in comparison to the amount of time invested.

The tragedy of Too Much Too Soon is seen in the aftermath of perceived rejection. Denise tearfully told me that in the last year she had

had seventeen "relationships" that didn't work out. After further discussion it was revealed that fourteen of the seventeen had been a maximum of two weeks in duration. These were men she had met in various singles bars where they danced and talked until leaving together to spend the night. There had been no formal dates and, except for his apartment or hers, there had been no time spent together outside the bars. Denise perceived these casual interactions as relationships.

The other three involved men that she had dated from six weeks to three months. Although more closely approximating a relationship, the whirlwind nature of these affairs and the sudden unexplained or casual disengagements indicated a lack of foundation.

Although Denise could describe each man physically and knew where each worked, she did not necessarily know their jobs. For the three she had known the longest she could describe a few personality characteristics and could enumerate categorically what they liked in terms of sexual technique. However, she knew little about family composition and background, friends, general tastes, or lifestyle. In spite of the fact that she had only interacted with fourteen of these men and become better acquainted with three more, she felt she had been rejected seventeen times (and lost seventeen relationships) in the space of one year.

Most people who feel they've had a series of lost relationships actually had no relationships. Instead, like Denise, they've had a number of high chemistry contacts and interactions that either ran their course or did not blend well within the two personality structures. Such interactions are not difficult to break off, by at least one party, because there is no true bonding beneath the chemistry. There is generally no explanation and quite often no formal ending. The remaining partner must remind himself or herself that one cannot lose what one has not had.

Because each person has more than surface feelings and attitudes, the process of healthy selection of partners requires a greater time factor than penguins realize. The early feelings of euphoria and electricity do not prove that a good match has been made. They merely indicate a beginning and a potential for a good match. In Too Much Too Soon that beginning is too often sabotaged by over-eagerness, over-contacts, and over-sex. In short, a couple tries to achieve all the emotional comfort and satisfaction of a long term romance within their initial contacts. More relationshit.

Jake, a 34 year old engineer divorced for three years, says: "I'm at the crossroads. I'm ready for a relationship. All I have to do is find the right woman and I've got it made!" Tall determined Madelyn says: "I want a relationship more than anything else in the world. I'm looking for it in all the right places, and sooner or later, I'll get it."

Although they think they're on the right track, both Jake and Madelyn have the wrong attitudes. The mental image of "having a relationship" is a great mistake. It is not something one "finds" connected with the right man or woman; it is not something one shops for in "all the right places". It is not a ready-made commodity that can be discovered, collected, or picked up. It is assemble-it-yourself, a step at a time. It is a work of art, a picture painted simultaneously by two artists each adding their own brushwork, and not completed until at least one artist opts out of the project. Thus it is a continuous process and the picture presented at one time may be quite different from what is seen either earlier or later in the time sequence because of the added brushstrokes.

Couples who actively work together to build and develop a mutually rewarding long term association together are Relationshipping. They do not "have" a relationship; they are working to build one. Whether they have been together for more or less than twenty years, they realize they are involved in a continuing process of exploration. Like skiers traversing virgin snow, they may look behind to the twin tracks which show where they have been, but they know progress ahead depends upon their own directions and energies.

Some of these couples have been divorced or have experienced the loss of one or more long term romantic partners. All have discarded the fanciful illusion that they will magically fall in love and live happily ever after without effort. They are called Relationshippers.

There are also Relationshippers who are single and who have dared to progress beyond their former penguin ways. Aware of the stages they are soon to experience, and the possible pitfalls, these Relationshippers seeking partners have a different approach to courtship. Their platypus pace is a little slower than the usual frantic self-marketing of the singles circuit. They know they are on a continuum and they tend to see each potential partner as an opportunity to be investigated rather than a make-it-or-break-it romance.

Visually represented, the Relationshipping continuum looks like this:

meeting recognition investigation	processing learning to get along	growing together	separating
Interaction	Testing	Negotiation	Termination

As can be seen, the Relationshipping continuum is not infinite. It has a definite beginning and it does stop. All Relationshipping comes to an ending, if not through an emotional termination then through a physical death. Although fear of that ending has led to many an anxious and premature demise, the actual process is gradual and consists of four stages.

The Interaction Stage involves meeting, recognition, and investigation. The Testing Stage requires processing of information and learning to get along together. The Negotiation Stage is a time of growing together, and the Termination Stage involves emotional separation and termination.

The Interaction Stage is the most exciting and the most dangerous of the four stages. It involves exposure to many self-destructive courtship customs practiced by penguins. Many demeaning and emotionally damaging patterns may inadvertently occur as a result.

George sits at the bar of a crowded singles night spot and strikes up a conversation with Ken who sits beside him and who has periodically left the bar to dance with a striking blonde. They begin to talk politics and Ken's attention turns from the dance floor to conversation and beer. Close to closing time, the blonde appears and says to Ken, "I'm going home. Do you want to come with me?" Surprised, Ken responds, "Hey, I just ordered this beer." As silence falls between the couple, George contributes, "Ken, you've got to be queer or an alcoholic to turn down an offer like that!" Given that choice, Ken takes a swig of his full glass, gives George a wolfish grin, and leaves with the blonde.

One week later our three heroes, along with several hundred others, are again present at the same bar. Ken is friendly to Blondie, but beyond asking her to dance shortly after he arrives, he does not show her any particular attention. He does not yet know who else he will meet that night, and he does not want to cramp his style by spending too much time with her. After all, he knows she is available. Blondie, in the meantime, is wondering what she has done wrong. She has faithfully followed the unwritten Law of the Singles Bar: she is attractive, enticing, and has proven her sexual desirability. As closing time advances she feels more and more panicky. She decides to pursue Ken, not realizing that by this second approach she and Ken will have reached a secret agreement (a covert contract) that specifies that she will be the aggressive party and that their interactions will be based on sexual bargaining.

George watches the action carefully. If Ken does not go home with Blondie, he will have the opportunity to move in and be sympathetic to her "rejection". Indicating an interest in her and in her feelings, George will be well on his way to scoring, as well as to having a secret agreement himself with Blondie: to wit, if the man of her choice does not return her interest, he will console her and neither will have to spend the night alone.

If this feels badly, it is not surprising. It is a typical relationshit covert contract and it feels relationshitty.

A covert contract or secret agreement is any set of behaviors that is not openly discussed and occurs to the extent that it becomes expected. The set consists of an initiating behavior and a response. This action-reaction need only occur on two occasions for it to become a pattern and an expectation between two people. When it has become an expectation, it has also become an agreement.

There is always an agreement which governs the actions and reactions between two people. The fact that it is not open and stated does not mean it does not exist. The two people have agreed to it by allowing it to happen — BY THEIR BEHAVIOR — and since it is a secret (undiscussed) agreement, it will continue regardless of the emotional penalty that is paid.

A person may have a covert contract with men or women in general. I remember Tammy who had a Great Test to which she subjected all interested males. Shortly after meeting and in general conversation, she would lead to the subject of ideal partners. She would then make it perfectly clear that any man who hoped to win her affections must want her for herself rather than for her body. She would state quite strongly that there was no question in her mind but that whoever pursued her sexually upon first meeting her was simply not the sort of man in whom she would continue to be interested. Her message would be clear and direct which is well and good. However, now to the test: if the candidate continued to be attentive and show interest after the above conversation, Tammy's behavior would become more and more seductive as the evening progressed. Many drinks later and back at her apartment, she would respond to any hugs, kisses, petting, etc. that the potential prince initiated. If he attempted to leave without any such approaches, she would initiate them herself. Most often, unable to resist her charms, the candidate spent the night, the most outstanding feature of which — no matter how marvelous the sex — was his obvious failure of the Great Test.

Tammy's covert contract with herself and the world of men could be verbalized something like this: "I will tell him what my thoughts and feelings are in this area and thus give him the responsibility as to whether or not we continue together. Since my behavior will be truly seductive, he will have to reject me to prove he's worthwhile. Anyone who rejects me is certainly worth my investment while anyone who accepts me on these terms is not."

Not surprisingly, the Great Test led to many one-nighters and a few experiences with men who not only rejected her initially, but who also continued to reject her regarding emotional investment. This was Tammy's own self-perpetuated brand of relationshit.

Les was much more subtle than Tammy. He was so subtle, in fact, that many potential partners were discarded without their knowing they had been considered. Les, 46 years old and a factual fellow who always preceded his actions with logical thinking, over-emphasized physical features and other externals to the extent that he excluded many women to whom he was attracted. He would not consider any woman who smoked, was blonde, or who had children under ten years of age. Her height must be over five feet, but under five feet, five inches, and he raised an eyebrow if she was ever known to have more than two drinks in an evening. He rarely expressed an opinion but encouraged his dates to express their preferences which he unilaterally evaluated in comparison to his own. His secret contract with women in general was the following: "I will pursue a mate by process of elimination and, giving her little feedback or imput, I will force her to guess what characteristics are important to me. Since her behavior and responses will therefore be completely "natural", I will find the perfect natural match."

In searching for a "natural match", Les's first mistake was in being overly rigid about natural features. A persons's size and height often is pertinent only in initial attractions. By his discounting people due to physical appearance and whether they smoked, had young children, etc., their personalities and compatibility ratios assumed an inappropriate last priority. However, Les's greatest mistake was depriving potential partners of crucial communication. Although his opinions and preferences were fairly narrow, most people have a wide range of interests which they develop more or less depending on their life situations and companions. These are negotiable items which provide for flexibility and development between two people. By assuming these attitudes and interests are carved in stone, Les left little room for Relationshipping. Women he dated had a sense of being off-balance, of saying or doing something wrong, and of not quite knowing how to please him.

Any game playing, Great Tests, manipulation, covert contracts, or with-held communication which leads to guesswork, anxiety, and negative self-images is relationshit. It is the greatest single factor in marital disruption and a major contributing force for those people who are unable to be successful with a partner. It is a result of a general courtship system which over-emphasizes sex and exaggerates the idea of personal risk. Defensive and protective in purpose, it instead creates victims of its participants. It is the product of simple ignorance of the Relationshipping process, and has become so much the custom in intimate interaction that there is little recourse without further education. Currently, if anything goes wrong between two people, the relationshit victim looks around confusedly and verifies that he or she is pursuing a partner in exactly the same manner as everyone else. The whole pack of penguins are relationshitting each other to oblivion!

The victim realizes it is time to leave the pack, to Shift to a more open and direct system in which one is aware of what is happening and why. Once aware, "rejection" becomes merely unpleasant information and "risk" becomes an adventure in communication and closeness.

CHAPTER II

"... And Then the Handsome Young Penguin ..."

"... and at the touch of love's first kiss, Snow White awoke. She saw the Prince and knew she loved him. And then he carried her off to his castle of Dreams Come True and they married, and lived happily ever after."

— *Grimm's Fairy Tales*

"... and at the touch of love's first kiss, Snow White awoke. She saw the Prince and felt the chemistry. Immediately she negotiated a simple initial contract in which she would have private quarters in his castle and see him regularly, but not exclusively, for three months so that they could evaluate if they also had compatibility and the same value system."

— *Relationshift*

In the original version of Snow White, the heroine never questioned if the Prince really was a prince before she rode off with him. The popular story of Cinderella indicates that the Prince was much more interested in who fit into the glass slipper than in determining whether or not he and she had established a meaningful relationship at the ball. Although being able to communicate ranks highest on the list of characteristics people seek in a partner, there is no evidence that any fairy tale couple sought to establish such communication. There are no indications that either Prince or Beautiful Princess attempted to evaluate whether their personality characteristics were compatible or whether their values and philosophies of life were the same. Instead, there are ideas of magic, love at first sight, and being rescued from a bad situation.

Despite disclaimers that expectations of love today have nothing to do with fantasy stories heard in childhood, the stories I hear from adults in my office have strong parallels.

Although successful at work, Cynthia hates her secretarial job. She also hates the responsibilities of rearing her two children alone and maintaining her own house and life. She has no interest in further training which would enable her to secure work utilizing her considerable artistic talent. Widowed three years, she is only working until her future husband (whom she has not yet met) will take over the responsibilities of income and maintanance. Cynthia is waiting for the Prince.

Laura met many nice men at the party the other night, but she is disappointed that there was no one really special. She can't describe exactly what she's looking for, but she will know *him* when she meets *him*. Laura is expecting love at first sight.

David is attracted to outgoing women, but complains they are too independent and don't seem to need him. He wants to rescue a damsel in distress.

Fairy tale situations and fairy tale attitudes do exist nowadays. It is the magic — the idea of instant love and happiness, occurring at once and never ending — that is the myth. Love grows and love can diminish. Love can develop and love can die. However, it neither grows nor diminishes, neither develops nor dies, without the influence of the two partners who together create or destroy it. No one person can control the process, but two people together have the power to create happiness. Relationshift replaces the fairy tale expectations by developing open, direct, and clear guidelines so that a couple may resolve or altogether avoid predictable problems.

These problems are predictable because Relationshipping grows and develops in stages and each stage has typical feelings, characteristics, and risks. In addition, each stage has certain developmental tasks which must be accomplished before a couple may healthily proceed along the next step of the continuum. Just as a child must learn to crawl and strengthen the leg muscles and develop co-ordination before having the best capacity to stand and walk, so must Relationshipping concentrate on early tasks in order to build a strong foundation to withstand stresses in the stages to come.

Relationshift is characterized by a shift in focus from the traditional fairy tale expectations. There is a strong emphasis on knowledge, logic, and emotional choices. It takes away excuses and encourages people to be responsible partners rather than allowing them to be helpless victims.

Educated, bright, and capable (also married) Adrienne hesitantly told me that she feared there was going to be an affair between herself and a man with whom she worked. Admittedly, there was a strong attraction between them as well as mutual affection and respect. As she described what she feared, it was as if some uncontrollable force were going to rob her of her volition in the matter. I reminded her of her emotional choices and stated positively that the Good Fairy, regardless of wishful thinking, was not going to pick them up and deposit them in the Holiday Inn. Her own voice would voluntarily agree to such a meeting. Her own feet would take her there. Her own mind, passively or actively, must make that decision. If she *actively decided* based on the advantages and penalties involved, she would be better prepared to deal with the situation itself as well as the dynamics involved. No longer a victim, Adrienne realized she had the power to control her emotions and her actions. Furthermore, she realized that by putting herself in the helpless victim status, she had been placing her potential lover in the awkward position of taking advantage of her. This active thought process is a part of the Relationshift.

In order to relationship successfully, partners must be responsible. Because they are on a continuum, they can therefore correct mistakes and change behaviors. It is important to accept that mistakes are made and that they are not irrevocable. Relationshift allows much more than The Six Hour Chance.

A further change in focus is whether the potential partner is appropriate rather than whether that potential partner will accept or reject the interested party.

Lisa, for example, sought therapy because she was convinced she was possessed of some terrible flaw in her character. "I want a man until I have him", she said. "I am obsessed by whether he likes me or not, whether or not he will call, and what I will wear on a date. But then when we've been dating awhile, I begin to pick him apart. I don't like the way he dresses or his attitudes or maybe the activities he prefers. I guess I just can't be satisfied."

Lisa's problem is not that unusual and it is not that she cannot be satisfied. It is simply that in the penguin society there is a great deal of emphasis on being accepted. The fear of rejection is so inappropriately high that there is a correspondingly false premium on acceptance. Once the acceptance is won, the competitor often finds himself or herself involved with someone who is not very compatible. The Shift encourages a more discriminating focus and searches out the compatibility factors before becoming so intensely involved.

Relationshift is the knowledge, mental attitudes, and thought processes involved in the successful developing of a long-term partnership. It is the study of the life cycle of caring.

Relationshipping is the application of that knowledge, those attitudes, and those thought processes openly and directly through the use of a contract or agreement. It is the practice and experience of caring.

Before one may practice Relationshipping, one must have a good grasp of the facts and dynamics surrounding the process. One must shift mentally to a new focus, to new attitudes, to a new system. One must be willing to become a platypus.

CHAPTER III

The Facts of Life about Relationshipping

There are four basic facts that must be understood and accepted before beginning the study of the stages of development in Relationshipping. Those facts are the following:
1. There are many different categories of Relationshipping.
2. All Relationshipping is on a continuum.
3. All Relationshipping involves contracts, either overt or covert.
4. Covert contracts will occur if overt contracts are not discussed and agreed upon.

Like all simply stated facts, these must be discussed and absorbed before their full importance emerges. They are natural law in human interactions and ignorance or disagreement with them does not alter their basic truth. They are the core issues on which Relationshift is built.

1. There are many categories of Relationshipping

When one thinks about the many people encountered in the course of one's ordinary day, it is immediately realized that one interacts differently and on different levels according to familiarity and to the role that each person plays in day to day living. Intimate information is not generally imparted at the check-out counter of the grocery store nor is the milk man generally asked to mail his customer's letters. Attitudes are different toward a policeman than toward one's secretary. There are people addressed by first names, people addressed by surnames, and people addressed casually without names. This is an automatic process and the mind does not actively compute which mode of address shall be used or in what manner the person shall behave. When these daily routine procedures are analyzed, it is easy to realize that one is not Relationshipping with all these people. One is interacting with most of them and probably shall not develop more than an acquaintance.

The major categories of actual Relationshipping in which one is involved are family Relationshipping, work Relationshipping, romantic Relationshipping, and friendshipping. A person automatically changes in his or her reactions from one category to the other. It goes without saying that the boss is not treated the same as senile Aunt Sarah, and best friends receive a different response than one's children.

In family Relationshipping and work Relationshipping, there is a defined and continuing bond. Even the most contentious family has a sense of identification and usually of solidarity. This is reflected in the legal system in which there are procedures for adoption and guardianship, but there are no petitions wherein one can "divorce" a mother, father, or sibling. Blood is usually seen as thicker than water, and family roles are seen as a continuing bond. Work Relationshipping has the added advantage of its role expectations being well defined either under a legal contract between employer and employee or in the printed form of a job description. Most companies also have a handbook of personnel policies so that any employee in doubt has ready access to the rules.

It is in the categories of friendshipping and romantic Relationshipping, where there is no common bloodline to insure a continuing bond and where there are no well defined job descriptions, that the most difficulties are encountered. It is in these areas that Relationshift is not only useful but crucial.

Friendshipping is the most discounted and underrated of the four major categories of Relationshipping, especially in terms of opposite sex friendshipping. Many people involved with a spouse or a romance do not feel they want, need, or have the time for the development of friends. There are others who are closely involved but do not intend to marry; they therefore often say they are "just" friends as if the lack of marriage prospects lessens the value of the involvement.

The idea of a friend has become further discounted and confused because it has become the custom to label as "friends" those former lovers and associations who not only are not often seen, but also would rather be avoided. Friendshipping is a more active process.

In their book *The Romantic Love Question and Answer Book*, Nathaniel Brandon and Devers Brandon said that the two major areas of personal happiness are in productive work and in romantic love.[1] They are quite right. However, people in desperate pursuit of Romance often deprive themselves of the personal validation and gratification that only a non-romantic friend can provide. With proper development and guidelines through Relationshift, it can be a most rewarding involvement.

2. All Relationshipping is on a continuum.

In Chapter I the first glimpse was seen of the Relationshipping continuum. It is a process which, all factors being ideal, begins upon the meeting of the two people and gradually builds and develops by their mutual and joint efforts. The continuum is represented visually by a line which is separated into four stages. The stages represent the focus of effort that needs to be done by the parties involved at those points of the continuum.

Interestingly enough, at early points on the continuum, strong emotional expectations or involvement are not assumed unless it is within a potentially romantic framework. There is an awareness of the continuum and of social roles when interacting non-romantically. When a possible romance is involved, however, one often thinks, feels, and reacts as if the continuum were totally unknown.

Bertha, for example, has for several years been involved in a community choir which meets once a week. On the first meeting night of each month, she and six fellow choir members meet for dinner prior to the choir rehearsal. Although she has enjoyed the entire group and would like to know some members better, she did not discuss her divorce last year with any of them, and did not expect them to call or nurture her during that time. She says she does not know any of them well enough to discuss her most personal feelings. However, her behavior upon meeting Roger last week was quite different from her behavior with her fellow choir members. Within several hours she had told Roger her innermost secrets and feelings, including sexual longings and frustrations. She immediately invested emotionally in a stranger that which she would not discuss with those she had known for several years. The difference is the possibility of romance.

Whether involving the work situation, friendshipping, or romance, such investment at the beginning of the continuum is inappropriate. It produces instant vulnerability because sensitive information is offered before knowing how that information will be handled. People essentially offer themselves in words with the hope that the self along with the words will be honored. This, like all magic, is tricky business.

The speedy investment syndrome comes in large part from the pressure of The Six Hour Chance To Impress Him (Her) That Absolutely Everything Depends On. The continuum offers many more opportunities than the Six Hour Chance. It is simply that since there are many more people with whom one is not compatible than with whom one is a perfect match, it is unwise to offer oneself so completely without progressing enough along the continuum to know whether the characteristics one seeks are present in the other person.

The continuum exists in all Relationshipping and proceeds in a pace of normal time and contact. Inner longings, intimate knowledge, nor furious impatience will speed the Relationshipping progress. There must be knowledge of personality characteristics, development of trust, and evidence of reciprocity in consistent and continuing forms.

3. All Relationshipping involves contracts, either overt or covert.

Relationshipping contracts are verbal or behavioral agreements which govern the conduct between two people. Most existing couples know most of those agreements. Close friends and families are generally aware of what is alright and what is not, even if it has never been discussed. In the work situation, many rules which are not written are quickly ascertained by observation. However, both at work and in social situations, agreements which are discussed openly and directly provide the clearest guidelines. Even if unpleasant, there is no doubt about the issue. If there is no discussion or if the discussion is indirect, a covert contract occurs by nature of the participants' behavior.

It is a universal truth that communication is much more than the spoken or written word. There are many instances of travelers interacting in countries without knowledge of the language. Children of different cultures play quite happily and communicate well without the benefit of prior instruction. Few adults need to tell someone they know well if they are angry for the other person to be aware of that feeling. A great deal is communicated by non-verbal behavior. It is the non-verbal and/or indirect responses to these non-verbal messages that creates the covert (undiscussed) agreements. It is a hallmark of human Relationshipping that most of the pleasant and enjoyable agreements are discussed while the unpleasant issues are avoided. They therefore evolve as covert contracts. Since it is impossible to discuss all issues — people would be in a constant state of negotiation — All Relationshipping involves a combination of both overt and covert agreements.

4. Covert contracts will occur if overt contracts are not discussed and agreed upon.

Not all covert contracts are negative. For example, Arthur sends Mattie one dozen long stemmed American Beauty roses every year on her birthday. He has been doing this for five years — more than twice — so his thoughtfulness is expected and anticipated. Their covert contract in this area is that he will send the flowers and Mattie will pretend to be surprised. Anyone who does not believe this qualifies as a secret agreement should observe Mattie's reaction if Arthur were to forget the flowers this year.

Other pleasant covert contracts involve sexuality. Since it is still difficult for many people to be sexy openly, there are certain behavioral agreements that signal sexual availability. It may be candlelight at dinner, a suggestion for a fire in the fireplace, or a glass of wine before bedtime. A woman may wear a sexy nightie instead of her usual granny gown. A partner observing such behaviors responds by initiating more direct sexual overtures.

The majority of secret agreements, however, are behavioral reactions to those issues which are uncomfortable to discuss. They often evolve innocently enough in the initial stage of Relationshipping and somehow get out of control. Feelings of resentment develop, and at least one partner usually begins to feel taken advantage of.

When Gwendolyn moved next door to Frieda she asked if she could buy a few stamps. A year later she continued to use Frieda as her private post office, including coming over with 57 Christmas cards for which she needed stamps. Frieda, having been irritated for at least six months and having anticipated the Christmas rush, steeled herself to say she had to go to the post office as she herself was out of stamps. Gwendolyn, adding insult to injury, immediately replied, "Oh great! Here's the money and you can take my cards when you go!"

Frieda never intended to go into the neighborhood postal business when she was courteous to a new neighbor and later began to develop Gwendolyn as a friend. She is now uncomfortable about confronting Gwendolyn because they enjoy many activities together. In this issue, however, Frieda feels abused. Gwendolyn, on the other hand, knows there is tension between them but she doesn't know why. She always pays for the stamps and Frieda has not complained. Gwendolyn assumes that Frieda's sometime ill humor is probably due to some marriage problems Frieda doesn't want to talk about. This secret agreement will continue, with Frieda feeling more and more abused and Gwendolyn feeling more and more confused, until Frieda comes clean and talks about it directly.

Although, like Gwendolyn and Frieda, covert contracts often begin innocently enough in the initial stage of Relationshipping, they may occur at any time along the continuum and develop into major secret issues between two people. The task is to discuss these issues while they are only uncomfortable and before they are highly emotionally and negatively charged. Since the party who initiates the covert behavior generally believes it to be right, it is the responsibility of the responding party to confront the covert contract.

After the birth of their second child, Brenda found herself too tired and too disinterested to be a participating partner in lovemaking. However, she never refused her husband's advances, thinking it better to lay like a stone while he attempted to practice the art. After this had gone on for some time, their secret agreement became obvious: Brenda will not verbally refuse sexuality but *by her behavior* indicates she wants no part of the sex act. He, in turn, will continue the activity, showing by *his* behavior that he doesn't care about her feelings. This is serious business until the concerned husband, who does care about her feelings but feels helpless, is able to bring this issue to the overt level and tell Brenda he would rather she say "no" with her mouth rather than with her body.

Behavior and attitude must be consistent for full communication to exist. A clear characteristic of the existence of a hidden agreement is a difference between thoughts and action, between attitudes and behavior. The higher the proportion of covert contracts, the more difficult it is for two people to communicate. Instead, they become confused, anxious, and fearful. Since contracts are going to occur anyway, it is important for them to be above-board, open, and consistent. Otherwise, the Relationshipping experience is predisposed to failure, and the partners become mired in the game-playing and guesswork of relationshit.

Armed with the facts of life about Relationshipping, there is no reason two people cannot find happiness along each step of the Relationshipping continuum. If one studies the stages of development and learns to apply the basic concepts, all the confusion, anxiety, and fear are replaced by open-ness and communication.

Relationshippers in the areas of romance and friendshipping are in particular need of the basic concepts because of a lack of a sense of security. Neither romance nor friendshipping guarantee blood ties, equal opportunity, or grievance procedures as do either family or work Relationshipping. Focus in the following chapters is therefore geared to non-related caring partners, those who would be lovers and those who would be friends.

CHAPTER IV

Separating the Penguins from the Platypuses

The Relationshipping continuum is separated into four predictable and identifiable stages: the Interaction Stage, the Testing Stage, the Negotiation Stage, and the Termination Stage. In friendshipping and romantic Relationshipping, there are three characteristics that are prerequisite for two people to advance along the full length of the continuum and be successful. Those three characteristics are chemistry, compatibility, and similar value systems.

The work and family situations are not included because obviously a person may continue at a job or may continue in a family whether or not the chemistry, compatibility, and similar value systems are present. But friends or lovers, however carefully they attempt to walk the tightrope of the continuum, will fall off if the chemistry, compatibility, and value systems do not match.

What is chemistry? Chemistry is the lightning bolt of mutual attraction. It is not limited to physical characteristics. It is the almost unexplainable unconscious matching process that creates someone for everyone. Tall, short, skinny or well-padded, thick glasses or crooked nose makes no difference to chemistry. The lightning bolt may knock one off the feet with excitement or it may provide a little electric tickle of interest. Whatever the intensity, it must be a *mutual* attraction.

There are penguins who are attracted to each other because they are both interested in the same person. Vickie and Turk, for example, were both interested in Turk. Because of the great chemistry she felt with Turk, Vickie could and did listen to him by the hour. On occasion she would clean his apartment and iron his shirts just the way he liked them. She was the perfect audience and the perfect date. They had been seeing each other regularly for almost three months before Vickie realized that while she was delighted to sit in the stands during his softball games, he had no interest in watching her women's volleyball team. Turk wanted Vickie's time, support, and attention, but saw no need to return the favor. He was not particularly interested in her job or any other aspects of her life that did not directly concern him.

When Vickie began to ask for more of an equal role in their Relationshipping, Turk perceived her as being unreasonable, demanding, and less interested in him. She began to feel she was receiving little return on her investment. As she began to give less, Turk did not give more. Instead, he found someone else who would focus completely on him to the exclusion of her own needs and wants.

Vickie and Turk did not have true chemistry. Everyone both wants and benefits from being appreciated by another person. However, a Relationshipping experience based on what only one person can receive from the other is an exercise in narcissistic self-gratification. For one partner it is an experience in self-abuse, even though it is an ongoing voluntary act. What Vickie and Turk had most in common was their mutual interest in Turk. When Vickie was no longer content to continue that focus, they no longer had anything significant in common. So, fortunately for Vickie, they fell off the continuum.

Chemistry is the great motivator. People will discard their own preferences or go out of their way for another person because of chemistry. It is the mutual spark that motivates giving to each other and leads to tolerance. However, it is not enough. There must also be compatibility. Without compatibility, too much strain is put upon a partner's ability to give or to tolerate.

Genevieve, for example, is "in love" with Eric but can't stand many of his personal habits. She tells her mother he eats "like a pig at the trough" and she is embarrassed to go to a nice restaurant with him. He sucks his teeth, smacks his gum, and can't sit still through a movie or a play. While standing to talk to people, he rattles the change in his pocket, and when walking with her, he often out-distances her by a good three feet. Unless she is in an exceptionally good mood, she is a nervous wreck after going out with him. She either has to swallow these irritations or spend much of the evening asking him to modify his behavior. Her constant comments make him feel picked on and criticized which, in turn, irritates her even more.

As Genevieve knows Eric longer, these behaviors will not bother her less. In fact, as the newness wears off and they advance further onto the continuum, the behaviors will bother her more. His assets of being out-going, energetic, and a giving partner will be taken for granted and she will focus more and more on the irritating characteristics. There are simply too many of them and they upset her too much.

Compatibility is each person's day to day habits and preferences being similar enough to blend together smoothly. Great amounts of tolerance and constant compromise are unnecessary when two people are compatible. A person who squeezes the toothpaste from the top can live quite happily with someone who squeezes from the bottom by buying two tubes of toothpaste. Tea bags and instant coffee successfully unite the tea drinker and the coffee hound. However, table manners, nervous gestures, energy levels, and different interests regarding activities and leisure time pursuits are not so easily reconciled.

Don doesn't believe it's art unless it's a traditional oil painting, would rather not associate with children until they're over eighteen, and his idea of a really big evening is making popcorn and watching the Saturday Night Movie on television. Joya, who he's currently dating, would go across the country to see an exhibit of Picasso, teaches preschool at marginal pay because "a day without children is a day without sunshine", and loves to be surrounded by people. Although they certainly have enough differences to keep boredom out of their Relationshipping, their differences are not within their partner's range of preferences. In these areas alone, a great deal of compromise and tolerance will be required for them to continue successfully along the continuum. The odds are it will be too much of a strain for them to make it successfully.

It must be understood that even under ideal circumstances, no two people are completely compatible. If Romeo and Juliet had waited awhile on the knife and the poison, they probably would have discovered that one or the other snored, was frivolous with money, or was a grouch in the morning. Every person in this world is a unique combination of personality and experience. No two people are going to approach all situations in the same manner. It is this uniqueness and these inherent differences that expand and enrich Relationshipping. However, too many differences, or having important priorities which do not fall within the partner's preference system, predispose the Relationshipping to excessive strain and probably to failure. There are very few couples who enjoy the luxury of ideal circumstances. Therefore it is important for people to be compatible enough to blend smoothly within everyday habits and preferences.

In addition to chemistry and compatibility, two people generally will not relationship successfully without a similar value system. Values are much less concrete than compatibility. Compatibility is how well two people's personalities and habits mix together. Similar value systems is a positive blend of their beliefs. Personalities and habits are often much easier to understand than beliefs and this is the sticky wicket: there is a tendency to be unaccepting of a partner's attitudes and beliefs if they are diametrically opposite to one's own. There are many couples who have learned not to discuss religion or politics and by avoiding these topics they successfully avoid challenging each other's beliefs and credibility.

However, there are other belief systems that cannot as easily be separated from everyday life. There is the handling of money, for example, and the question of whether a couple should live below their income, within their income, or beyond their income. Maggie considers Greg a positive skinflint because he banks and refuses to spend one third of his income each month. According to her value system, they unnecessarily deprive themselves of various material items and activities which they can easily afford. Greg, on the other hand, sees Maggie as an economic idiot and does not think she should be trusted with grocery money. Neither can understand the other's attitudes.

Another example is the discipline of children. Lorraine, the mother of four pre-school children (one set of twins) definitely believes that sparing the rod spoils the child. Her partner Leo, a gentle soft-spoken man, believes in catching flies with honey. She sees him as a disgusting push-over who is easily manipulated by the children, and he has real concerns that she might be a potential child abuser. Neither has any doubt that the partner is dead wrong regarding discipline.

A person's value system encompasses beliefs in religion and the practice of it, government and the participation in it, handling of economics, care and discipline of children, interactions with the extended family, male and female roles, work habits, and goal-setting, for starters. In short, it includes nearly every "should" in a person's framework of ideals. We should pay our bills; we should avoid caffeine; we should visit Mother on Sunday; we should go to work every day; we should vote; we should be physically fit; we should mow the lawn once a week; we should be good neighbors, etc.

For most people personal beliefs go without saying and certainly without argument. If friends and lovers have similar value systems or do not feel strongly about their individual beliefs, there can be mutual understanding and acceptance of the partner's framework. However, for each difference in strongly held beliefs, there is a resulting loss of respect and closeness. Relationshipping can tolerate a few differences, but the more that exist the less successful the chances for the long-term. It is difficult to continue to befriend or to live with a partner who is seen as stupid, ignorant, irrational, or weird. The partner loses in respect and esteem, and there is no confidence in his or her judgment. A strong and continued loss of esteem and confidence erodes the chemistry factor.

Contrary to popular myth and song, "Love" (chemistry) is not enough. Chemistry provides attraction and motivation, but it is compatibility and a similar value system that enables people to live and interact successfully together over the long term. People who are sincere in Relationshipping need to begin to evaluate the existence of these factors in the Interaction Stage at the very beginning of the Relationshipping continuum. Penguins generally believe that love will see one through, that all one needs is love, that if one only has love all other problems will resolve themselves. This is why there are packs and packs of lonely unhappy penguins.

It is a simple fact that if one continues to do the same things in the same ways, one will generally have the same results. Evaluating chemistry, compatibility, and value systems is the first step in separating penguin ways from platypus ways and leads to the difference in penguin results from platypus results.

CHAPTER V

The Interaction Stage

Fall-outs and Fall-ins

The exciting Interaction Stage begins when two people meet and/or recognize a mutual interest in each other. At that point they take their first step along the Relationshipping continuum. In the majority of situations a couple only advances a few more steps before one or the other jumps, falls, or is pushed off the continuum. Most initial interactions do not progress to Relationshipping.

There are reasons for these stalemates. First of all, when one thinks of the number of people with whom one interacts, it is quickly realized that no one is attracted to everyone one encounters. Including sales people, bus and taxi drivers, colleagues at work, and fellow customers in stores, one not only is not attracted to most of these people, but quite often does not notice them as one goes about business. Many people are eliminated from Relationshipping goals simply because of a lack of chemistry. This is fact and no insult. Different characteristics appeal to different people and it is not something one can control.

Secondly, not everyone one meets is a compatible partner. Tina declined to continue interacting with Marco Polo because she becomes airsick on a thick rug and he, owner of his own plane, wants to fly some place exotic every weekend. Harvey didn't ask Trixie out for a second date because he is a quiet sort and she is so bubbly and out-going that he feels overwhelmed and inadequate. All four of these people are desirable, enjoyable personalities, but they do not blend well together as couples. They quietly step or fall off the continuum.

Sometimes a person has a "shopping list" which blinds him or her to many potential partners. Martine, for example, is looking for a successful professional man with money. When she interacts she is alert for three piece suits, expensive cars, and prestige addresses. She can hear the chime of a gold Seiko watch within three floors of any building, but will not notice a man standing next to her if he hasn't the trappings on her list. Les, in Chapter One, has a list which specifies height, smoking habits, and no young children. Any woman who doesn't fall within the limits Les has pre-ordained doesn't have a chance with him regardless of her sterling qualities. Martine and Les won't get on the continuum unless they see what they want.

Even when there does initially appear to be chemistry and compatibility and even when one initially does pass muster on someone's shopping list, the fall-out rate of the Interaction Stage is still amazingly high. Why? Because with the sure appearance of everything coming up roses, penguins become frightened and screw everything up.

The Interaction Stage is the most exciting stage of the Relationshipping continuum. In it one feels one's feelings more intensely than in any other stage except Termination. It is a time of euphoric high adventure, equally high anxiety, and very little control. If it were possible to put emotions on a graph, there would be a line of mountains and valleys reminiscent of the Swiss Alps. Once it is realized that penguins are attempting to deal with a new person as well as with this turmoil of emotions and anxiety, it is understandable why people make so many mistakes.

The tendency toward screw-ups is such that a well-intentioned potential partner quite often shoves the other off the continuum. This compulsive, repetitive behavior has become a hallmark of the penguin society. Quite a bit of relationshit is a reaction to constant (and expected) pushing and shoving. Many penguin courtship customs are rationalizations and protections against it which (because they're penguins and don't know any better) usually lead to more screw-ups instead of less.

The biggest screw-up of all, both literally and figuratively, is sex. It has become a penguin custom in recent years, practiced primarily in singles' clubs and bars but an underlying concept wherever singles meet or get together, to attempt to seduce a partner into Relationshipping. Axiom I of the Penguin Society By-Laws reads: "If I am an enjoyable companion for a few hours and prove I am GIB (good in bed), this person will fall in love with me." Grandma's old adage that the way to a man's heart is through his stomach has simply shifted a good six inches downward. Unfortunately, these days nearly every woman is GIB (or at least pretends to be) and men, who have a tendency to discount premature sexuality anyway, begin to view women as walking vaginas rather than potential partners. Since the current unspoken question within one hour of meeting is not, "Will we go to bed?" but "Shall we go to bed now or later?", the focus mistakenly establishes sexuality as the prime criteria for interacting together.

Those who fall in bed together do not necessarily stay together. In fact, those who go to bed together too soon practically guarantee they will not stay together. They have focused on an artificial *act* of closeness rather than on the areas that produce true intimacy. They gamble their self-esteem and their emotions on Axiom I which is a lose-lose situation. Regardless, within the penguin society there is no tendency to discard an axiom that does not work. Rather, there is the philosophy that if this time did not work out, the next one will. Self-esteem erodes and confidence dwindles, but the axiom lives on.

One Night Stands

Since the axiom is not true and does not work, it cannot survive without rationalizations to support it. One Night Stands are the most colossal rationalizations of all. For purposes of this book, a One Night Stand is defined as a sexual encounter, usually with a new acquaintance, on a one time basis with little if any basis for follow through with further contact. The favorite rationalizations for this de-humanizing activity are:
1. "Sex is a natural need just like eating or drinking. Why shouldn't I satisfy my needs?"
2. "I don't know this person. I'm never going to see him (or her) again. Why not let myself go?"
3. "I'm so lonely. I just want someone to hold me for a little while."
4. "I had too much to drink and didn't realize what I was doing."
5. "I've been used by so many people so many times, I just think I'll do a little using of someone else for awhile."
6. "Sex is all-American fun and fun should never be turned down."
7. "People who say 'no' are uptight and inhibited and probably have sexual problems."
8. "I've never had really good sex. I need experience so I'll know it when I find it."
9. "Maybe it will turn into something, and even if it doesn't, I've still had a nice evening."
10. "If I don't have sex, then he (or she) won't be interested in me any more."

Logically speaking, One Night Stands, and the rationalizations that encourage the custom, are dangerous, both physically and emotionally. Venereal disease is epidemic with some strains having no cure. People who are infected do not usually tell their friends, much less a partner for the night. Physicians and health departments have not noticed any great surge towards sexual responsibility in this area. Also, when engaged in the sexual act, a person is physically at his or her most vulnerable. Participants in One Night Standing generally do not know each other or do not know each other very well. To be beaten or robbed or forced to perform acts one would rather not perform are normal occurences. In spite of these possible hazards, physical dangers inhibit very few sexual encounters. After all, there are enough rationalizations to support the practice and enough practice creates an acceptable custom.

Although there is no proof that every One Night Stander will be exposed to physical danger or violence, there is a great deal of proof that emotional damage goes hand-in-hand with the One Night Stand. Lovemaking is an act of cooperative intimacy by two people who are expressing their emotional closeness. If one subtracts the emotional closeness, one must also subtract the intimacy, and what remains is sex — a cooperative act by two people. These two people have shed their clothes and, all too often, their self-respect and their goals.

Sex for sex's sake is vastly over-rated. Lorette says, "The best lover I ever had was Earl. He was a real cocksman. Actually, he wasn't really a lover; he was a technician. If anyone ever deserved the description of playing a woman like a violin, he did. I went to bed with him twice and then I didn't want to any more. . .That was all there was to Earl. But the best sexual experience I ever had was with a man who couldn't perform. He was so upset he cried, and he didn't try to hide it. We were really close and it was a very human experience."

In spite of the rationalizations, penguins are really looking for closeness. To those who have been unsuccessful in finding it, the facsimile of intimacy of a One Night Stand is better than nothing. The underlying admission is that the participants are incapable or undeserving of the real thing. The rationalizations help justify the behavior and are an attempt to feel better about it. However, a logical look at the rationalizations reveals the flaws in penguin-style thinking:

1) *"Sex is a natural need just like eating or drinking. Why shouldn't I satisfy my needs?"*

Sex to the extent people talk about it is really more of a "want" than a need. Sexual "need" can be taken care of manually or mechanically. When sex is viewed as a need like eating or drinking, the Self is placed on the same level as a fast-food restaurant. Who wants to be a quick burger and coke to be gobbled up quickly and then forgotten?

2) *"I don't know this person, I'm never going to see him (or her) again. Why not let myself go?"*

The idea of not seeing another person again is often thought to provide the safety of anonymity until, like Linda, one goes to a Christmas party and sees, happily grouped around the punch bowl, three of one's One Night Stands. All of a sudden, a person doesn't feel so anonymous.

3) *"I'm so lonely. I just want someone to hold me for a little while."*

All single people without well-matched partners (and many married people) are lonely. This rationale is the closest on the list to the real conflicts experienced. A person who uses number three is much more in touch with his or her feelings, but complicates the loneliness by using the One Night Stand. Being physically held for just one night emphasizes all the nights unheld, both those nights past and those to come.

4) *"I had too much to drink and didn't realize what I was doing."*

The decision not to realize what one is doing usually takes place before taking the first drink. Everyone who uses this rationalization knows it for a colossal cop-out . . . and so do the people on whom they use it.

5) *"I've been used by so many people so many times, I just think I'll do a little using of someone else for awhile."*

No one is "used" without cooperation. This rationale is sex as anger, and whoever uses number five gets to be both victim and the abuser.

6) *"Sex is all-American fun and fun should never be turned down."*

Of course, sex can be fun. So is hang-gliding, spelunking, and climbing the Matterhorn. Yet, people more often than not would turn down these "fun" activities.

7) *"People who say 'no' are uptight and inhibited and probably have sexual problems."*

People who say 'no' to sex with strangers (strange sex?) are discriminating rather than inhibited, and generally they are in much better shape mental health-wise and sex-wise than those who say 'yes'.

8) *"I've never had really good sex, I need experience so I'll know it when I find it."*

If Lorette's word is valid, really good sex has little to do with sexual technique. It is closeness and emotional involvement that give meaning to sexuality. In addition, in terms of technique alone, it is interesting to note that the sexual adjustment period for two partners to attune one to the other is from nine months to a year. The chances of having "really good sex" with a One Night Stand are therefore minimal.

9) *"Maybe it will turn into something, and even if it doesn't, I've still had a nice evening."*

This rationale is based on Axiom I of the Penguin Society and basically entraps the user into a series of disappointing experiences.

10) *"If I don't have sex, then he (or she) won't be interested in me any more."*

This rationale is a variation of Axiom I and is related to mistaken expectations. Christopher and Hugger are one of many couples who dispute this myth. Meeting at an out of town convention, they spent the evening together but not the night. Three months later and in spite of 150 miles distance between them, Chris contacted her to develop Relationshipping. Chris admits he continued to be interested in Hugger because she declined premature sexuality. The rationale that no sex is equivalent to no interest is a variation of Axiom I of the Penguin Society and is a result of mistaken expectations.

After analyzing all the excuses, people who continue to feel comfortable about One Night Stands have developed some that are not on the list. The key issue is that placing sex on a casual throw-away basis places the *self* into the casual throw-away category. Self-esteem and sex — no matter what the excuses — are too closely intermingled for people to get away with One Night Stands and still feel good about themselves.
The rule is: There is no incident of One Night Standing that is not emotionally damaging.

The Incredible Carlos Murphy

While most of my patients and students logically agree with me in my anti-One Night Stand attitudes, I hear vehement objections when it comes to Carlos Murphy. As a therapist who focuses on facts, feelings, and problem solving, it has taken me years to admit his existence. However, though he is rare, he has definitely been sighted and experienced, and these experiences are unforgettable. Jeannine encountered him most recently and it is from her account that he takes his name:

It was at a special out of town seminar that Jeannine met this every-woman's-dream who took her to dinner at Carlos Murphy's Irish Mexican Restaurant. Witty, bright, and obviously skilled in his career, he was also personally interested in Jeannine. Their conversation was a combination of work-related topics, personal discussion, and fanciful ideas. He even showed her how to hold a filled wine glass to the light of the fireplace to watch the fairies dance in the flames through the glass. Though there was no urgency, there was chemistry nonetheless. After dinner, quite naturally and almost magically, he gave her a night of the most incredible sexual fulfillment she had ever experienced. He being married and each living in different and far distant communities, Relationshipping did not develop. However, Jeannine will never forget her "Carlos Murphy". She will never hold a wine glass beside a fireplace without thinking of him. She continues to look for him in each man she meets.

Carlos Murphy is what a woman would like to think that Robert Redford or Paul Newman would be like. He is that highly skilled and equally sensitive sexual partner who can communicate caring along with technique. He is an enriching experience and rather than chipping away at a partner's integrity, he builds her self-esteem.

Even with Carlos Murphy there are disadvantages. Once having experienced him, it is more than difficult to let him go. On the other hand, if both parties are not absolutely available, it is unwise to pursue Carlos Murphy. He nearly always belongs to someone else and he takes this "belonging" most seriously. One Night Stands are not his usual style and if the night and the woman herself had not been touched by magic, the whole incident would not have happened. Also, having once experienced Carlos Murphy, it is difficult to be interested in ordinary men. They cannot quite compete. Carlos Murphy is the modern day Prince in the old fashioned fairy tale. Women whose lives he has touched, like Jeannine, wait and look for a similar touch. Unfortunately, he is as rare as the restaurant — only eleven in the United States — and the chances against duplicating the experience are thousands to one.

There is no female equivalent of Carlos Murphy. It is curious to me that in spite of the myths surrounding female sexuality, none of my male patients or students have ever reported a female Carlos Murphy experience. Perhaps women are expected to be caring, sensitive, and sexually responsive. If so, the discovery of one who is a combination of these characteristics is not particularly remarkable.

The Demon (Instant) Sex

In the Interaction Stage the goal is to establish Relationshipping. Since One Night Stands do not lead to this goal but instead contribute to some damaging self-concepts, it is important to side-step the demon (instant) sex and concentrate on other issues that will lead to successful Relationshipping. It is not that people should become puritanical stick-in-the-mud foes of sexuality. After all, sex is only a demon with the wrong partner or under the wrong circumstances. Sexuality should be restored to a meaningful place in peoples' minds and emotions. It is as George Burns says, "Timing is everything."

Without proper timing premature emotional investment is encouraged at a point when cognitive reasoning is more important. Like all stages on the Relationshipping continuum, the Interaction Stage features certain typical feelings, characteristics, and risks. There is also a time factor, and there are developmental tasks to be accomplished. It is logic, not emotion, which intermingles the feelings and characteristics with the time and the tasks. It is the processing of information, not premature emotional investment, which detects predictable risks. It is peoples' minds, not their gonads, which determine their eventual and continuing success.

Primary Feelings of the Interaction Stage

If people can avoid the push for sex, the primary feelings of the Interaction Stage are anxiety, erratic mood swings, and "false" intimacy. Everyone beginning on the Relationshipping continuum experiences these feelings to a greater or lesser degree. They are exasperating, but they are also typical, expected, and normal.

Anxiety

The Interaction Stage is a time of interacting together when the traditional concept of "a relationship" does not yet exist. Anxiety, however, is so prevalent that many people associate this primary feeling with being in love. The amount of anxiety experienced depends upon the amount of chemistry between the two potential partners and also upon the strength of the desire to relationship together. If there is not that much chemistry or not that much desire to be acceptable to the other person, there will be very little anxiety. In this way, anxiety acts very nicely as a personal barometer regarding whether or not to be involved. Anxiety is fear: fear of not being accepted, fear of the unknown, fear that one won't have what is wanted so badly. The anxiety itself is not unusual and not terribly important. It is the control of the anxiety which is important because people often embark on foolish behaviors as a result of it. Attempting to seduce a partner into Relationshipping, jumping into Too Much Too Soon, and testing for reactions are a few of those anxiety provoked behaviors which screw up the whole process.

Erratic Mood Swings

The erratic mood swings are a reflection of contact with the potential partner. If one sees or hears from him or her, one is excited; one feels good. If one does not, one is moody-blue, irritable, and depressed. It works somewhat like a temporary battery charge. Contact with the desired person reassures the fears and sends a brief but stimulating charge of energy and hope. The fears shortly re-emerge and another contact is needed to re-charge.

"False" Intimacy

The feeling of intimacy and closeness is so strong that it is difficult to believe that it is false. Although it feels real, it must be labeled as "false" because there has not yet been enough time for a foundation of true closeness to be established. Although people feel as though they have known each other forever, the fact is they have only known each other for a short while. The current feeling of intimacy is a good sign, but true closeness is developed after experiencing time and events together. The feeling of intimacy in the Interaction Stage is actually due to mutual attraction and mutual newness.

Time Factor

A couple can begin a continuum together at meeting or, having known each other for awhile, can begin a continuum upon discovering a mutual interest in each other. Two people continue interacting for three to six months of *normal time and contact* before the traditional idea of "a relationship" exists. It cannot be just time nor just contact. A couple will continue in the Interaction Stage for three to six months or its equivalent in normal time and contact.

For example, Billy and Marie met and spent a marvelous week together before he returned from military leave. For the next two years, they have corresponded several times a week, called each other periodically, and spent a week-end together every six months or so. In spite of the fact they have known each other for two years, they are still in the Interaction Stage. They have had the time, but not the contact. Also, neither the time nor the contact has been "normal". They have not had the opportunity to see each other regularly under normal and every day circumstances.

Another example is Paulette and George who "clicked" instantly when they met at the local singles spot two weeks ago. They have had seventeen dates and forty-two telephone calls since then. They are still in the Interaction Stage although they feel they've known each other for years. They have had the contact (too much contact) but not the time.

A third example is Sam and Marilyn. They are married, each to someone else. They have been secretly seeing each other at least twice a week for three years. They have the time and the contact but it is not normal time. They are still in the Interaction Stage of Relationshipping.

Primary Characteristics of the Initial Stage

Primary characteristics are differentiated from primary feelings in that the feelings are emotions while the characteristics are mental or physical acts. These well-known and predictable characteristics are guesswork, waiting, communication, and "special" behaviors.

Guesswork

Guesswork is the result of anxiety, attraction, and not knowing a potential partner well enough to anticipate his or her feelings and responses. In guesswork, a person attempts to mind-read and asks oneself unanswerable questions. The questions often begin with, "I wonder . . . (fill in the blank) . . .". "I wonder if he (or she) is thinking about me . . . I wonder if he (or she) will call . . . I wonder if he (or she) will show up . . . if he (or she) will be at the party . . . how much he (or she) likes me . . ." In the Interaction Stage people wonder if they do this, will the potential partner do that. Those who have had prior negative experiences, especially those who have known the Magician, have more anxiety and do more guesswork than others. The more unanswerable questions, the more the anxiety and guesswork feed themselves.

To combat this characteristic, the Relationshipper must answer all the questions, even if the answer is "I don't know". Other answers to defeat the 'I wonders' are: "He (or She) might be thinking about me and he (or she) might not . . . He (or she) will call when he (or she) gets a chance . . . He (or She) has not stood me up yet . . ." To stop as much guesswork as possible, one must rely on the facts.

Waiting

Waiting is more uncomfortable than guess work and often increases it. This is the most difficult characteristic of the Interaction Stage. To slow down for the dangers of Too Much Too Soon; to wait for the next telephone call; to wait for the next contact sometimes seems like more than the human personality should be expected to bear. Dr. Daniel Cappon, in his book *Coupling: Understanding the Chemistry of Close Relationships*,[2] says that withstanding uncertainty is a powerful test of mental health. By withstanding uncertainty trust is developed and established. A person learns that a potential partner will follow through without one's interference. The follow through inspires confidence, and the development of covert contracts is inhibited. The primary characteristic of waiting is an uncomfortable but necessary evil.

Communication

The third primary characteristic of the Interaction Stage is communication. At this point on the continuum, two people talk to each other more often and more deeply (excepting those topics which might offend the other or endanger the Relationshipping) than at any other time. There is the urge to tell the potential partner everything that one has experienced, thought, or dreamed. Each person therefore quite naturally obtains a great deal of information which is useful to evaluate compatibility and value systems. One also uses this time of mutual outpouring to develop a feedback system which keeps people closely knit and in touch with each other along the farther reaches of the continuum.

"Special" Behaviors

The final typical characteristic of the Interaction Stage is "special" behaviors. The problem is that there is no way of knowing if these behaviors are unusual for the potential partner until arriving well into the Testing Stage. If the behaviors disappear in the Testing Stage, they were probably "special" in the Interaction Stage. A "special" behavior is one that a person would not ordinarily do unless his or her mind were temporarily boggled by a potential partner.

For example, when Leonard and Sally first met, he sent her cards and bought her Valentine candy. She was expecting candy the following year but it didn't come. Then she realized it had been a long time since he had sent a card or done anything extra special with no particular reason. Cards and candy were early courtship behaviors for Leonard. Danny, on the other hand, is always picking up a little something for Niccole and they have been Relationshipping for four years. Leonard is considerate in other ways, but for him these behaviors are "special". For Danny, who is considerate in almost every way, these behaviors are an everyday part of his personality. If the behaviors continue well into the Testing Stage, they are usual behaviors rather than an Interaction Stage characteristic. Potential partners therefore should enjoy them while they last without necessarily expecting them to continue into the future.

Primary Risks of the Interaction Stage

Those who would sincerely relationship must be aware of three major risks that are typical of the Interaction Stage. Knowledge of Relationshipping theory and use of contract communication make it possible to negotiate these predictable risks. However, to negotiate them successfully, the Relationshipper must be certain the mind is engaged as well as the emotions. The Interaction Stage is a vulnerable time. One is relating to an unfamiliar person and tends to rely too readily on characteristics hopefully possessed rather than waiting for facts to be demonstrated. A person is then unpleasantly surprised unless he or she realizes that certain dangers are inherent and natural in every new beginning.

High Drop-Out Rate

The first major risk is the high drop-out rate. Most initial interactions do not lead to Relationshipping. Quite often, as disappointing as it may be, there is a lack of mutual chemistry or a mis-match in compatibility. Sometimes it is a matter of the right point in time. Dora is convinced that she and Ned are perfect for each other. He is so preoccupied with the pain of his divorce that he isn't romantically interested in anyone. It is the wrong point in time for him with Dora and if she pursues Ned, she will be linked in his mind with the divorce time. Todd, another eligible male, was divorced two years ago, but he is intent on making up for all the women he didn't sleep with during a faithful twenty years of marriage. He is looking for action, not Relationshipping. It's the wrong point in time.

Whether the high drop-out rate results from a lack of chemistry, a mis-match in compatibility, or simply a matter of bad timing, it is one risk that cannot be avoided. A person's negative reactions, however, can be controlled to the extent that the dropout rate is no longer threatening. Penguins forget that the matching process requires random sampling and feel as if they have failed. They continue to interact, and the list of potential partners they have "lost" becomes longer. They then project that the process of failure will continue forever and begin also to feel cynical and bitter. People must accept the high drop-out rate as a normal characteristic of the Interaction Stage and cognitively fight any feelings of hopelessness and helplessness. There truly is someone for everyone although sometimes considerable time may be needed before one encounters the other. People who allow themselves to become cynical and bitter will not be psychologically available when the encounter occurs.

Too Much Too Soon

Too Much Too Soon is the second risk of the Interaction Stage. People who completely immerse themselves in each other frequently burn each other out. Also, Too Much Too Soon is often the result of encountering either the Clinger or the Magician.

The Clinger is easily recognizable because he or she instantly falls is love and doesn't want the potential partner out of sight or sound. It is more than affection and companionship that the Clinger wants from a potential partner; the Clinger wants that person's life's blood. Dependent and insecure, the Clinger will attempt to absorb the potential partner if allowed. Initially, all of this attention is flattering and gratifying. Soon it begins to feel demanding and stifling. The only hope with a Clinger is to develop a contract. Clingers like contracting because it guarantees interactions. Potential partners like contracting with Clingers because it gives them information that is not obvious under the penguin system. For example, no matter what is contracted, it will not be enough for the Clinger. He or she does not want to be a part of one's life; he or she wants to *be* one's life. Another advantage to contract communication with Clingers is that the system offers the opportunity to renegotiate to a different category of Relationshipping. Clingers who can accept friendshipping instead of romance often become loyal friends. Finally, if re-negotiation is not possible, contracting provides a natural ending after a few interactions. It is notoriously difficult to extricate oneself from the Clinger unless people have agreed in advance to a natural ending point.

David re-met Lucille at a singles party. He had originally met and danced with her at a party about five months previously and thought her an attractive and interesting woman. This time they spent most of the evening together and exchanged phone numbers. About a week later Lucille called him just to talk, and David found her attention very flattering. They began to talk fairly often on the phone and he supported her regarding some personal problems she confided to him. It was not long before she wanted to come over to his house, fix dinner, etc. Within a few months David was hiding in his own home while Lucille banged on the door demanding to be admitted. A few phone calls a week had advanced to four or five a day, and a visit to fix dinner for him developed to demands to eat nearly all their meals together. Lucille wanted David's every waking moment, and it no longer felt flattering. When he quit answering the phone, she laid siege to his house, became vindictive, and called his friends with wild stories and accusations. A contract could have held Lucille at bay and provided a framework for discussion and definition of their Relationshipping. Instead, David found himself being forced to be as vicious as Lucille in order to extricate himself from the involvement.

Most Clingers are more pitiful than aggressive. Typically they will say, "I'm not angry. I'm just hurt." The covert contract they will attempt to establish is for the potential partner not to hurt their feelings. As there is more normal time and contact together, it becomes almost impossible to avoid hurting their feelings unless one acquiesces to a Siamese-twin sort of existence. If the potential partner objects, he or she becomes the unfeeling villain in this piece and the Clinger becomes the poor victim. Potential partners can look forward to being at fault for whatever unpleasant events occur. That is, it will be their fault unless there is a contract. With contracts one has the opportunity to discuss events and come to agreements either before or after the case in point. Contracts defeat the Clinger's indirect maneuvering, create the opportunity for re-definition of the Relationshipping, and also provide for a graceful exit if necessary.

Contracting with Clingers is both preventive and protective. It prevents the evolution of covert contracts and helps protect against feelings of blame and guilt. If one wants to relationship with a Clinger, it protects from being swallowed up. If, on the other hand, one doesn't want the role of being totally responsible for another's feelings, contracting also offers the way out.

If one runs into the Magician, it feels very different from interacting with the Clinger. The Clinger has "forever" in mind (every moment of forever) while the Magician is known for his or her disappearing act. The Magician comes in two varieties: temporary and permanent. The temporary Magician is incapable of more than superficial Relationshipping for a particular period of time, usually because of a recent or unresolved event. People in the midst of separation and divorce are classic examples. Many seek new companions but are unable to connect emotionally because they are preoccupied with the on-going termination. Feeling emotionally intimate with the new companion raises fears that the separation process may have to be endured again in the future. They often consequently disappear as the Relationshipping becomes more indepth. Other examples of temporary Magicians are people emotionally preoccupied regarding problems at work or school, illness of a dying relative, or other situational troubles. The temporary Magician is usually easily identifiable because the causative factor is either conversationally or visibly obvious.

The permanent Magician is identifiable only by his or her behavior patterns. He or she does not usually have a history of long-term Relationshipping and can be very elusive. The permanent Magician is incapable of healthy bonding. Because of deep seated conflicts formed at an early age, the permanent Magician can be dependent but can never truly love.

Both varieties of the Magician are incapable of in-depth Relationshipping. The Magician thrives on the excitement of new potential partners. Somehow he or she has confused the initial thrill of discovery with true love. The Magician therefore loses interest when the emotions are less tumultuous and, unfortunately for the Magician, when true loving has a chance to develop. In a rare piece of feedback, one Magician told a woman with whom he was terminating, "I prefer the excitement of creating new relationships to the work of maintaining ones I have." Despite his many romantic forays, this man was basically relationshipless because he never went beyond a somewhat superficial Interaction Stage.

Contracting with the Magician is important because he or she often vanishes without warning. In fact, his or her Great Disappearing Act often occurs shortly following an event of extraordinary closeness.

"I don't understand it", said Caroline who had been dating Tim just over six months. "We had a wonderful time driving to the East Coast together, and I even met his parents who live there. He told his mother he hoped she liked me because I just might be around for a very long time. It's almost like he was talking about marriage. But then since we got back, I've hardly seen him, and my girlfriend said she saw him out with someone else last week."

Randy says, "It was the funniest thing. It's like she just sort of went cold. In December with all the Christmas parties and everything happening, we were together almost every day and night. We had a super time and everything felt so natural. Maybe we were together too much. I don't know. All I know is in January she wasn't that interested in being with me. She still went out with me, but it was like her heart wasn't in it. She was just going through the motions. And then she was too busy to go out with me, and then I knew it was over."

In addition to their unpredictability, another trouble with Magicians is their distractibility. They are often developing two and sometimes three potential partners simultaneously. For a few years there was a fellow I called Flynn (after the swashbuckling Errol) who wreaked emotional havoc among the women in the area. Although I never met him, I came to feel I knew him well. I had that feeling because upon terminating with a woman, he would send her to me for help in getting over him. An eligible bachelor who had charm, good looks, and a well-paying job, Flynn could (and did) burn ten women in one year. No matter how delightful his current companion, he was continually distracted by what he had waiting in the wings.

Magicians often like contracting because it is new and different. Initially, they are quite involved in the principles but as the Disappearing Act looms imminent, they are less interested in communicating or negotiating. This attitude provides a valuable clue to the partner of what is to come. Also, a partner who has fulfilled all the terms of the agreement need not wonder what went wrong or have self doubts regarding his or her contribution to the disappearance.

The Magician can be a gift. There are many who believe the pleasures of interacting with the Magician are well worth the pain of dealing with the loss. This attitude is prevalent only among those who have learned to identify possible Magicians from their contracting behaviors. Since Magician fans are alert and aware, the Great Disappearing Act does not take them or their egos by surprise. They make the choice of involvement fully aware of the probable and eventual loss.

Those who do not contract with Magicians and Clingers, those who otherwise are caught up in Too Much Too Soon, and those who personalize the high drop-out rate nearly always fall victim to the third major risk of the Interaction Stage.

Perceived Rejection

It is impossible to be rejected the number of times rejection is perceived. It is as if a person expects to be rejected so greatly that he or she mentally manufactures it. Almost any excuse will do. Not being asked (or being turned down) to dance, being alone when others are in couples, not having a date for a big event or a holiday or just a Saturday night. Rejection is more of a felt attitude than an actual event. People who are lonely will cause themselves to feel rejected simply because they have no partner. Being alone does not equal rejection. Being accepted by just anyone does not resolve the issue. People who over-perceive rejection, however, over-value acceptance. They often become involved with unsuitable potential partners who do not match in terms of chemistry, compatibility, and/or value systems. When the mis-match is apparent and the potential partner withdraws, they then feel rejected *again*. Rejection simply does not occur the number of times people perceive it to happen.

Developmental Tasks of the Interaction Stage

Decide and Define

People who would abandon trumped up fears of rejection are delighted to discover that the first developmental task of the Interaction Stage is to decide whether a Relationshipping situation is desired and then to define what category of Relationshipping is appropriate. This means actively seeking potential partners instead of passively keeping a tally of how many one doesn't have.

Since the desire to relationship is based on the criteria of chemistry, compatibility, and similar values, it is necessary to devise methods of acquainting oneself with the potential partner before a decision can be reached. It would be nice if a person could walk into a made-to-order situation like the old fairy tales depict, but this is impossible. Instead, the preferred method of acquainting oneself with a possible partner is to become involved in a regular on-going task-oriented group. Translated into English, this means that a Relationshipper should join a club or organization that meets regularly with basically the same people and focuses on something the members have in common besides being single, lonely, and basically unhappy about being single and lonely. The regular meeting times allow developing acquaintances while the outside task provides structure without pressure.

Classes from local community colleges on skills, hobbies, or basic information are ideal. So are similar classes and lecture series offered by museums, stock brokers, and local businesses. One woman took a course from a local lumber yard and in addition to learning how to build her own redwood deck also developed a rich contract with a fellow do-it-yourselfer. Little Theatre groups, choirs, civic organizations, and special interest groups all equally qualify. In addition to obtaining exposure to possible romantic partners with similar interests and values, a person also has the opportunity to develop new friends and increase skills and knowledge. No law requires one to commit for life to these groups. If no one interesting or available participates, or if the activity is not enjoyable, another organization may be visited.

The singles bar/club is the worst location to seek a potential partner. In spite of the usual self-lies and rationalizations ("I just like to dance" or "I just like to listen to the music and have a drink" or "I just like to talk with my friends"), the driving common denominator is loneliness, and the success or failure of the evening depends on how well a person can sexually market himself or herself. It is not impossible to find a potential partner, but it is necessary to transfer from the singles bar/club atmosphere as soon as possible in order for the Relationshipping to have as much chance as possible to succeed. Interactions that are begun in a sexual-based atmosphere rarely evolve beyond sex based interactions. It is difficult to avoid the bedroom implications in locations where Axiom I of the Penguin Society is so dominant.

Many of my students use the singles bar/club to hunt. Their rationale: it has the highest concentration of Relationshipping candidates available. Their short-term goal is to identify interesting men and women who they can then invite to activities in a different environment. Audrey, Beatrice, and Faye use this system to accumulate a list of people who they invite to periodic casual no-trouble parties. Audrey likes to have wine, cheese, and conversation get-togethers. Beatrice has subscription television service and has the list over when a good movie is being run. Faye organizes groups to go to see events together — a play, a football game, a popular entertainer. In this way, they develop a group situation wherein they can become acquainted with potential partners out of the sexually charged bar atmosphere. Even here the population is constantly changing. Last year it was Hazel, Rosa, and Mary (each now friendshipping and Relationshipping with partners developed from the lists) who used this system.

The developmental task of decide and define places an active focus on determining compatibility, chemistry, and value systems within a framework in which these characteristics are apparent. It allows potential partners to become involved cognitively rather than the penguin system of being swept away by chemistry.

Develop Trust

The second developmental task of the Interaction Stage, developing trust, is basic and essential to successful Relationshipping. It is much more than sexual fidelity and it is at the core of true intimacy and closeness. Quite often in marriage counseling cases, one or the other troubled partner will cry, "He (or she) broke our wedding vow!" I always respond with the question: "Which one?"

Generally, when one marries one makes four vows: a person promises to love, honor and cherish, and keep oneself to the partner only . . . It is in the first three as well as in the fourth that trust is a real issue. There are many couples who are absolutely faithful but for whom there exists little trust because of the lack of honoring and cherishing. To love someone is to make oneself vulnerable, and because of that vulnerability, it is important to feel honored and cherished.

In the Interaction Stage communication is one of the primary characteristics. One tells the potential partner almost everything one thinks and feels (that won't hurt their feelings or cause them to "reject" one). As a part of the primary feeling of "false" intimacy, one tells one's mistakes, one's regrets, one's failures, and one's sore spots. Trust involves not having the potential partner misuse that information in the future. It involves trusting one will receive humane treatment, not only in the social customs, but regarding feelings, opinions, and decisions. Trust involves confidence that the potential partner will do what he or she says he or she is going to do . It involves consistency. It involves taking one's side in public — even if a person is maybe just a little wrong — because that person is more important to the potential partner than the stranger or friend who is on the other side. The trust issue begins in the Interaction Stage and is reinforced or destroyed as people interact with each other over time.

Develop Behavior Contracts

As people continue to interact and evaluate the trust factor, behavioral contracts are developing without their conscious awareness. It is simply a matter of responding to each other and it happens quite naturally. In the Interaction Stage, almost anything a potential partner does is alright with the other. However, as has been stated, any behavior that is repeated twice comes to be expected, and there are some behavioral contracts that partners would rather not develop.

If Jethro is late several times and met with understanding behavior by Matilda, they then have a behavioral contract that tardiness is acceptable. If Ann often drinks too much and Perry acts tolerant, then getting drunk is okay. If a couple generally does the activity only one partner prefers, the two people agree to one partner's dominating the couple.

Develop Feedback

The development of behavioral contracts cannot be prevented, but they can be influenced to be positive contracts by utilizing feedback, another developmental task. It is not as easy as it sounds. Penguins like to do their business in an indirect manner.

"Harris knew I disapproved of his behavior at the party because I kept frowning at him", said Penny. "That's not true!" said Harris. "I thought you had a headache."

Belinda shows her disapproval by not speaking to Rodd for three days. He knows he's done something wrong, but he's not sure just what it was.

Early on the Relationshipping continuum, most penguins don't want to rock the boat so they do not disapprove either physically or verbally, thinking that a change will occur later. Instead, they guarantee themselves more of the same. Feedback prevents misinterpretation, confusion, and inadvertent behavior that causes a negative effect. It is a verbal system that informs one's partner how one views his or her behavior and how one is feeling about other people and events. Penguins do not realize that if a person is consistently provided with positive feedback, that person will tend to be open rather than defensive when the time comes for negative feedback. If there is a consistent system in which both positives and negatives are exchanged regularly in order to move toward compromise together, a couple develops a mutual system of communication and working together.

Feelings cannot currently be measured and thoughts cannot be read. Perhaps a futuristic society will indeed develop these skills. One of my patients is hopeful that a mad scientist will invent a gadget that will flash colored lights and register feelings of happiness, praise, irritation, anger, and approval. She would like to have it surgically installed in her husband's forehead. They have never developed feedback.

A mad scientist cannot substitute for a person's own work. Feedback is an information system that only each person can provide. Since thought and feeling processes are internal, effort is required to present those thoughts and feelings in an external direct manner. It must be done verbally because behaviors are open to misinterpretation. Like Penny, who thought she was clearly disapproving, and Harris who as clearly thought she had a headache, one can never be positive that the partner will guess exactly what one wants to convey unless the information is provided directly and verbally.

Feedback does not imply that the information will be pleasant. In fact, the fear of unpleasant feedback is precisely why penguins avoid such open communication. There is the idea that a potential partner's feelings might be hurt, that one person might think badly of the other, or (Heaven forbid!) that there might be conflict. Thus the potential partner is deprived of knowing valuable attitudes and feelings which might otherwise produce quite different behavior. If the potential partner reacts badly to the information, if he or she views the other as stupid and/or unreasonable for having those feelings and attitudes, then the originating potential partner receives valuable feedback. He or she realizes that this person is not worthy of trust and is not willing to participate mutually in Relationshipping. This data is necessary to evaluate whether it is a good idea to proceed along the continuum with this person.

Unpleasant information is nonetheless information. Although the penguin society would label it top-secret and withhold it from the person who could most use it, silence inhibits compromise and closeness and forces potential partners into relationshit. Feedback is the burglar alarm announcing invading unhealthy behaviors between two people. It keeps potential problems in the open where they can be discussed and resolved. It provides for the safety of the Relationshipping.

In spite of sometimes receiving unpleasant information, establishing feedback is often the most enjoyable of the Interaction Stage developmental tasks. Relationshippers are surprised to discover that most potential partners have attitudes of "Tell me what you like and I'll do it again!" as well as "Tell me what you don't like and I won't do it any more!"

Joel says, "The thing I like about Margo is she lets me know what's going on. I can't correct what I don't know about. I'm making less mistakes with Margo than I have with anyone else and it's because she tells me what she likes and what she doesn't."

No one wants to duplicate past unhappy experiences which occurred for the most part out of ignorance. Most partners therefore appreciate any information which will prevent their having to make the same mistakes again. They also enjoy having their positive points reinforced. Mutual interchange happens so naturally in the Interaction

Stage that it is the ideal time to develop a system to insure that feedback will be natural along the farther and more crucial stages of the continuum.

Since the Interaction Stage is highly emotional and permeated with penguin customs, help is needed to aid the Relationshipper to focus on developmental tasks and resist being drawn into relationshit. This help is provided with the use of certain questions which each person should ask himself or herself in regard to the potential partner. Satisfactory answers to the questions provide data as to whether Relationshipping with this person is a viable possibility.

Interaction Stage Questions

1. *Is this person open to new ideas?*

    A partner who is rigid or inflexible has a major handicap in Relationshipping. This is a person who is convinced that there is a certain way to do a certain thing and that there is no other way. He or she will have difficulty appreciating another person's point of view and will not generally be accepting of a shift from indirect penguin systems to open, direct, and mutual Relationshipping. The need to be open to new ideas is often mistakenly dismissed in the tide of a high chemistry attraction. However, being a couple nowadays is a complicated enterprise often involving former mates, here-again, gone-again children, and pre-existing commitments. The key to survival is often innovation and flexibility, and chemistry cannot compensate for an inability to adapt.

2. *Does this person make commitments?*

    A potential partner who has difficulty making commitments will have trouble bonding and will not be able to progress along the continuum beyond superficial interactions unless he or she is very dependent. Evaluating prior Relationshipping experiences (both romantic and friendship) and other social commitments such as clubs and organizations provide clues to a possible Magician. Such evaluation also gives a general idea about capacity for emotional investment.

3. *Does this person follow-through on commitments?*

    A potential partner who does not follow-through on commitments can never be completely trusted. People who do not give their word seriously generally do not regard Relationshipping seriously. However, a person who makes commitments and follows through on those commitments is genuinely invested and can be trusted to respond.

4. *Does this person communicate directly?*

To avoid relationshit there must be open and direct communication. Otherwise, potential partners are reduced to guesswork and mindreading and are vulnerable to distortions and misinterpretations. If the potential partner does not communicate directly, he or she will often be defensive and evasive, and there will be difficulty identifying and resolving problems. Unless the person is trainable, vital communication will be missing.

5. *Does this person communicate honestly?*

A potential partner who does not communicate honestly will say what one wants to hear rather than what he or she really thinks and feels. This person is over-eager to please and overly fearful of rejection. One can rarely know his or her true attitudes until it reaches crisis proportions. The innocent party will then be resentfully accused of taking advantage and of being selfish.

6. *Is there a difference between philosophy and action?*

A potential partner who has a difference between thoughts and actions will give mixed messages and will have mixed expectations. It will be difficult to evaluate compatibility because opposite attitudes often exist simultaneously. For example, a man may indicate an intellectual support for women's rights and may verbalize an admiration for independent women while his dating behavior — making all the decisions, not understanding why she would want to go without him, and generally "taking care" of a woman so that she has little independence — indicates a preference for dependent women. Interacting with such persons creates confusion as to their real attitudes. The easy rule to remember is: When there is a difference between what a person says and what a person does, the true attitude is always what he or she does. If there are many such contradictions, it is better to seek another possible partner who will be more consistent.

Individually applied to each Relationshipping candidate throughout the Interaction Stage, the answers to the six questions give valuable data as to the capacity for being open, for emotional investment, and for communication. Evaluation of the resulting information provides good indications as to whether Relationshipping with this person is viable.

Interaction Stage Summary

The Interaction Stage is a time of excitement and anxiety that at first features a changing kaleidoscope of prospective partners. Upon mutual selection, a couple begins a series of interactions together on a Relationshipping continuum to determine if they have the appropriate chemistry, compatibility, and values for a successful match. As the two people venture along the continuum together, they experience certain typical and predictable feelings, characteristics, and risks. By reacting to these feelings, characteristics, and risks in current acceptable but destructive patterns, they often make penguins of themselves and predispose the Relationshipping to failure. These mistakes are avoidable if the parties focus on the developmental tasks required of the Interaction Stage and if the parties are willing to shift to a healthy and more open system of interacting. Creating open direct agreements instead of allowing covert behavioral contracts is a hallmark of that successful system, and should begin immediately within the Interaction Stage.

CHAPTER VI

Contract Communication: Interaction Stage

Those who resist contracting as communication often say they have difficulty with the word usage rather than the concept. The word "contract" has legal overtones, they say, and it also sounds much too final and committing. However, upon further discussion, I find that few actually have courtroom concerns, and the real difficulty is their strong penguin indoctrination. The penguin system is indirect and requires its participants to shy away from giving or receiving information that could intellectually be used to understand and adjust. The basis of their system is to protect against personal risk. The tragedy and contradiction is that by not being direct, the same personal risk is guaranteed and magnified.

Applying contracting to Relationshift theory is the only effective alternative to relationshit. It is the only vaccine against chronic and recurring personal pain. Carefully matched to the feelings, characteristics, and risks involved in each stage of development, contracting minimizes anxiety and provides for understanding of what is required for a successful match. Instead of floating helplessly on a current of misdirection and manipulation, a couple is guided by a series of agreements to experience the natural gifts of communicating and interacting together. There are no victims in the Relationshift: either a match is viable or the participants understand why it is not.

The effect of contracting is to create an atmosphere of mutuality and non-defensive negotiation. When two people are working together instead of pulling against each other, the common dangers and disruptions are easily avoided. It is especially important to begin healthy habits in the Interaction Stage when patterns of communication and interaction together are being established. It is the foundation which will either crumble or which will remain beautifully bonded when later predictable difficulties arise.

The two forms for Interaction Stage contracts are the simple initial contract and the interim contract. These Interaction Stage contracts are not threatening and they are not difficult. They do require follow-through and a short-term commitment because part of their purpose is to defeat the anxiety and mistakes of penguin practices, such as The Six

Hour Chance. Both contract structures provide for the opportunity to acquaint each other with a potential partner, set up some basic ground rules, and begin the rudiments of open communication through feedback. For people who are sincere in Relationshipping, it is a no-lose situation.

Simple Initial Contracts

A simple initial contract contains six basic clauses: a definition of purpose, a time and contact period, a privileges clause, a cancellation clause, a sex clause (when applicable), and a feedback clause. Depending on the individuals involved and their primary concerns, there may be more clauses included, but these basics must always be present as they provide for security, understanding, and communication.

Definition of Purpose

The definition of purpose is the extremely important guideline that keeps the emotional involvement consistent with footage on the continuum. There is no confusion as to why two people are doing what they are doing because they have defined it in advance. There is no fear as to where they are going because clear limits are set. Each knows the intentions of the other at that particular point in time on the continuum. Typical definitions of purpose in simple initial contracts are as follows:

"To get to know each other better to decide if we want to develop friendshipping or dating."

"To determine if we are compatible and have similar values to go along with our chemistry."

"To find out if we want to develop a supportive friendshipping outside the office."

"To see if Relationshipping long-distance is workable."

"To set up ground rules for . . . (a specific task) to see if they work."

In simple initial contracts, the phrasing of the definition of purpose always indicates the exploratory nature and trial-and-error reality of the new joint venture. As a result, fairy-tale expectations recede and attention is given to the purpose at hand.

Time and Contact Period

For a simple initial contract, the recommended time and contact period is four interactions in six weeks with a variety of activities. This is a little less than an average of once a week and provides for some "settling down" distance following interactions. The pre-planned series of time together greatly reduces anxiety and protects against the Too Much Too Soon syndrome. Initial contractors report that their greatest fear — "losing" the potential partner — rapidly disappears with the agreement for a series of contacts. Of course, there is the risk that the potential partner will not honor the agreement and will simply not appear for the scheduled interactions. In this case the initial contractor discovers that the potential partner is not trustworthy and does not follow through on commitments. Such a person is not a good risk for sincere Relationshipping.

For those who insist on more frequent contact, it is not outlandish to see each other once a week or, in extreme circumstances, twice a week. However, in these cases the contract period should be shortened to one month rather than the usual six weeks.

Privileges Clauses

Privileges may be included in one clause or in a series of clauses as long as they are clearly enumerated. Typical privileges discussed are telephone access (frequency and length), financing (Dutch treat or otherwise), and exclusivity (other friends and dates are, or are not, allowable). A "say no" privilege is also often included which states that each party has the privilege and the obligation to "say no" to any activity that is inconvenient or uncomfortable for that person. Other privileges may be added according to the individual concerns and preferences of the contractors as long as there is agreement by both parties.

Cancellation Clause

This clause provides for the necessary cancellation of pre-arranged interactions due to illness or unexpected events such as a death in the family or unexpected out of town business. *It is not a provision for cancellation of the contract* since the initial contract itself is very short-term. There is the assumption that two people will not agree to contract initially if they are not sincerely interested in knowing each other better. Therefore this clause provides only for cancellation and re-scheduling of activities in case of emergency. People who fear the partner will not appear for a planned interaction may reassure themselves with this clause.

Sex Clause

Sex too soon has damaged more people and lost more opportunities regarding romantic Relationshipping than any other behavior or attitude. Since early sex confuses the issues and places an inappropriate focus, a "no sex" clause is strongly recommended for initial romantic contracting. Partners agree not only that they will avoid sexual intercourse, but also that they will not be seductive with each other. In this way they can concentrate on truly and seriously getting to know one another without the artificial intimacy and sexual politics of the penguin society. People become oriented to being close in other ways. The ability to express caring through other behaviors increases the trust factor and reinforces that partners are appreciated for themselves rather than primarily for sex. It is best to begin possible romances with a "no sex" clause. However, it is not too late if sex too soon has already occurred. Couples in the Interaction Stage may voluntarily agree to abstain sexually while focusing on other issues of compatibility and similar values. By giving up sex at this stage, one partner says to the other, "You are a special and valuable person in and of yourself. I want to know you and be with you with or without secondary benefits to myself."

The sex clause is always present in opposite sex Relationshipping or same sex Relationshipping if the participants are gay. There are too many people who confuse closeness with sexuality for the sex issue to be bypassed. Even if the definition of the Relationshipping specifies friendshipping, the sexual aspects should be clearly stated.

Feedback Clause

The feedback clause, last of the required clauses, provides for information and communication. It takes advantage of the Interaction Stage characteristic in which potential partners have the urge for verbal outpour. With feedback this outpouring becomes directed and honest. The feedback clause provides for discussion following each interaction, and a summary discussion at the end of the contract period. Focusing on compatibility, values, and chemistry, each gives the other impressions of their time and activities together.

Ray's discussion with Barbara is typical of feedback at the end of a first activity together:

"Gee, Barbara, you are a good listener. I have really enjoyed our time together but I feel a little uncomfortable because I did all the talking. I don't know if we have a lot in common but you're certainly easy to talk to and you're nice to look at, too. Do you feel I monopolized the conversation?"

"Well, you did talk a lot and I would like you to get a chance to know me, too. And I liked the things you had to say, like what you're looking for in Relationshipping and how you don't want to make the same mistakes again. I've enjoyed our time."

Barbara's feedback indicates she liked what she heard from Ray, and he now has the opportunity to be sure in their next interaction that he does more listening and encourages Barbara to talk. However, Barbara's feedback could have been of a different variety:

"Well, you did talk a lot, but I learned what's important to you and frankly, I don't think we have that much in common. You like the out-of-doors and I like in-doors things. You're allergic to cats and I have three of them. I really couldn't think of too much to say because I'm afraid we're so opposite."

Ray now has the opportunity to negotiate instead of perceiving himself as rejected. He says:

"Listen, Barbara, those are only a few of the things I'm interested in. I bet if we had talked more together instead of me being a motor-mouth, we could have found more things in common. Besides, seeing different viewpoints and talking about them is important. Maybe we'll end up being friends instead of dating, but let's really get to know each other and find out."

If Ray had merely asked Barbara if she had enjoyed the evening, she would in either case have said yes. However, by offering her feedback and by her direct responses, both are more in tune with the thoughts and reactions of the potential partner. Both know where to focus their efforts in the next interaction together. Neither has to guess what the other is thinking and feeling, and the beginnings of true communication have been established. At the end of their first activity together, there is already an atmosphere of mutuality.

In addition to these six basic clauses, a written simple initial contract is dated, has a definite expiration date, and is signed by both parties. It is not necessary to be fancy or eloquent. Simple initial contracts have been sent to me which were written on the back of restaurant placemats, cocktail napkins, and purse sized notepads. It does not matter if they are handwritten, typed, or marked with crayons. It is not the medium but the message that counts. The important item is the clear understanding of two people with regard to: why they are seeing each other, how long it will last, what is allowed and what isn't, what to do in case of emergency, the limit of sexual involvement when applicable, and how impressions and information will be passed from one to the other. How each understands and follows through on these agreements determines the beginnings of trust and communication.

Many contractors do not use a written form of the simple initial contract. Because of the short time period and the few clauses, it is not difficult to remember what has been agreed, and they find a verbal form works well for them. However, it is preferred to become habituated to the written form because later longer contracting periods are not as easily recalled to mind. Clauses are added and there is more time to interact. Although a verbal form is better than no form, those who begin their contracting in writing usually continue in writing and there can be no confusion later as to the actual contract.

Jerry and Jackie's contract is an example of a verbal simple initial which was reported to me on the telephone and later written down. It is a basic agreement and eaily negotiated in conversation.

Contract between Jerry and Jackie
October 28

Purpose: To get to know each other in a safe system to find out if we want to develop a long-term dating situation.

1. This contract will last six weeks and we agree to see each other four times in that six weeks with a variety of activities.
2. Arrangements for each date will be made in-between times by telephone by Jerry.
3. Jerry will assume financial responsibility for each activity and Jackie will be considerate of his finances.
4. If cancellation is necessary, either party will call the other as soon as possible and another date will be scheduled at that time.
5. There will be no sex.
6. Both can date other people.
7. Feedback and evaluation will be on Dec. 12 at 8:00 pm at Paddy's Paddock and will be Dutch Treat. We will meet there.

This contract briefly contains all the basics and includes a provision for Jackie to be considerate of Jerry's finances. Other simple initial contracts, like the following one by Rick and Sue, contain a few more personal provisions.

Separated for a year, Rick and his wife were discussing settlement (not amiably) and were approaching finalization of their divorce at the time of this contract with Sue who had been divorced for seven years. In spite of Rick's tendency to ventilate for hours about his unhappy marriage and his wife's current "unreasonable" demands, Sue decided to break her personal rule of not becoming involved with a man in the midst of divorce. The chemistry was high and the stress level was comparable. Through the contract Sue attempted to keep the emotions separated.

First Contract between Rick and Sue
August 15

Purpose: To determine if we are compatible enough to establish romantic Relationshipping.

1. There will be a minimum of four dates in six weeks to be set up from one date to another with a "say no" privilege in regard to activities planned.
2. If something comes up and a date has to be broken, an explanation will be given if not at that time, then as soon as possible, and a new time will be arranged.
3. It's okay to date other people.
4. One half-hour of any given date will be spent on past events. If something comes up at times other than those times set aside for us, we can meet and discuss what is bothering us, but this will be a separate time and not on time which is set aside for us.
5. Either person may call the other at will during the period of this contract.
6. No sex during the time of this contract, with the right of one person to tell the other to take a break if things get carried away.
7. This contract will end on Oct. 1st at which time we will meet at Sue's house at 7:30 pm to discuss the effects of contracting together.

Signed:

Clause four reflects Rick's current emotional turmoil and Sue's concern regarding basing their conversation, and thus their Relationshipping, on events rising from this difficult time in his life. This clause restricts Rick from using their date time to ventilate. His divorce as a primary topic of conversation would give them little opportunity to discover each other. However, the clause also provides for separate and distinct "support" time if either is under stress regarding past situations. Clause six is a compromise. The other clauses are standard ingredients.

Some simple initial contracts are very specific. D'Artagnan and Meg were very cautious about emotional involvement and insistent on feedback. Their otherwise general simple initial contract was very specific in those particular areas. D'Artagnan and Meg had met while enrolled in the same night class. Meg, divorced for two years and not yet having dated, was immediately attracted to this good looking charmer. D' was separated from his wife of 18 years but not totally committed to his lover of two years. Both D' and Meg realized they could learn a great deal about themselves and the opposite sex from each other.

Relationshipping Contract:
D'Artagnan and Meg

Purpose: To get to know each other in a comfortable system to determine whether we want to develop a friendship or dating situation.

1. The contract will begin on Oct. 24 and end on Nov. 12. We will meet three times. On Nov. 12 we will give each other final feedback and decide where we want to go from there.
2. It is further agreed that there will be involvement with no emotional commitment nor exclusivity.
3. We agree that personal and confidential matters will not be discussed with anyone else.

4. Communication must be open and honest without fear of hurting the other's feelings. We will have a minimum of ½ hour feedback at the end of each of the three meetings. We must have both positive and negative feedback — the goal here is growth!
5. Either person agrees to unlimited phone calls, but never past 11:00 pm.
6. Finances will be Dutch Treat.
7. There will be no sexual involvement.
8. Each party agrees to be flexible regarding date, time, and activity with a "say no" clause.

Signed:

Vickie and Elaine's simple initial contract was specific in a different way. It concerned defining ground rules for a particular task. Vickie and Elaine had been on the singles' circuit so long they had it down to a science. They were close friends but had no intention of letting their friendshipping interfere with their endeavors to meet men. This contract was developed to provide safety factors, enhance their individual chances, and prevent each from stepping on the other's toes in the process.

Vickie and Elaine's Hunting Contract
January 9

Purpose: This is to set up ground rules for when we go out to meet men.

1. Unless specifically discussed before hand, only Vickie and Elaine will go and no other women will be invited to sit at our table.
2. We will go in our own separate cars and meet in the parking lot and wait for each other if necessary.
3. We will walk in together and sit together. Neither will leave the bar without telling the other.
4. We will not invite any man to sit at our table. If either wants to sit and talk with a man, we will go to his table or somewhere else other than our table.
5. Our code sentence is: "Did I tell you my aunt in Georgia has to have surgery?" That means one of us has a problem, and as soon as possible after hearing it, we will meet in the ladies' room to discuss it.
6. We will plan to go out every Thursday night unless discussed in advance and another night scheduled.
7. On Friday we will contact each other by telephone and discuss the previous night's events, especially if one of us has broken these rules.
8. We may also do other things together as arranged.
9. This contract will continue for three months. We will meet at Vickie's house on April 12 to give feedback on how it has worked for us.

Signed:

Clarice and Diane were friends at work and their contract involved evaluating the further development of that friendshipping. They had known each other several years but had never had any contact outside the office setting. Clarice was a widow and Diane had been divorced for about eight months. Diane's recently changed marital status was the motivation for the contract. She was trying to enrich and expand her resource group.

Clarice and Diane's Contract
April 2

Purpose: To find out if we want to develop a supportive friendship outside the office.

1. We agree to planning and following-through on six activities outside the office in the next two months.
2. Two of these activities will include our children and be family-oriented activities.
3. The other four will be a variety for the two of us such as seeing a show, shopping, having dinner, or going to a Parents Without Partners meeting.
4. All activities will be Dutch Treat.
5. Clarice will keep Diane's children the last weekend in April, giving Diane a free week-end.
6. Diane will keep Clarice's children the last weekend in May, giving Clarice a free week-end.
7. This contract will end on June 15 and we will meet for a feedback session on June 20 with particular emphasis on what activities we enjoy most, how the children get along, and to decide if this system works for us.
8. We shall also have feedback the last half-hour of each activity.

Signed:

Some simple initial contracts provide for understanding and clarity in the out of the ordinary Relationshipping situation. Christopher and Hugger met at a convention (see Chapter V) and wanted to relationship in spite of living 150 miles apart and in spite of their active and involved lives. Chris balanced a full time job, graduate work, and joint custody arrangements for his seven year old son. Hugger had sole custody of her two grade school aged daughters and was also an active officer of several organizations in addition to her own full time job. Both Chris and Hugger were concerned about the miles between them. Both were also somewhat guarded with the fear that developing romantic Relationshipping at this point might interfere with their individual goals.

Christopher and Hugger's Long Distance Contract
February 18

Purpose: To determine if it is possible to develop loving, limited long distance Relationshipping.

Term: This contract is for three months with a June review.

Frequency: Only one weekend a month with next month's time being planned one month in advance.

Romance: We want the natural growth and development of romance and passion with each person verbalizing when and what is uncomfortable for that person. Sexual intercourse is prohibited for the term of this contract.

Phone: Either party may call to change arrangements or share experiences and/or feelings.

Cancels: There is to be no change unless it is an unavoidable high priority situation but arrangements can be changed without penalty.

Finances: Chris will assume financial responsibility but Hugger may contribute.

Feedback: During each interaction each partner will feedback behaviors that are liked and disliked with no obligation toward changing those behaviors.

Playing: We agree to play during each interaction with a combination of physical exercise and leisurely activities which will include a wide variety to be mutually planned and discussed.

Signed:

A simple initial contract is by definition the first contract that two people negotiate together. Although there is always an agreement resulting from the final feedback session, an ensuing contract is not automatic. Some simple initial contracts are time limited from the beginning. The following contract between D'Artagnan and Rand and the agreement between Toni and Bill were never intended to progress beyond the prescribed period. Their circumstances are self-explanatory.

A Contract between D' Artagnan and Rand
November 10

Purpose: To express the feelings of loneliness and loss of self-esteem as each of us is going through a divorce.

> We are to meet three times over a one month period for coffee, breakfast, or lunch for no more than two hours per visit. At the end of each meeting we will allow one half-hour for feedback.
>
> The term of the contract is one month only as both of us feel we should be able to have obtained confidence within that time.
>
> As we both realize it is difficult to communicate openly and honestly, we will make every effort to overcome this obstacle. Divorce and divorce feelings will be our only topic of conversation.
>
> We both agree we can have unlimited phone calls at any time of the day or night.
>
> Each is responsible for his own expenses.
>
> Emergency cancellations are to be re-scheduled as soon as possible.
>
> Both parties agree to the above terms written this tenth day of November:

Contract for a Summer Romance
July 10

Purpose: Toni and Bill agree to be partners for the summer, realizing that our geographical distance from each other as well as other emotional investments prohibit long-term Relationshipping. We agree to the following:
1. We shall see each other at will for the length of our mutual stay at this resort.
2. Our activities will be by mutual consent with "say no" privileges.
3. Bill assumes financial responsibility except when Toni wants to treat and that is to be at her invitation.

4. We shall be exclusive sexually for the term of this contract.
5. The contract will terminate on Saturday before Labor Day.
6. Feedback session will be at 2:00 pm at the dance pavillion on the Saturday before Labor Day.
7. We agree not to try to contact or see each other after the contract expires.

Signed:

Several options are available upon the expiration of the simple initial contract. The first option is to decide to continue no further. People may have identified obvious mismatches in chemistry, compatibility, or values. One or the other potential partner may not be able or ready to pursue further contracting. Also, people may have noticed that the potential partner consistently did not follow through on commitments during the course of the contract period. If one or both partners decide to continue no further, they discuss their reasons in the final feedback session. They also talk generally about how they will respond to each other should they run into each other in the future. People who choose the first option come to a feedback agreement.

The second option is to continue together under a different definition of purpose. Many Relationshippers begin contracting with romance in mind but renegotiate to friendshipping at the expiration of the simple initial contract. The reverse is also true of friendshippers who renegotiate to romance. If the second option is chosen, continuing potential partners discuss their feelings and reasons for renegotiation in the feedback session. They then progress to discussing provisions for the next step along the continuum: the interim contract. They leave the feedback meetings with their new interim contract agreement.

The third option is to continue together under the same definition of purpose in order to continue the evaluation process. During the feedback meeting, potential partners discuss their Relationshipping and add or refine clauses for the next time period together. Relationshippers continue along the Interaction Stage continuum together under a series of interim contracts.

The word interim implies an interval period between one step and another. A series of interim contracts focuses attention on developmental tasks, encourages open direct communication, ingrains feedback, and provides a medium to enter the Testing Stage without succumbing to remaining Interaction Stage pitfalls. Interim contracts build on the original simple initial agreements with opportunities to modify according to information obtained through interaction and feedback. Definitions of the Relationshipping may be expanded or completely changed. Time periods are extended from six weeks to three months. Contact is increased to once or a maximum of three times a week. A couple begins to negotiate preferences and to seek compromise.

Like the simple initial agreement, interim contracts contain a definition of purpose, provision for time and contact, privileges clauses, cancellation clause, sex clause (when applicable), and feedback clause. They also contain clauses relating to negotiation of any disagreement of opinion or preference that was noted during the simple initial contract period.

Examples and Progressions

The different potential partners who developed simple initial contracts earlier in this chapter chose different options at the expiration of their contracts. Some continued, some terminated, and some re-negotiated. The following are examples and progressions of what transpired in their Relationshipping.

Jerry and Jackie's simple initial contract had proceded without unusual incidents. They had observed no obvious differences regarding compatibility or value systems. Their chemistry level remained high. Both wanted to continue to explore Relationshipping.

Interim Contract between Jerry and Jackie
December 12

Purpose: To continue to get to know each other to evaluate our compatibility for long-term romance.

1. This contract will last three months and we agree to see each other for a formal date at least once a week with a maximum of three times a week.
2. Arrangements for the next date or time together will be made at the end of the current date. Spontaneous calls are okay with "say no" privileges. A variety of activities will be explored.
3. Jerry will continue to pay; low cost events will be encouraged.
4. Same cancellation clause as last time.
5. Sex is allowed.
6. Neither will begin dating anyone new, but can continue to follow-through on other existing contracts.
7. Either can call each other at will.
8. Feedback will be at Jackie's house on St. Patrick's Day. She will fix dinner and we will devote the evening to discussing likes and dislikes about our activities and time together.

Note: We agree to written contracts and also to jot down special items for feedback as we've learned that we forget the best parts.
Signed:

Feedback Agreement: Rick and Sue
Oct. 1

Whether or not we are compatible, we agree this is a bad time for Rick to pursue a romance. Instead of dating, we are going to be friends without any formal arrangements. If Rick needs someone to talk to, he can call or stop by Sue's house. If she needs an escort to an event, Sue can call Rick and if he is available, he will take her. After Rick is over his divorce, the option is open to try dating again and this is open to discussion at a later time.

During their simple initial contract D'Artagnan and Meg decided they liked each other too much to stop seeing each other, but the chemistry was not right to seek a romance. Also, Meg felt that D' was going through an irresponsible period in his life and did not feel he was interested in long term commitment. They therefore changed their definition of purpose and focused on supportive activities.

Interim Contract D'Artagnan and Meg
November 12

Purpose: To develop friendshipping and encourage each other's personal growth.

1. This contract will be for three months, beginning tonight and ending on February 12.
2. We will talk to each other on the phone at least once a week and plan two activities a month together.
3. We will help each other out. During this contract period, D' agrees to fix Meg's toilet and help her wallpaper the kitchen. During this contract period, Meg agrees to repair D's favorite sport coat and sew on some missing buttons on other clothes.
4. If either needs a date to a Christmas party, either will accompany the other if nothing is already scheduled. Limit: one party per person.
5. Our personal and confidential matters will not be discussed with anyone else.
6. Our communication will continue to be open and honest without fear of hurting the other's feelings. Formal feedback will be on Feb. 12, but if either does something the other doesn't like or especially does like, there will be immediate feedback.
7. It is recognized there is no romantic involvement and we are certainly not exclusive.
8. Unlimited phone calls are still okay, but not past eleven.
9. Finances will continue to be Dutch Treat except for office or Christmas parties and then it will be the treat of whoever's associated with that function.
10. There will be no sexual involvement and no kissy-face either. The object is to be friends.
11. We will continue to be flexible regarding date, time, and activities with "say no" privileges.

Signed:

Vickie and Elaine's Feedback Agreement:
April 12

Since Vickie has begun Relationshipping with Darryl and since they have recently agreed to an exclusive contract, we won't be going hunting together anymore. However, we will keep in phone contact and do other things together. If Vickie and Darryl break up, we will go back to the old contract which has worked very well for us. If Elaine develops Relationshipping with anyone, we will do some things together as couples.

Interim Contract: Clarice and Diane
June 20

Purpose: To continue our super supportive friendshipping outside the office.

1. We shall continue all provisions of our first contract for another three months with the following additions:
2. Money will be left with the hostess to cover costs of the children on the free weekends.
3. Discussions about other people in the office and about our personal lives will be kept confidential.
4. Each of us will keep the other's children one weekend during this contract period, times and dates to be arranged.
5. This contract will end Sept. 20 and feedback will occur at that time when we go out to dinner together.

Signed:

Sometimes simple initial contractors approach the feedback session with different ideas in mind: one wants to continue and one wants to stop. Such was the case with Christopher and Hugger.

As contracted, Chris and Hugger saw each other on only three occasions from March through May. However, with contact being from Friday evening through Sunday afternoon, they were together virtually every minute and the time was intensive. This was dissipated somewhat by periods of working on professional and academic projects which was not consistent with the "playing" clause in their contract. There was no deviation on other clauses. Both noticed a dramatic increase in telephone bills. In progress, the sending of cards and notes was added to the list of privileges. During feedback after each interaction, Chris remarked on Hugger's smoking which was uncomfortable for him. He did not remark on it at any other time and provided ashtrays for her use when interactions were in his geographic area. During each feedback session Hugger remarked on the intensity of Chris's schedule: it seemed he had at least ten tasks to accomplish for any given moment and there was an underlying sense of crisis. All other feedback was positive. Hugger was therefore surprised during the final feedback session when Chris stated a preference for not negotiating a new contract. Concerned with their developing closeness and afraid it would interfere with his time with his son (who would be living with him during the summer), Chris's initial reaction was to withdraw from interacting together. Realizing that he was a possible Magician, Hugger suggested the options of redefining the purpose of the Relationshipping and providing for flexibility. Pleased with their compromises and their ability to talk honestly together, they developed the following interim contract.

Interim Contract: Christopher and Hugger
June 1

Purpose: To be resources to each other and have periodic times together to enjoy each other in various activities and to be of mutual support to each other.

Term: Three months with a September review.

Frequency: Skip June. Hugger will come to Cleveland the evening of July 5, returning home the morning of July 9. August: We will attend the state Folk Festival with the children. Bonus time: Bonus time may be arranged as agreed upon by both partners.

Romance: Same as last time, but sex is allowed.

Phone: Either party may call, but considering the expense of long distance, a 30 minute time limit is imposed. However, the called partner may offer to call back and extend for 30 more minutes, but this is the option of the called party.

Cancels: Same as last time.

Finances: Same as last time.

Feedback: Same as last time.

Playing: This time we are going to *play* during each interaction as previously planned. Children can be included.

Talking: Parenting to be a topic of conversation. Also, Chris agrees to be more verbal regarding stating preferences.

Smoking: Hugger agrees not to smoke in a closed car and Chris agrees to stop the car at any time at her request so she can get out for emergency cigarettes. Hugger agrees to generally cut down on smoking when with Chris.

Language: Chris agrees to lessen the usage of his 4-letter Anglo-Saxon vocabulary when with Hugger.

Others: This is a non-exclusive contract.

Signed:

Feedback Agreement: D'Artagnan and Rand
December 10

After calling each other every time we had a new feeling, thought, or reaction to our divorces, and analyzing our situations over meals together, we feel we've gotten over the crisis and it is time to go on with our lives. We may call each other from time to time for a beer or to go fishing. We will not develop a new contract but will agree to generally keep in touch. We both appreciate the other's support and never realized before how nice it is to talk like this with a male friend.

Feedback Agreement: Toni and Bill's Summer Romance
Labor Day

We agree it has been a wonderful summer. Both of us feel refreshed and renewed to work toward making our other emotional commitments better. We will not contact each other again unless both of us "happens" to be here next year.

Some couples do not begin contracting until they are well into the Interaction Stage and have already established patterns of contact and being exclusive. Rather than attempting to manufacture a new beginning with less contact and intimacy, their first contract together identifies current patterns and establishes privileges and obligations which are pertinent to their present interaction.

Lena and Bud had been dating five months when they learned about Relationshipping and decided to try its concepts. Although Lena had been divorced for two years, Bud had only been separated for seven months at the time of the contract. Their high chemistry level and desire for communication provided for rich Relationshipping which they wanted to continue. In addition, both were motivated not to repeat past mistakes and were already beginning to notice creeping concerns in several areas. Lena and Bud were able to clarify their thoughts and expectations regarding each other in the areas of Lena's children, little surprises, opposite sex friendships, and sexual interaction. Although it is their first contract together and open ended instead of time limited, it is considered an interim contract because of their point of the continuum and the issues it concerns.

Contract between Lena and Bud
May 10

Purpose: Open ended exclusive romantic contract. With the goal being to explore the possibility of our compatibility.

1. We will see each other a minimum of two times a week.
2. We will see each other Sunday and Thursday of one week and Friday and Saturday of the following week, alternating with the weekends Bud has his son.
3. It is understood that there will be times when one or the other will have another commitment that does not include the other, at which time an alternate date will be offered.
4. One minimum two hour period will be spent with Lena's two sons every two weeks doing some activity.
5. Each of us can phone the other as desired.
6. When out with Lena's boys, Lena pays for her boys expenses unless Bud wants to and states his intent in advance of leaving for the activity.
7. Bud has no discipline authority with Lena's boys except when there is a safety factor or when they are doing something against Bud, his property, or his apartment.
8. Lena and Bud would like one surprise a month in the form of a card, an inexpensive gift, or a surprise appearance under appropriate circumstances at one or the other's functions.
9. Each may have and cultivate friends of the opposite sex. However, these friendships are not to be allowed to interfere with our days except in an emergency.
10. Either party can initiate sex, the other has "say no" privileges.
11. After sex, both good and bad feedback is encouraged.
12. We agree to try one new sex technique per month.
13. This contract will end on the day Bud is divorced and we will have feedback to decide where we go from there.

                    Signed:

As is evident from these examples and progressions, the differences effected by contracting from the usual penguin system are communication and information. Relationshippers *know* the goals of their interactions and also know *why* they should or should not continue together. In the Interaction Stage they find that even the worst information is not so terrible; it is merely not what one would rather hear. To know that a desired potential partner is not capable of Relationshipping at this time or that another would rather be a friend than a lover should not be desolating. It is infinitely preferable to know the reasons than to be in the uncomfortable position of wondering why contact did not continue, not to mention wondering how to act upon unexpectedly seeing the former partner. What the penguin trained mind imagines to have happened is immeasurably worse than the reality.

The following are the ten most common items of reality which lead to feedback agreements instead of interim contracts:

1. We don't have that much in common.
2. There's something missing – just not the right chemistry.
3. You want to get married and I'm not ready.
4. I've met someone else.
5. You drink too much.
6. You're too jealous (possessive).
7. You don't follow through on commitments.
8. I'm too busy to relationship right now.
9. You don't like (want) children.
10. You've got more problems than I can handle.

This important information, also known as "The Ten Sentences Penguins Like Least to Hear But Need Most to Know", serves to prevent the assumption of rejection and also provides for self growth. Relationshippers realize their success potential depends upon a match in chemistry, compatibility, and value system. They also realize they are dependent on the other person for feedback on the impression they make. If several potential partners decline to continue contracting because of a relationshipper's jealousy or other insecurity, that person would do well to seek professional help to overcome the problem.

Hearing the same feedback more than once provides a personal check regarding how potential partners view the prospective relationshipper. It also equips one with the opportunity to correct any little insecurities and instabilities which might interfere with one's abilities to relationship in a healthy and successful manner. Sometimes feedback is a parting gift one would otherwise not have received without contracting. At other times it exists as a continuing communication system to provide insights and understanding of each other as a couple progresses from the Interaction to the Testing Stage.

CHAPTER VII

The Testing Stage

There is no clear-cut demarcation between the Interaction Stage and the more mellow Testing Stage. There are, however, several signs of passing the border which are at first noticeable in terms of time and emotions.

After a couple has been interacting for three to six months, there is a conspicious difference in the emotional tone between the partners. Contrary to those mountainous peaks and valleys depicted by an emotional barometer in early interactions, the lines smooth to gently rolling hills as the Testing Stage is approached. If an emotional graph could be drawn, the striking absence of anxiety would be immediately apparent. Although so prevalent in the Interaction Stage, apprehension decreases to minimal amounts as a couple continues contact over time.

The three to six months range of time is due to each couple's individual circumstances. Long distance interacting will often require the entire six months (and sometimes more) while those who interact regularly within the same setting (such as a small town) often reach the same point much more quickly. The amount of stress in a person's life also affects the time factor as well as the number of negative experiences which have occured prior to the current Relationshipping.

Mary Jane and Alton, for example, began dating after working together on a union bargaining committee. Neither had general problems in their lives and both had a variety of friends and interests. They saw each other two to three times a week, and in a little over three months, they realized they were approaching the Testing Stage.

Blake had just officially been placed on six months probation when he met and began dating Nadine. The boss said his work was good enough; it was just that everyone else's work was superior. The company was over-staffed and there was going to be a general cut-back in the coming months. Blake had no idea where he would be working and living beyond the next few months. He enjoyed his time with Nadine and found her to be very supportive. However, he was anxious and preoccupied with job instability and had little left over for romantic investment. Blake and Nadine continued in the Interaction Stage until the employment question was settled about eight months later.

Gloria, on the other hand, had no particular stress in her life. She had a good job, several close friends, and managed her finances well enough so that she had no money troubles. She had, however, had a series of unfortunate romances and when she met Ace she was convinced he was too good to be true. She told her friends he was too considerate, too entertaining, and too good-looking to be really interested in her. She spent their first six months waiting for the ax to fall. Eventually, his demonstrated interest, consistency, and follow-through enabled her to relax her guard and her fears.

The disappearance of anxiety and insecurity regarding the partner is one of the first signposts to mark entry into the Testing Stage. The second signal is a major, and often dramatic, conflict. Hopefully, this occurs as an overt and direct disagreement which can be resolved by communication. Unhappily, it sometimes transpires in so covert a form that one of the partners may not even be aware of what the fight is about. Regardless of the method, the ability to disagree indicates that the initial issues of acceptability have been settled and the work of blending together has begun.

In the Interaction Stage arguments are abnormal and should be viewed as danger signs. Initial relationshippers are eager to please and the flow of communication provides plenty of guidelines. It is important to express one's viewpoints, and disagreements in the Interaction Stage are primarily a matter of information exchange regarding ground rules and behavioral contracts. Initial relationshippers are notoriously tolerant of their potential partners and if they are not, a raised eyebrow is totally appropriate.

Contrary to the Interaction Stage, periodic disagreements in the Testing Stage are positive signs. This is a time of testing in which two people begin to establish a couple identity without totally giving up the separate individuality to which each has a rightful claim. As a couple blends and harmonizes, some of the rough edges are worn away by friction. Periodic disputes are necessary to provide for smooth integration of the two personalities, to enable each to maintain integrity, to be overtly away of what is expected, and to minimize or completely avoid the predictable risks of the Testing Stage. In this second stage, the tremendous need for verbal outpour no longer exists, and it is through disagreement that much major communication takes place.

A couple who therefore has been together from three to six months who has noticed a decrease in general anxiety but an increase in disagreements need not be overly concerned. These symptoms are signs of passing into the Testing Stage where efforts need to be focused on quite different feelings, characteristics, risks, and developmental tasks than were experienced in the foregoing stage.

The Testing Stage Time Factor

The time factor for the Testing Stage is from six months to one year. Whether a couple completes this stage in six months or in twelve months depends on the amount of attention given to the developmental tasks and on how well they overcome the typical risks inherent in this stage. Accomplishing Testing Stage developmental tasks completes the resolution of the trust issue which is so important in the Relationshipping foundation.

Penguins react with shock and surprise that such a long time is required. They can immediately list numerous couples who have met and married in less than a year. So can I. They comprise about twenty per cent of my practive. These people have little sense of commitment. They have mistakenly expected temporary Interaction Stage feelings and communication to be a permanent state of affairs. They feel disappointed and cheated when reality inevitably appears with the arrival of the Testing Stage. Since the trust issue has not yet been resolved and couple bonding has not yet taken place, there is a tendency to jettison the partner whom they feel has somehow betrayed them. Interacting together over time, before commitment, answers many questions regarding the validity of chemistry, compatibility, and similar value systems. It is the simplist and most time-honored method of evaluating romantic Relationshipping; if a couple can stand the test of time together prior to formal commitment, they usually have the best chances for the long-term.

Primary Feelings of the Testing Stage

The primary feelings of the Testing Stage are security and comfort, and the urge "to do something". The Testing Stage features the first glimpse of that elusive "relationship" for which people yearn. Reaching that point is reflected in the warm feelings of security resulting from no longer having to seek a partner and from the comfort of each other's companionship and support. Hardly does a couple reach this relaxing state when, consistent with penguin practices, it is rapidly accompanied by a need to formalize it in some way.

Security and Comfort

In the Testing Stage, earlier feelings of anxiety are replaced by feelings of security and comfort. Since neither partner has disappeared (so far), partners feel reassured and accepted by each other. Having someone available for general support and concrete help in times of trouble enhances feelings of safety. Also, couples fit better into the social system than unmatched individuals. A person is no longer alone; he or she "has a relationship" and can depend on it. Partners begin to relate to the world on a couple basis. Each person feels taken care of.

Urge "To Do Something"

Since penguins tend to think "a relationship" can be found rather than developed, they also tend to do something with it once they think they have it. Premature marriage and premature co-habitation are the usual urges that must be resisted since the couple is not yet fully developed. Those who enter into a joint living situation at this point are thinking of themselves rather than of the two of them as a unit. They are seeking the gratification of their own needs rather than of developing a joint venture. The developmental tasks of the Testing Stage must be accomplished to complete the Relationshipping foundation. Otherwise, the newly obtained idea of couplehood quickly disintegrates when individual needs are not met.

However, not realizing the nature of these dynamics, penguins usually begin to think how nice it would be to have all of this warmth, acceptance, and security on a twenty-four hour basis instead of in segments. It makes sense economically and it also makes sense in terms of their own best self interests. These feelings are strong and it is difficult to wait for a healthy period of time to pass unless partners focus on other issues such as the developmental tasks.

Primary Characteristics of the Testing Stage

If one were recording the life cycle of Relationshipping with a movie camera, certain observable characteristics different from the Interaction Stage would be apparent in the film of the Testing Stage. The first difference would be a noticeable routine between partners rather than separate episodes of interacting. The two people would also be seen together more often. In addition, there would be a noticeable lack of "special" behaviors so often present in the Interaction Stage.

Routine

By the Testing Stage, couples have established habit patterns which produce a noticeable routine in terms of the partners' activities and interactions together. Instead of a flurry of excitement preceding contact, there is a calm expectancy. The relationshippers know each other's preferences and schedules, and have begun to assume time together. They have established certain activities they both enjoy, and they have developed couple habits. There is no longer an attitude of discovery; there is instead an easy familiarity. They are relating on a normal day-to-day basis without the Interaction Stage euphoria, and they are now relating realistically.

Couplehood

Not only would a movie camera record ease and familiarity within an established routine, but the film would also show the increased visibility of the two partners as a unit rather than each operating independently. The development of the couplehood is beginning. One partner does not generally make plans without consulting and/or including the other. Friends and relatives view them as a unit; an invitation to one is an invitation to both. Although each partner retains individuality, there is less independent action and more functioning as a team. The blending of the two personalities has begun to form a third personality: that of the couple.

Disappearance of "Special" Behaviors

The third typical characteristic revealed by the Testing Stage camera is the general disappearance of "special" behaviors. Any behavior or attitude that was especially adopted by a partner, either consciously or unconsciously, as a result of the pressure or excitement of the Interaction Stage usually disappears with the advent of the Testing Stage. Typical "special" behaviors include studio cards, love letters, poems, flowers, presents for no reason, frequent telephone calls, and events planned far in advance. Although these behaviors are usual attributes of many people's personalities, they are only courtship customs for a large proportion of the population.

Victor is a good example of a man who almost seemed to have a different personality from Interaction to Testing Stage. At 47 years old, he felt that some behaviors were appropriate to winning a woman which were unnecessary once she was won. Upon beginning Relationshipping, Vic made it a point to call the object of his attentions at least once a day just to tell her he was thinking of her. He often stopped at the florist for a single carnation on the way to a date. He mentally stored tidbits of gossip and other news to pass along, and he watched for interesting movies and other events which they might attend together. However, after several months on the continuum, Victor relaxed to the point that he didn't call unless he had specific information, and he no longer thought of flowers unless a friend was hospitalized. He preferred to spend quiet evenings at home unless his partner requested otherwise. Since he was perfectly willing "to go along" but didn't seem to have any ideas, his partner gradually took responsibility for their activities. Vic generally had great success in Relationshipping until about the middle of the Testing Stage. The women he dated then began to wonder what had happened to that stimulating and attentive man they had originally met. With the absence of his special behaviors, Vic was perceived as boring and passive.

For some people tolerance is a courtship custom and the Testing-Stage reveals them as wanting to mold and change the partner to their own preference system. When Ginny and Pete began dating, Ginny couldn't do anything wrong. Four months later, she couldn't do anything right. She was the same, but Pete's attitudes had changed.

"Special" behaviors include not only those traditional tokens of new romance, but also those attitudes that are influenced by the newness of Relationshipping. It is not until the Testing Stage that the normal and usual reactions can be evaluated because at this point the specially adopted behaviors begin to disappear. Any which appear on the Testing Stage camera film are characteristics which are a regular everyday aspect of the partner's behavior.

Primary Risks of the Testing Stage

The risks of the Testing Stage revolve around certain attitudes and behaviors which are common to the point that not only are they expected but erroneously encouraged in the general penguin society. Except for "The Great Disappearing Act", penguins seldom complain about such risky couple conduct as centering, making irrational assumptions and expectations, or goal-orienting their Relationshipping toward marriage. Few have realized the dangers produced by these couple attitudes and behaviors.

The Great Disappearing Act

The Great Disappearing Act is a trick for which the Magician is famous, but it is also a common exit strategy for those shy or cowardly penguins who cannot face a fellow relationshipper with bad news. Some do not know how to withdraw gracefully and others do not want to hurt anyone's feelings. They therefore avoid the situation by simply disappearing. Terminating by default, they cause more pain than if they had dealt with the matter openly and directly. The Great Disappearing Act occurs so frequently that the *fear* of it has become a common factor in most initial Relationshipping.

It quite often happens in the Interaction Stage that one date is not followed by another contact and the potential partner is neither seen nor heard from again. This is the usual processing of potential partners. It is not to be confused with The Great Disappearing Act which happens much later on the continuum when there has been more time together and a consequent much greater emotional investment. The Great Disappearing Act is usually a surprise to the disapearee who is left with a feeling of unfinished business and self doubt. The general vague but certain belief is that some terrible offense which can neither be discussed nor pardoned has been committed. This belief is nearly always incorrect. Most often people who disappear from Relationshipping do so because of their own problems rather than from any affront by the partner. They are unwilling to discuss the issue because discussing it involves admitting those personal problems.

Rob says, "Sure, I like Betsy. I more than like her. But I just don't have that feeling of commitment with her. I don't think I've ever had it with anyone. Maybe I won't ever have it, and it worries me to think that. I don't like to talk about it, so whenever I run into her I just tell her I've been really busy and I'll call her sometime. Then I feel like a real heel because I know I'm not going to call her again."

"I just don't have any intestinal fortitude", whines Ilene. "I knew a long time ago that we weren't particularly compatible, but I kept on going out with him because there wasn't anyone else. I just *have* to have a man in my life. I don't like that about me, but it's true. So when I met Perry, I just dropped Stu. If I tell him all that, he'll think I'm awful."

Rob and Ilene are examples of people with personal problems who chronically disappear on their partners. In lying to Betsy, Rob is trying to spare his own feelings. She, however, knows he is lying, and she also senses his general discomfort. Whatever she did must have been so terrible that he doesn't even want to talk to her or be around her any more. Since they were so close just a short time ago, his behavior is doubly confusing and doubly painful. She doesn't realize that Rob has trouble with intimacy and commitment. Ilene is also trying to spare her own feelings. She knows she misled Stu, but doesn't want to admit it. Overly dependent, she passes from one man to another as something better comes along. She is a floater and has trouble being honest in Relationshipping. Stu might feel foolish if he had that information about Ilene. However, he would also realize that continuing with her would have been an exercise in dishonest communication and a poor emotional risk.

A percentage of those who disappear have reasons but not the courage or social skills to pass that information along to the partner.

After all, penguins are supposed to *be nice*. Heaven forbid that anxiety or self doubt might be alleviated or some useful data exchanged if feelings might be hurt in the bargain. This information, though unpleasant, is important. It is used to grow and develop so that as different people are experienced, each person becomes richer from the association. The trick is to obtain that information. It becomes the responsibility of the disappearee to obtain the data since the one who disappeared would obviously have volunteered it if he or she were that comfortable about it.

The recommended method of pursuing missing information is to allow a passage of time so that the emotional turmoil is somewhat settled and then to engage the former partner in one-to-one conversation. Face to face contact is preferable although telephone conversation is accepted if there are no other options. A typical conversation would be the following:

J. "Hello, Dave? This is Janet. How's everything going for you?"
D. "Oh, okay. I've been really busy lately."
J. "Listen, Dave. I want you to know I'm not mad at you. It's alright with me if we don't date anymore."
D. "What do you mean?"
J. "Well, you haven't called me in four weeks and we used to talk or be together all the time. And when we run into each other, you seem so uncomfortable. I just hate to see it all go down the tube. We could still be friends, you know."
D. (Pause) "You know something, Janet. You are one terrific person."
J. "Well, that's nice of you to say that. It makes me feel better. I've been thinking I did something terrible that offended you."
D. "Hell, no. You're a super person. It just didn't work out, that's all. As much as I like you, we're just not compatible, Janet. Listen, this sounds terrible, but I just don't think you fit in with my friends and my lifestyle. You don't play golf or raquetball and you're not interested in learning. Everybody in my group has been to college. You don't have anything to say when we're all together. Maybe I'm a snob, but my friends are really important to me and you don't seem to be happy around them."
J. "Gee, Dave, you're right. I always felt like an odd ball, and couldn't wait until we were by ourselves. If I went back to school and tried to change that about myself, would it make any difference to you?"
D. "I don't know. It might. My better judgment says just to let well enough alone."
J. "Thanks for telling me, Dave. I admit I don't like hearing it, but

at least I know what's going on. I'm going to think about it. Maybe it's time for me to make some changes. But regardless, let's you and me not go out of our way to avoid each other. We had some good times and I'd hate for either of us to be uncomfortable when we run into each other."

D. "That's okay with me. In fact, I think it's great. I'll buy you a drink sometime. And Janet, I should have told you this before. I'm sorry I just disappeared like that. I didn't treat you right by doing that. Thanks for calling."

J. "I'll see you around. Bye."

D. "You better believe it! Bye."

Dave, like many partners who disappear because of lack of courage or social skills, appreciated the opportunity to tell Janet his perception of the problem. Once he realized that she was not going to be emotional or rejecting, he gave her the information which she can now evaluate as to her options. She can decide to extend herself (take some night classes and develop some athletic skills and interests); she can accept Dave as a snob who doesn't appreciate her virtues; or she can realize it was a bad match. She can simply wait and see if she receives the same feedback in her next Relationshipping experience. If so, she either needs to change her skills and interests or her taste in partners. She has information to grow on.

Periodically, former partners refuse to be enlightening regardless of how non-threatening and openly they are approached. In this case, Field's Law (usually credited to W. C. Fields) is brought into effect. It simply states, "If at first you don't succeed; try, try, try again. If you try, try, try again and still don't succeed, then forget it and don't make a fool of yourself." One must accept the situation as not having worked out, draw on what data one has from prior overt communication, and one must go on.

Those who contract in Relationshipping report much fewer Great Disappearing Acts. Contracting has built-in communication evaluation periods and also has natural ending points where options are considered and discussed. There is less fear involved when partners contract: not because there is less risk, but because there is more communication, information, and structure.

Centering

Centering, another risk of the Testing Stage, is that couple state in which one's lifestyle, comfort, and gratification all center on the partner. It can be a mutual centering of two people like Scott and Emily who exist only in each other's world or a single centering like Theresa whose total thoughts and actions revolve around her husband Bill. All Scott and Emily have right now is each other. Scott was laid off five months ago, and finances are tight. There is no extra money for entertainment or for anything that is not absolutely necessary. Except for going to the grocery store together, they rarely leave the house. No one comes to visit since they never developed outside friends even when Scott was working. Scott and Emily take care of their two preschool children, watch television, and talk about all the wonderful things they will do together when Scott is called back to work. In the meantime, they are supportive to each other and never leave each other's sight. Bill and Theresa are involved in a different type of centering. Since they married, Bill has not written a letter nor made a nonbusiness telephone call. He has not shopped for himself nor shined his shoes. He has not attended an event not to his preference nor voiced an opinion not supported by his wife. Theresa is involved in nothing unless it is an extension of one of Bill's activities. He is the center and purpose of her life.

Centering is the natural concommitant of "Too Much Too Soon" in the Interaction Stage. In the Testing Stage it is encouraged by the penguin society who acts as if it were unusual and abnormal for one partner to be present without the other. There is the pervading myth that those who love each other want to be with each other constantly; if they are not a reasonable imitation of Siamese twins, it is almost as if the quality of their love is questioned. It may be cute to see a couple whose only interests and thoughts concern the partner. However, centering involves responsibility and dependence as well as love and companionship. In centering, one or both partners look to the other as the only source of gratification and support. One or both may work, but essential satisfaction comes from the partner. One or both may be distressed to appear socially without the partner or to belong to an organization as an individual instead of as a couple. Each is dependent on the other as well as responsible for the other's emotional well-being. Centering is a symbiotic form of blending and people who center become totally isolated and deprived if there is trouble between partners or if the partner is absent.

David and Marylou met at a Christmas party last year and people fondly say they've been inseparable ever since. David used to like to downhill ski, but Marylou does not like heights. They both took up cross-country skiing instead. Marylou likes to sail but David cannot swim and feels uncomfortable in a boat. After a few unsuccessful sailing attempts, Marylou sold her Laser. Each has stopped going to church because they can't decide which church to go to. They both say their work is their outside interest.

Well into the Testing Stage, David and Marylou are over-blending to the point of centering. They are excluding their individual tastes and preferences to the point of eventual deprivation. They are proceeding under the myth that two people in love should spend all their time together and share all their interests.

Centering can occur as a reaction to a prior situation. Joannie, for example, is a vibrant woman of many interests who during her marriage had a husband who was constantly on the go. He traveled for business and also was a Cub Scout leader, member of Jaycees, and referee for local school sports. In addition, he went deer hunting in November and took night-school classes from February through May. In the summer he coached Little League. They were basically incompatible but Joannie misinterpreted his constant activities as signs that he didn't love her. Currently, she has decided she is not going to make the same mistake. In her new Relationshipping with Brian, she insists that they are either jointly involved or not involved. She has given up all her individual interests and friends in favor of joint time together. By being constantly by his side, she believes she can satisfy all his needs. Reacting to her failed marriage, Joannie wants to center because she mistakenly believes centering is a sign of loving. She has yet to learn that it is the quality of the time together rather than the quantity that determines loving Relationshipping.

As blissful and socially desirable as it may appear to be, centering is destructive to Relationshipping. It subjects the couple to the erosion of constant contact and to the disintegration of individuality. It provides for over dependency on each other and isolation from others. It also produces a total responsibility to make the other person happy which no sane partner should accept; those who fail in the attempt must then accept the responsibility of the reverse: that of making the partner miserable. Each partner must have interests, activities, friends, and sources of fulfillment in addition to the couple bond which nuture the individual and enrich the Relationshipping.

Assumptions – Expectations

The second risk of the Testing Stage is having irrational assumptions and expectations which are destructive to Relationshipping. It involves much more than neglecting small courtesies between partners popularly known as "being taken for granted". This risk concerns mental approaches to the Relationshipping and to the partner which can seriously affect the course of the continuum. These mental approaches create a distorted image of people and events and can be categorized in three areas: past thinking, wishful thinking, and defeatist thinking.

Those who utilize past thinking tend to create irrational assumptions and expectations based on what they have experienced in the past rather than what they are experiencing in the current situation.

Joellen says, "Everything is going well with Rocky and me right now, but I'm scared to death. Every other man I've dated has pulled something on me and I'm sure Rocky is going to do it too. I'm nervous and irritable and I'm afraid I'm going to drive him away, but I just can't get comfortable. I keep waiting for the other shoe to drop."

Joellen admits that she has dated Rocky longer than any other man and that he has not "pulled anything" common to the other men she has known. However, it has happened in the past (more than once) and she irrationally both assumes and expects that it will happen again regardless of the indications of Rocky's innocence. He, in turn, finds it impossible to prove that he will *not* do something that she is sure he will do.

The Relationshift requires awareness of potential danger signals and profit from prior Relationshipping. Nevertheless, one partner should not be penalized for a prior partner's actions. Each step along the continuum together must be evaluated under its own pure merit. Otherwise, one is under the control and influence of the past which inhibits ability to be open in the present. Without attempts to defeat past thinking, the assumptions and expectations of disaster often create a self-fulfilling prophesy.

In past thinking, it is assumed that the positive elements seen are irrelevant or invalid, and tragedy is irrationally expected. In wishful thinking, it is assumed that the negative elements seen all have reasons for being there, and it is expected that they will change or go away.

April and Gene have been dating for eight months. He is very active in sports and in the outdoor life. She enjoys watching him play baseball, but has little interest in sports or camping herself. There was a tournament on her birthday and Gene forgot to buy her a present, but April is not concerned. She is sure that after they get married Gene will give up sports for his family, and he will also be more considerate.

Deb and Howard have been dating for 28 months. All their friends say Howard is so tight he squeaks, but Deb knows better. The first year they dated was his last year in college, and (according to Deb) he was afraid he wouldn't get a job right away so he saved all his money in case he would have to live on it until something came along. Of course, he did get a good job right away, but he couldn't know that in advance. Then he had to start saving for a new car. He's just driving that old clunker until he finds a car he really likes that gets good mileage. They rarely eat out because Howard says Deb cooks better than the chefs in nice restaurants and besides, she loves to cook. They haven't gone to the movies in a year because there's nothing worth seeing. People just don't realize that Howard is a man of strong personal tastes, and when he finds something he likes, he'll spend the money for it with no problem.

Rex and Polly have been dating for 16 months. They are compatible in every way except sex. Except for some occasional heavy petting, there really hasn't been any sex. Polly says she's still a virgin at 25 and she wants to be a virgin when she marries. Rex has quit pressuring her because she actually gets the shakes if he persists in touching her anyplace between the neck and knees. He's talked to some of his friends about it, and now he understands that many women are like that until they get married; then they go crazy! He wants to set a wedding date, but Polly wants to wait a while longer.

April, Deb, and Rex are all fooling themselves with wishful thinking. The Testing Stage provides a good reflection of everyday normal behavior; what one sees is probably what one is going to get. If Gene is so involved in his sports that he forgets a birthday, he will probably also forget anniversaries, dinner, and social events if his sporting interests conflict. April's expectation that he will give up his interest for family life is unrealistic. Howard is definitely tight. He would rather put a nickel in the bank than anywhere else. Believing Howard's excuses and being willing to provide some of her own are proof only of Deb's loyalty. The input of friends is objective and valuable data that Deb's wishful thinking is ignoring. As for Rex, his wishes are no different from any man's, but there can be little basis for his belief from the behavior he has observed. Like it or not, it is abnormal in contemporary society for a woman to reach the age of 25 with no sexual experience beyond kissing. The possibilities are much higher that Polly has some fairly ingrained sexual problems than that she will go crazy with passion on her wedding night.

For one reason or another, all three assume that the negative behaviors seen are invalid, and they expect that eventually the behaviors they wish will appear. Their assumptions and expectations prevent them from realizing that wishes, no matter how strong, no matter how pleasant or how well-meaning, do not alter the real situation.

Past thinking assumes that the positive elements seen are irrelevant or invalid, and tragedy is irrationally expected. Wishful thinking assumes that the negative elements seen all have reasons for being present, and irrationally expects that these negatives will change or go away. Defeatist thinking assumes that the behavior or the situation has always been thus-and-so and irrationally expects that it will always be thus-and-so. With defeatist thinking, there is little motivation for compromise or change.

Conversation overheard in a restaurant between a tall good-looking man and a not extraordinary but reasonably attractive woman:

TG-LM: "You know, I don't send cards or like to talk much on the phone. I'm not good at remembering birthdays, and I'm lousy at anniversaries. (Teasing tone) Do you think you'll like me as time goes on?"

RAW: "I don't know, but I think I'll pass on finding out."

TG-LM: (Taken aback) "What do you mean!"

RAW: "We've had a lot of fun together and I think you're a nifty guy. But it's your attitude that bothers me. Why should I set myself up for something like that? We've just started dating and already you're telling me that you're not going to call me much or send cards and you're practically promising to forget my birthday and anniversaries. I like those little things and you don't sound like you have any intention of changing."

The rest of TG-LM and RAW's conversation was lost as the pianoplayer returned from his break. However, RAW had focused quite nicely on her dinner partner's defeatist thinking and on an attempted covert contract which she refused to accept. Obviously a platypus, she was actively processing information and giving feedback in the Interaction Stage.

Defeatist thinking can apply to one's own behavior and attitudes or to the partner's behavior and attitudes. As in the example above with TG-LM's own attitudes, there are often hints of defeatist thinking in the Interaction Stage. However, it is in the Testing Stage that it is much more apparent and becomes a problem. One who practices defeatist thinking will have difficulty resolving conflict. In the first place, such a partner assumes the worst about the other's behavior and attitudes and does not usually communicate complaints, depriving the other partner of the opportunity to change. In the second place, when a complaint is communicated by the other partner, a defeatist thinker will often respond about his or her own behavior or attitudes, "Well, that's just the way I am" as if there were no options and no other possibilities..

Defeatist thinkers have been encouraged by narcissistic penguin attitudes that say one must be accepted "as is" as if people were damaged articles placed on sale in a gift shop; once the bargain price is paid, the item (or the person) can't be exchanged or returned. Defeatist thinking prevents the blending necessary to form the couplehood. It denies the fact that many possible behaviors exist and sabotages feedback which determines what behaviors help partners function better as a unit. Even with a high compatibility ratio, there are few partners who automatically jell in all aspects of their usual behaviors. Blending requires compromise and change. Defeatist thinking stifles the growth of the couplehood and gives a partner the unfortunate choice of liking it or lumping it.

It is not difficult to recognize the defeatist thinker. Sentences such as, "That's just the way I am", "You can't teach an old dog new tricks", "He (or she) won't change so it won't do any good to talk about it", and reasonable facsimiles are symptomatic of the condition. These sentences reflect closed and rigid attitudes and people who seek open viable Relationshipping must realize the handicap when confronted with such attitudes.

All three thinking systems — past, wishful, and defeatist — involve assumptions and expectations that are not valid and that are significant risks in the Testing Stage. Partners must confront and discuss these attitudes to determine the difference between assumptions and expectations versus reality, their true compatibilities, and the possibilities of continued growth together.

Perminize or Terminize

The risk of "perminize or terminize" involves the belief that as soon as partners feel comfortable with each other, they should legitimatize the Relationshipping in some way. For most penguins this means marriage. Perminize or terminize goes hand-in-glove with the erroneous philosophy of finding that ready-made package: "a relationship"; once found, something has to be done with it. Peers compound the error. After a couple has been seen together for several months, they begin to be greeted by the question, "Aren't you two married yet?" This and similar remarks remind the couple that the penguin society has cultural expectations of them. Pressure grows and the goal becomes to make it permanent or to terminate.

Unfortunately, there is a tendency to feel comfortable with a person before knowing all the facts relating to compatibility and value systems. People are comfortable as soon as they are reassured that the chemistry is mutual and sustained, and as soon as they believe that this potential partner probably won't go away. They may or may not have a great deal in common and they may or may not have enough similar items in their value systems. Although it quite often occurs, marriage at this point is premature. Precocious commitment explains the recent phenomenon taking place in mental health centers and marriage counseling agencies across the nation: an epidemic proportion of new marriages with major problems. People are marrying before they have their facts and information, and society is rapidly becoming sequentially polygamous.

Stella comments, "I look back and I can see it now. We dated three months and everything seemed perfect. Art was staying at my place every night anyway, and we started thinking how much cheaper it would be to live together. So he moved in, and after another three or four months it just seemed silly not to get married. I mean, everyone kept asking why not, and we really didn't have any reasons why not, and there were the children to consider. After a while, it was almost as if his personality changed. He says mine changed, too. And on our first anniversary we had a terrible fight and started talking about divorce."

To escape the trap of inappropriately considering marriage at an early point in the Testing Stage, a couple needs to focus on developmental tasks and on the other options available. There are many people for whom marriage is not the optimum choice.

Charlene is 42 years old and holds a responsible position in the publishing business in a large metropolitan city. She has been divorced for 11 years and her children are grown and live independently. She works 12 to 14 hours a day and loves the excitement of her job. She says she does not want to give up the time or take on the responsibility that marriage involves. She is in love with equally busy Patrick but they have no intent to marry. They instead have open-ended romantic Relationshipping with contractual guidelines.

Harrison has been married three times and pays alimony to three former wives and child support for five children. He says he can't afford to marry again. In reality, Harrison is filled with self doubt regarding both his judgment and his ability to Relationship successfully. He and Clarissa have an open-ended loving friendship, and they have been happily Relationshipping for five years. They have no plans to marry.

Thea's kids need braces and half of her department has already been laid off. Her car is seven years old and it just developed another ominous whine. Even though Ab has been asking her to marry him, she knows better than to marry him now. It would solve her financial worries, but not answer her questions about day to day compatibility. She is focusing on developmental tasks before thinking about commitment.

Marriage is no longer a social pre-requisite for continuing couplehood. It should not be an automatic evolution of the boy-meets-girl-process, but a carefully considered decision in view of all the facts, information, and options available. Rather than responding to the risk of permanize or terminize, a couple needs to focus on the developmental tasks of the Testing Stage to further evaluate the viability of their continued Relationshipping.

Developmental Tasks of the Testing Stage

The Testing Stage is a time of testing and blending together, of discovering the limits of what behaviors the partner and the partnership allows. The developmental tasks of establishing ground rules, determining goals, identifying non-negotiable issues, learning to resolve anger together all reflect that testing and blending.

Establishing Ground Rules

Establishing ground rules occurs in all Relationshipping among penguins and platypuses alike. It transpires actively or passively, usually behaviorally, and is the basis of all couple behavior. Penguins try to develop imaginary sensors and antennae-like detectors to determine if their own behavior meets the approval or disapproval of the partner. According to their unilateral evaluation, that behavior then becomes a ground rule for the couple.

Grant, for example, perceived that something might be wrong with Arlene. She wasn't as warm as usual toward him and didn't have too much to say. When he asked, "How was your day?", she responded, "Fine." (That was it — just "Fine." Nothing else.) He concluded that her period was coming, and he should stay out of her way. They spent a very quiet evening watching television, and he went home early. Two days later, everything seemed normal again, and Grant congratulated himself on handling the situation right. This must be the way to handle Arlene when she is moody or upset.

Denny and Rachel had the same situation. However, when they were together two days after the event, Denny said, "You seemed upset the other night, and I didn't know what to do so I kind of stayed out of your way. Was anything wrong? And if there was, is that a good way to handle it? My ex-wife just wanted to be left alone, but I don't know if you do." Rachel responded, "I had had a terrible day at work and I wanted to talk about it, but I didn't want to ruin our evening together. I finally talked about it to my best friend the next day. I wish you had probed a little because I ended up feeling not very close to you and thinking you didn't care about my feelings. In the future, I'll try to be a little more direct and why don't you help me out a little by asking a few more questions? You see, my ex-husband never wanted to hear about it — he said I was just complaining."

Most people have had different backgrounds and everyone has had different experiences. When people begin guessing, like Grant, they have to remember there is at least a fifty percent chance of being wrong. The art of developing healthy ground rules involves discussing behaviors with the partner. Each person is capable of many reactions. Part of blending together is letting the partner help pick the best multiple-choice response. Without his or her input, a person will tend to react as he or she did either to parents or former partners which may or may not be appropriate and comfortable for this different companion.

Many penguins prefer to use their sensors and antennae instead of their mouths because of a fear of criticism or an irrational fear of conflict. It is important to differentiate between information and criticism. To comment that one does not like a behavior is not to reject the person, but rather encourages the person to explore alternative behaviors. If conflict ensues, the task is to make that conflict creative by resolving the issues together. Healthy ground rules are developed one at a time through discussion and comment, and sometimes through anger.

Determining Goals

Because of the tendency in the Testing Stage to want to terminize or permanize, most couples mistakenly begin to look toward marriage as a goal. This may be a long term possibility, but there are many more immediate goals that are much more appropriate. There are some general goals upon which every couple should focus. All partners who are considering long term commitment should first concentrate on becoming involved in the partner's extended environment, on involving the partner in one's own extended environment, and on developing short term projects together. Working toward these goals, common to all potential long term couples, provides further information about how a partner relates to others and how a partner is accepted by others. It further generates data as to how the two people work together as a team. In addition to general goals, there are other goals which each couple must pinpoint according to each couple's unique situation.

For example, Warren and Carrie were well into the Testing Stage when Carrie realized that Warren and her 14 year old son not only didn't really get along, but actually disliked each other. Before continuing to consider marriage, they established the goal of developing positive Relationshipping between the man and the boy. For this couple, it required seeking therapy for all involved.

Each couple's situation is different and the goals established depend upon the way in which one partner interacts with the other and with the partner's friends and family. Couples are able to identify trouble spots and pinpoint them for further work.

Virginia, for instance, is calm about everything. She is not overly affectionate and can be silent for days when angry or otherwise upset. Tony is Italian and emotional over anything, even Ground Hog's Day. He finds it difficult to understand her, and his excitability sometimes frightens her. They are compatible in all other areas and have very similar value systems.

Walton is from a very large and very close family. Joy is an only child born when her parents were in their late forties. He can't imagine a holiday without "going home". She'd just as soon skip all the noise and bother.

Lois is quite expressive when she's angry. She throws things: cups, plates, potted plants, and anything else that comes to hand. Needless to say, Webb feels intimidated about initiating anything that might bring about this reaction.

All Rose and Harry's friends are single and into the bar scene which no longer interests Rose and Harry. They don't have any companions for different activities and find themselves centering.

Sonya and Cameron have discovered they have almost nothing in common. It is their differences that have attracted each other. Attempting to plan activities together often ends up with their watching TV because they can't agree on anything else.

In spite of their strong affection and attraction for each other, major problems are germinating for each of these couples. The tendency among penguins is to ignore these early warning signals and/or assume that these problem areas will (by magic) work themselves out or disappear. However, the reality is that they become worse over time as they become too emotionally charged for the partners to discuss. The Testing Stage offers the opportunity to practice problem solving by focusing on the friction. The couple not only continues to learn about the partners' compatibility by this blending process, but also learns about the partners' capacity to resolve issues together. No two people, regardless of the extent of their love and attraction for each other, can survive as a couple without that capacity.

Each of these couples — unemotional Virginia and Italian Tony, Walton and Joy, Lois and Webb, and Sonya and Cameron — have particular trouble spots that are not common to all couples and that should be identified as immediate goals for work together. They are examples of partners who react differently to people and events. Often it is these differences which have initially attracted each other. People feel more complete because personal gaps are filled and personalities are rounded out. However, different is also scary. If attempts are not made to blend differences, couples often find the very characteristics which attracted them become sources of chronic friction.

For these couples to be successful, each partner must bend toward the middle. The contractual framework is ideal in creating trial and error avenues to reach that middle ground. Regardless of the method utilized, it is the marvel of communication that productive discussion of an issue leads to resolution. Once a problem area is identified and steps to correct it suggested, the issue often disappears.

In addition to goals each couple must pinpoint according to its own unique situation, there are general goals common to all couples which should be established in the Testing Stage. One of these general goals is to become involved in the partner's extended environment. By observing how he or she interacts in work, family, and friendshipping, one has a fairly good idea of the partner's values, attitudes, and respect for people. One also has a fairly good idea of how that person will interact with oneself as a partner in the future. Furthermore, there is the opportunity to evaluate compatibility within this extended system: can family members be accepted? Are the established friendships liked and enjoyed?

It is important to realize that it is not enough only to *meet* these people. A partner must become *involved* with them to obtain the needed information. Ingrid, in retrospect, says she met the members of the motorcycle gang with whom Ramsey had been associated. She and Ramsey even went camping with them over Labor Day weekend. However, with this one interaction she never realized the importance this group held in her partner's self concept and attitudes. Underneath his smooth and acquired professional manner, he was still "The Ram". His identification with the gang (and her revulsion to it) eventually made it impossible for them to continue together. Ingrid believes that earlier identification of the issue could have have avoided much later pain.

A similar but second general goal in the Testing Stage is to involve the partner in one's own extended environment. It is important to know if he or she is acceptable in one's own work, family, and friendshipping situations. The opinions of relatives and friends carry weight. There is an adverse effect if they think the partner undesirable or foolish. The couple identity is forming and any negative attitudes attached to one partner are also uncomfortably felt by the other.

Three different people recently realized that partners take on a different color in the outside world. At a bowling banquet Minnie realized she was embarrassed by Wesley's appearance. He looked really out of place. She realized he was habitually careless in his dress. Morton thought Lani came across as a silly clown at the department picnic. Cooky was shocked by Tad's off-color jokes at a family get-together. In all of these situations, family and friends commented. As a result of the comments and resulting embarrassment, Morton saw Lani more realistically while Minnie and Cooky approached their partners in a problem solving manner. Two couples were able to establish goals in these areas, and one couple recognized an incompatibility.

A final general goal for the Testing Stage, developing short term projects, helps partners evaluate how well they work together as a team. Short term projects are fun and productive, and they enrich the

Relationshipping by providing opportunities for mutual efforts and mutual achievements. One couple developed a part time summer lawn care service to earn money for a color television set. Others have taken courses in Chinese cooking, disco dance, and photography to develop skills together. House maintenance, building something (anything from a scooter for the children to a deck or screened-in porch), co-sponsoring a Little League Team are all projects which are time-limited and which focus on a couple's ability to work together.

When Ida announced her intention to paint the interior of her apartment, Lee offered to help her. In the actual effort, it became apparent that Lee's definition of "help" was for him to do all the work while Ida remained available to hand him brush or tape when needed, and to make general admiring sounds. Although Ida greatly appreciated the work he did for her, she resented being excluded from her own project. As the Relationshipping continued, Ida realized that they did not work well as a team. Lee was either chief worker and boss, or he did not work. Neither did their Relationshipping as Ida was an independent woman with strong opinions of her own. She did not function well in a chronically dependent position. Lee's attitude, first clearly manifested in "helping" her paint, did not allow equal efforts. Eventually, she did not include him in her projects or decisions because he tended to take them over. They became distant because of their inability to work as a team. With another partner, Lee's system may have been perfectly acceptable. With Ida it was a non-negotiable issue.

Identifying Non-Negotiable Issues

Identifying non-negotiable issues is the third developmental task of the Testing Stage. A non-negotiable issue is a strongly charged difference in opinion or belief between partners to which neither can reconcile or compromise. It can be accepted or tolerated but not resolved. The question is whether or not the partner can endure it or work around it without undue complaint.

Hemingway is a hunter. He has enjoyed hunting since childhood. He plans to continue enjoying hunting. Tess strongly believes it is wrong to kill anything. She organized the local chapter of the animal society and is its current president. To hunt or not to hunt is a non-negotiable issue between them.

Non-negotiable issues are not usually clearly visible until the Testing Stage, that time of friction, blending, and couple comfort. Interaction Stage euphoria prevents the objective evaluation of a potential partner's characteristics, but the vista from the routine of the Testing

Stage is much more reality oriented. No two people are completely compatible. Non-negotiable issues exist for everyone, and it is imperative that they be recognized and discussed. The acceptance of these differences is crucial for long term Relationshipping.

Non-negotiables are highly charged disputes. They are usually found in the areas of religion, politics, finances, and sex roles. Partners, though diametrically opposed, usually each believe themselves absolutely right with many examples and philosophical proofs to support their opinions. They find it impossible to understand or respect the other's position. Most couples can accept and/or tolerate some non-negotiables if partners are able to agree to disagree. Five to seven non-negotiables are not unusual in Relationshipping and can be tolerated without severe difficulty. As the number of items increases, however, the chances for successful Relationshipping decreases geometrically. Couples with more than seven non-negotiable issues need to re-evaluate their compatibility and differing value systems.

The contracting framework is ideal in identifying non-negotiables and in determining how a couple may deal with them. These examples, taken from Testing Stage contracts with background material added, illustrate how some couples have handled some very strong differences.

Art enjoys his beer and also likes something a little stronger on social occasions. Maureen could qualify for membership in the Temperence Union. They decided that nothing with alcoholic content would be kept in the house and there would be no drinking at home. Art, however, can have a few beers with his friends after work or bowling, and a cocktail or two when they go out to dinner or to social events. He takes the responsibility of monitoring himself so that he never comes home drunk.

Gary's full beard is his manhood. Constance liked him in spite of it when she met him. Although deep down she believes it makes him look dirty and anti-social, the beard is his choice and she has agreed she will make no more comments about shaving it.

Joy hates the uproarious holiday visits to Walton's family and all the work it entails for her as a woman to prepare food and clean up after everyone. Walton offers that for every holiday trip "home", he will shortly thereafter take her on a long weekend mini-vacation for just the two of them.

Gene can't stand Carolyn's housekeeping, or rather, her lack of housekeeping. In addition to dust and accumulated debris, she also has ceramics in various stages of completion scattered around the house. Although his mother taught him that "a messy house is a sign of a messy mind", he realizes this is part of her zany character that he otherwise adores. (She claims she's a true Aquarius). He figures to budget money for a cleaning lady if they should marry or live together.

Mario is a self-proclaimed atheist and believes religion exploits people. For Bonita, her church and its activities are an important part of her life. They have agreed that religion will not be discussed and that she will not attempt to involve him in her church life. She, however, may attend as she likes and will give Mario advance notice when she will be gone for evening activities.

Some of these couples were able to work around their non-negotiables. Others found it necessary to accept the differing viewpoint without forcing their own upon the partner because they could not strike a balance. In all cases, however, there was the ability to accept the other's feelings as valid though different. This is the key item in bridging the gap between the diversity of background and experience which often attracts one to the other. The willingness to work around or, at worse, to accept an idosyncracy, provides for closeness and continued bonding as a couple progresses along the Relationshipping continuum.

Resolving Anger Together

In discussing non-negotiables couples often find it necessary to deal with anger, a giant bug-a-boo exterminated by Relationshift. Although a normal and necessary part of the Testing Stage, the penguin tendency is to view this natural feeling as an unwelcome boat-rocker that will ruin everything.

Anger, the so-called negative emotion, has solved more problems and met more challenges than the sum of several of the more positively considered feelings. Anger is strong and powerful. (That's why it's so scary.) It is a motivator and an attention-getter. It is the psyche's early warning system. Properly channeled, anger produces direct communication of feelings and deals with issues efficiently and productively. It's virtues are rarely recognized, however, because anger has a bad reputation.

Penguins identify anger with rejection, war, and catastrophe. They thus view this human and everyday emotion as undesirable and unacceptable. They deny it ("We never fight"), lie about it ("I'm not angry, I'm hurt"), discount it ("You're being silly"), and call it by other names ("upset, nervous, high-strung"). They avoid its overt expression with partners and force it underground so that it manifests itself in petty little games of being late, forgetting, becoming "ill", drinking, or having a temper tantrum over a totally related (and completely safe) item.

Frustration, annoyance, resentment, and irritation are all accelerating levels of the same emotion: anger. The ideal system is to discuss the question with the partner at the frustration level. This is dealing with anger in its mildest form when there is the least emotional charge and the most possibility of resolution.

Unfortunately, the frustration level is also that point when one can most easily avoid the problem. People make excuses for each other and refrain from *bothering* the partner about such little nuisances. The result is a building of tension and the unexpressed emotion accelerates to a far more threatening form. One then has to deal with an explosive situation rather than an unpleasant one. The chances of resolution decrease significantly.

Dr. William S. Bach and Peter Hadyn have given valuable aids toward resolving conflict in their book *The Intimate Enemy*.[3] Their method, which has met with tremendous success, involves rules for fair fighting which reduce feelings of threat and intimidation associated with anger. Much simplified and with some alterations, these rules appeared in *Social Work* (July, 1978)[4] in an article about treatment of hostile married couples:

1. Make a date to fight at a convenient time for both partners when there are no distractions.
2. Tell the partner in advance the subject for discussion.
3. Fight by the clock with a time limit set in advance.
4. Only fight about one issue at a time.
5. Stay on the subject.
6. No intimidation techniques allowed.

Couples who resist fighting by these rules usually complain that the method is too structured and does not provide for spontaneity. With further thought they tend to realize that it is those "spontaneous" remarks in fighting which they most regret.

Lois, who used to smash everything in sight before a disagreement with Webb could really get started, was at first reluctant to abandon this intimidation technique. In fact, she agreed to consider other options for fight behavior only when Webb seriously threatened to terminate with her if she did not, in his words, "get her act together". He was not, he said going to go through the rest of his life dodging flowerpots and cleaning up pieces of crockery. This was far too spontaneous for him. Lois's fear of losing him was greater than her fear of losing an argument, and she agreed to try fighting by the simplified rules for a three month period. To her surprise, disputes were easily settled, and her points were listened to and accepted more often than not. She learned that there is no loser in a fight if the issue is resolved.

Other intimidation techniques are not as dramatic. Women often use crying, rushing from the room, developing a headache, or not speaking at all. With men there is usually a symbolic show of force: fist-shaking, fists through walls, or angry pacing and pounding. For men of large physique it is sometimes their style only to stand and loom over the partner. For both men and women vulgar language and name calling is not uncommon. All of these behaviors are unnecessary and do not contribute to resolving the issue. They instead create subject matter for future disagreements.

To jettison those methods is to step toward mediation. Partners who chose their timing so no children or other adults are in adjoining rooms, who inform each other in advance and therefore don't rely on the element of surprise, who focus on the subject at hand rather than bringing extraneous material to confuse the issue are partners who are working toward non-defensive negotiation. They form a couple who can truly achieve intimacy together and for whom the natural and normal feelings of anger hold no threat.

Learning to resolve anger together, at whatever level, is an individual task for each couple. Continued closeness for the long term depends on success in achieving this developmental task of the Testing Stage.

Relationshippers who focus on developmental tasks of establishing ground rules, determining goals, identifying non-negotiable issues, and learning to resolve anger together find they have little if any difficulty with the primary risks encountered in this stage. In addition, as they test and blend together, they discover their ability to resolve issues and to compromise without consequent catastrophe. This assurance of being able to go forward together regardless of problems encountered provides for strength, in-depth intimacy, and real confidence for long term Relationshipping.

Testing Stage Questions

Following the achievement of the Testing Stage developmental tasks is the ideal time to marry or to otherwise commit to a partner for long term Relationshipping. Those tasks have been successfully accomplished when each partner can completely and positively answer each of the following questions.

1. *How does this person get along with my significant others?*
2. *Can I disagree with this person?*
3. *Does this person "fight" fairly?*
4. *What are the non-negotiable issues? How many? Can I live with them without resentment or comment?*
5. *Except for the non-negotiable issues, are disagreements resolved?*

Testing Stage Summary

The Testing stage is a time of testing and blending that is quite different from the euphoria of discovery that is typical of the preceding stage. Instead of anxiety, Testing Stage couples find themselves feeling the routine of comfortable couplehood. That comfort often misleads couples into mistakenly considering long term commitment at a time when they do not yet have valuable information concerning how the partners can survive together in future upheavals. Instead of premature commitment, couples must concentrate on developmental tasks to determine if they can successfully resolve anger together and live with non-negotiable issues. In the Testing Stage people look most like themselves. It is not until they lose that rosy glow of initial interaction that they can realistically evaluate the potential success of long term Relationshipping. In the Testing Stage a couple develops the strength necessary to withstand the constant changes of the upcoming Negotiation Stage. Avoiding the primary risks and successfully accomplishing the Testing Stage developmental tasks completes the foundation and provides for true pairing.

CHAPTER VIII

Contract Communication: The Testing Stage

It is an occupational hazard of the continuum that couples tend to try harder in the Interaction Stage and settle into a comfortable routine in the Testing Stage. Contracting at this point involves insurance that negative covert contracts do not intrude, and provision of a structure in order to work on essential developmental tasks. It must be remembered that at this stage, as in all four stages, the basic purpose of contracting is to provide a communication system. Contracting does not guarantee successful Relationshipping; it does guarantee answers and information.

"Your system doesn't work!" accused an angry and obviously unhappy Ruth in a middle of the night crisis call. "I have done everything right. I have contracted every step of the way. But two hours ago I walked in on him in bed with another woman and then we fought and now I think it's all over. We agreed to be exclusive and he said he is except he did it because I flirted with Chad at the party Friday night, and he was getting me back. I didn't even know he was mad at me about Chad, and I never would have done it if I'd known. Contracting just doesn't work and now it's probably over and I don't know what to do."

Ruth was so upset that she did not realize that contracting had indeed worked for her. She was in possession of a great deal of information as well as answers to several Testing Stage questions. The information and answers were not those she would like to hear, but they provided important data about her partner that she needed to evaluate. The contract also provided an avenue of approach if she were to decide to continue Relationshipping with him.

First, Ruth learned that her partner did not keep a major and important agreement. He had agreed to be sexually exclusive with Ruth. She has seen a difference in what he has said he would do and what he has done. She needs to take a look and evaluate his general consistency. Second, he has said his action was in retaliation to her behavior of a week ago which she did not know annoyed him. If this is true, she realizes that for some reason, he did not feel he could openly disagree with her. Also, by his behavior he has shown himself to be a dirty fighter. The trauma has told Ruth that as a couple they are neglecting developmental tasks upon which they must focus if they want to continue together. Her approach to her partner should not be the general issue of infidelity but the fact that he has broken the contract. Their future focus needs to be in the areas of open and direct disagreements, resolving anger, and fair fighting. Although the contract did not guarantee her partner's behavior, it has provided Ruth with a communication system to confront that behavior and proceed toward resolution of the conflict.

Unfortunately, except for information and communication, there are no guarantees in Relationshipping. Not even a contract can turn inappropriate partners into a better match. A contract can, and does, however, focus on areas for work so that the indirect penguin system does not destroy the successful matching of those partners who do have chemistry, compatibility, and similar value systems.

Testing Stage contracts are called term contracts. Like Interaction Stage contracts, they contain a definition of purpose, a duration period, a feedback clause, and a review date. They may include previously agreed upon clauses from prior contracts or they may simply refer to those earlier contract clauses as remaining valid. Testing Stage contracts reflect and build upon earlier contracts just as Testing Stage Relationshipping reflects and builds upon earlier interaction together.

With the basis established from earlier contracts, Testing Stage contracts include areas connected to developmental tasks and expand to include any problem area which has arisen between the two partners. The Testing Stage is a time of actively working and blending together which is reflected in the solutions and compromises offered in the individual clauses. For some issues there are neither solutions nor compromises; these non-negotiables are identified and accepted as such. The expanded time period of six months gives partners the extra room to live within the framework of the contract and further evaluate viability of the couple.

Bud and Lena's term contract is a good example of Testing Stage contracting. It builds on their prior interim contract and also focuses on their individual problem areas as well as developmental tasks of this stage. It also reflects new circumstances (financial stress and limited access to his son John) created by the finalization of Bud's divorce.

Term Contract between Bud and Lena

Purpose: To mark a new point in our Relationshipping; To have an opportunity to integrate families; To alleviate financial worries; To learn to resolve anger; To further evaluate compatibility.

Contract Communication: Testing Stage

Term: Six months. All prior agreements apply except those we are specifically changing.
1. We will see each other every other weekend and two days during the other week instead of the prior schedule.
2. A minimum of one activity will be planned each month to include all five of us.
3. Expenses for these activities will be split 50-50.
4. Discipline of the children will be primarily the responsibility of the parent. If a child from each family is involved, discipline is applied equally to both.
5. At the time we are angry we will verbalize it. We then have a maximum of 24 hours to discuss the problem (no pouting.)
6. Financial Obligations:
   A. Each person is responsible for at least one suggestion of a free activity each month.
   B. We will help each other with loans or moral support when needed and when possible. Loans will be re-paid by next payday or other arrangements made.
   C. Bud agrees to provide more help to Lena in getting her house ready to sell.
7. **Non-negotiable Issues:**
   A. Bud refuses to cut his beard.
   B. Lena feels Bud's drinking is excessive.
   C. Bud is close to his famiy and will see them frequently. Lena agrees to accompany him whenever possible except when she really needs to stay home which Bud will accept.
   D. John is a priority with Bud. Lena will accept that they need time together and that they will do things that do not include her.
   E. Bud likes to be on time in certain situations. He will make these times known to Lena and she will make every effort to be punctual.

Termination: This contract will end September ninth at which time feedback will be given and modification made.

Signed:

Rosalie and Fritz's contract also builds on earlier agreements and focuses on areas particular to their individual Relationshipping. It is another typical term contract.

Term Contract between Rosalie and Fritz

Purpose: To expand our Relationshipping to include other people and other areas of interest, to resolve little trouble spots we've noticed, and to accept non-negotiable issues.

Term: 6 months with a review on November 19.
1. When Fritz is in town the whole week, we will have two nights a week when we do not see each other so we can have time with our own families and activities and personal chores. The usual nights will be Monday and Thursday but these nights can be changed depending on special events that come up. We will have a brief telephone call at some point during each evening.
2. We will do two projects during this six months:
   a. We will paint and repaper Rosalie's dining room.
   b. We will build bunk beds for Fritz's children.

3. We agree not to commit each other for any project or activity (even with our families) without checking with the other first.
4. We agree to call at the earliest opportunity if one or the other is going to be late.
5. We agree to go out once a week even if it's just window shopping or to McDonald's to eat.
6. We will take the next class offered by the public education service on simple automobile mechanics.
7. We will do an activity with another couple once a month.
8. Fritz will mention what is bothering him *when* it bothers him. He will make strong efforts not to stew over it and eventually blow up over something else. If Rosalie notices something is wrong and Fritz is not telling, she can nag him until he tells her.
9. All our agreements are still in effect except how often we see each other.

Non-Negotiables:
1. Rosalie is a little overweight and knows it. Fritz does not have to remind her and will stop urging her to go on a diet.
2. Fritz is not going to quit his job even if it involves many out of town trips. He will call Rosalie each night he is away.
3. Rosalie reserves the right to have nothing to do with Fritz sexually when he is drunk.

Feedback: We reserve November 19 for a whole evening of feedback but agree to feedback to each other on a weekly basis how we feel about the new projects and activities as we undertake them.

Signed:

Some term contracts are more specific. Stacy and Micky decided to concentrate only on their non-negotiable issues in a last ditch effort to combine their totally different preference systems. Since they were going to do this by living together, they did include some basic definitions of responsibility for co-habitation.

Stacy and Mickey's Try-To-Make-It-Work Contract

Purpose: To focus on our non-negotiable issues (there seems to be so many of them) to see if they can be tolerated or to determine if we really are incompatible.

Term: Six months.

1. Because it's a good idea economically and because we believe we can focus better on our problems by closer contact, we agree to live together for six months, January through June.
    a. We will each pay half the groceries in terms of basics. Mickey will independently pay for his cigarettes and junk food and Stacy will independently pay for her wheat germ and health foods.
    b. We will each pay half the rent, utilities, and half the basic phone charge.
    c. We are each responsible for our own laundry, personal property, and long distance calls.
    d. We will share the chores for meals and clean up, and for maintaining the apartment.
    e. Mickey will assume financial responsibility for social outings unless Stacy wants to treat and says so in advance.

2. **Non-Negotiable Issues**
   a. Stacy can dress any old way when we're at home or when she goes out without Mickey. When we go out together or when she is to meet Mickey someplace, she will dress up a little, wear make-up, and fix up her hair.
   b. Remembering that Mickey is allergic, Stacy will not bring home any stray animals and will not keep anyone's pets for them regardless of the circumstances.
   c. Mickey will limit his going out with the boys to one a night a week. He will also only play golf once a week unless we play together.
   d. We will each try new recipes and not make negative comments about each other's cooking or about health food or junk food in general. Hopefully, we can find some dishes that both of us like.
   e. We will visit each other's family one weekend a month: Mickey's in January, Stacy's in February, Mickey's in March, etc., and go by our parents' house rules. If they don't want us to sleep together, we won't. The person whose turn it is for a family visit can decide to skip it that month, but neither of us will make negative comments about each other's family.
   f. Stacy will not demand attention and affection as soon as Mickey walks in the door. She will give him wind-down time, Mickey will try to be more affectionate.
   g. Stacy will not flirt with other men. Mickey will not make demeaning remarks about women such as "Look at the jugs on that one" or "I wouldn't kick her out of my bed for eating crackers".
   h. We may each watch our favorite TV shows and play our favorite records on the stereo even if the other doesn't particularly like the shows or the music. Neither of us will make sarcastic remarks about the other's taste in records or TV.
   i. We agree to be pleasant to each other's friends even if we don't like them.
   j. Stacy will put her clothes away in a reasonable time period and not take up the whole bathroom with her stuff. Mickey will be less picky about everything in its place.
   k. Stacy agrees to plan at least one activity a week in advance. Mickey agrees to do at least one activity a week impulsively.
   l. We will solve our disagreements by the "fair fighting" rules instead of constantly picking at each other. The rules will be posted on the refrigerator.
   m. This is an exclusive contract. Neither will date anyone else and neither will tease about wanting to date anyone else.
   n. All clauses from our previous contracts are still valid.
   o. We will review our progress and have a feedback session on May 14 so we will know whether to renew our lease together or whether we just ought to admit that it doesn't work.

Signed:

Even when there are major differences such as with Stacy and Mickey, the transition from Interaction Stage issues to Testing Stage issues occurs quite smoothly for those contractors who seriously apply Relationshipping principles. Those who have contracted from the outset find they have a built in bridge of communication which helps them focus on problem solving. Those who begin applying Relationshipping principles through contracting at this stage on the continuum report less disillusionment with each other and more of an ability to work together toward compromise. The contract framework gives them a guide to work through those problems which had been terminal in prior experiences without contracting.

However, the effect is quite different for those persons who are not sincere and who are contracting merely in order to humor a partner, to keep the peace, or to use the contract as a control technique. These persons usually find their partners reacting to the motivation and attitudes behind the stated agreements. Since the Testing Stage involves expressing and resolving anger, the transition is not only less than smooth, but also blows their cover.

Ernie went along with contracting from the beginning. If it made Carrie more comfortable, it was alright with him. In fact, he thought she was adorable when she presented her opinions so earnestly. It was easy to let her have her way even if it involved a silly system. Besides, it ended up with her being less demanding than women usually are. He had more time for his own friends and interests without being nagged like other women had nagged him in the past. Since he was just going through the motions, Ernie sometimes forgot their agreements and never took them seriously. In a Testing Stage confrontation, Carrie accused him of humoring her, of treating her like a child, and of laughing at her behind her back. She was reacting to his attitudes that women are silly frivolous creatures who should be humored and pacified. Carrie wanted validation and participation. In fact, Carrie *demanded* validation and participation. The ultimatum she issued was that he either take her seriously or he could take off permanently. Rudely awakened and faced with those options, Ernie gave contracting a sincere effort. He was surprised at how smoothly he and Carrie were able to blend together. It was the same result he had sought by humoring and pacifying; however, Carrie's system had produced mutuality while his approach had produced disaster. Although contracting did not begin in a synchronized fashion, Carrie and Ernie became able to intermesh when contracting was seriously utilized to communicate and problem solve rather than as a tool to keep the peace.

Judd, 34 years old and separated from his wife of two years, sought contracting as a tool toward control. Bea had left him after eight months of constant verbal and physical conflict. Both wanted to continue the marriage, but each felt it was impossible to talk to the other. Although not interested in Relationshipping theory, Judd studied the form and prerequisites of contract communication and presented the following proposal to his estranged wife:

Purpose: To set some guidelines to help us get along better and enrich our relationship.

    1. No alcohol, including beer and wine, is to be kept in the house unless Judd is present.

2. Bea will not drink any alcoholic beverage, including beer and wine, unless Judd is present.
3. Bea will not enter any establishment that sells alcoholic beverages unless Judd accompanies her.
4. Bea will not speak to any man who is not a relative except in the performance of her job unless Judd is present.
5. Bea will not stay out past ten o'clock p.m. unless Judd is with her.
6. Bea will always answer the phone instead of just letting it ring.
7. Judd will call home every night he is working out of town.
8. Judd will not hit or push Bea.
9. Judd will be more prompt about household chores.
10. Any departure from this agreement is grounds for immediate filing for divorce.
11. This contract will last for six weeks and we will see each other at will and at least twice a week. At the end of the six week trial period, we will either move back in together or we will file for divorce.

Although extremely difficult for her, Bea did not accept this proposal. She felt it unnecessarily restricted her movements, left her little room to exercise her own judgment, and showed an absence of trust. She pointed out that Judd was out of town an average of three nights a week and she saw no reason why she couldn't go to a movie or visit a friend past ten o'clock on those evenings. Since there were no children to supervise, she felt no responsibility to be so home-bound. Judd accused her of being unwilling to negotiate and uninterested in the home.

He did not realize that he himself was demanding instead of negotiating, and that the primary item in his proposal was control of Bea's behavior. His underlying fear was that Bea would become involved with another man. His proposal therefore reflected efforts to restrict any such opportunities rather than attempts to resolve real issues between them. Bea reacted to the restrictions, and they could not reach an agreement concerning a reconciliation period.

A proper contract *form* does not insure proper contracting. The essence of the agreement is to provide overt working conditions which will allow room for compromise. Except for a few non-negotiables, clauses should be seen as short term behavioral options. A contract is an avenue for communication and problem-resolution, an opportunity for trial and error negotiation. It is not a threat. Those proposals which threaten and/or demand rather than adjust and expand are those whose primary purpose is to control.

There is no need for control measures in healthy Relationshipping. Accomplishing Interaction Stage developmental tasks provides the foundation for trust. Testing stagers thus safely engage in time limited behavioral experiments which nourish mutual growth, develop continuing compatibility, and avoid unnecessary debilitating frustrations which usually evolve under the penguin system.

When Bud and Lena decided to live together, they attempted to anticipate most eventualities by introducing a *set* of contracts: one between the two of them, and one which included themselves and the three children, all boys. Since living together required adjustments on everyone's part, feedback periods were emphasized and the contracts were of short term. The contract between Bud and Lena also reflected their prior contracting and their growth and development from one agreement to another.

Contract A: Term Contract between Bud and Lena

Purpose: Exclusive, romantic contract to explore, test and further evaluate compatibility with the goal being marriage. Also to evaluate further integration of the families. To insure financial stability.

1. Bud and Lena will arrange one weekend a month by themselves.
2. A minimum of two activities a month will be planned for just Bud and Lena.
3. When a problem arises that is not resolved for one person, that person will chose a mediator and we will abide by the decision of the mediator.
4. New Non-Negotiable: Kissing members of the opposite sex is limited to friendly hello's and goodbyes. Friendly meaning brief. This applies whether we are together or not.
5. Integration of families:
    a. A minimum of one activity per month to include all five of us.
    b. A minimum of two activities per month to include all four of us.
    c. A minimum of one activity per month for Bud and Lena's boys.
    d. A minimum of one activity per month for Lena and her boys.
    e. When either of us is having a problem with feelings concerning the other's children, we will discuss it before discussing it with the children.
    f. We will post a set of house rules which we agree on.
    g. We will back each other up in front of the children. If we do not agree, we will discuss it privately.
    h. Decisions concerning the family will be discussed privately before they are decided or presented to the children.

6. Financial:
    a. Rent, phone, utilities, and cable TV will be split 50-50 with each person responsible for his or her own long distance calls.
    b. Food costs will be split in this way: Bud $25.00 and Lena $75.00 per week. (Not included are Diet Pepsi, Beer, cigarettes, dog food which are personal items at personal costs.)
    c. Major purchases will be discussed and agreed upon before the cost is 50-50. If not agreed upon, the person wanting the item can buy it with his or her own money. A list will be kept of agreed-upon purchases and their costs.
    d. Money borrowed from each other or from the cookie jar must be paid back by pay day unless otherwise agreed upon.
    e. An additional $10.00 will be paid by Bud for food on weekends when John is with us.
    f. Lena will pay the $10.00 extra charge per month for pets because Jawa is her dog.

g. Money not spent for groceries will be placed in the cookie jar to be used in an agreed upon way.
h. All prior contract provisions are still valid re: sex, surprises, feedback, and anger.
7. This contract will be discussed, evaluated and revised at least every three months or sooner if necessary.

Signed:

Contract B: Term between Bud, Lena, Danny, Mike, and John

Purpose: To promote compatibility between the five of us and to establish individual responsibilities and expectations. This is a short term guide for living together.

1. Privacy
   a. No one goes into anyone else's room unless invited.
   b. No one will borrow anything without the owner's permission.
2. Authority
   a. Adult authority is split 50-50 between Bud and Lena. Each have the authority to hand out punishment to all three boys.
   b. In the absence of either, the other will have full authority.
3. Responsibility
   a. Each person will be responsible for his/her own bedroom which will show some effort of being presentable.
   b. Individual personal items such as toys, tools, clothes, books, etc. will not be left lying around when not in use.
   c. Each person will be responsible for the job assigned or chosen on the job chart.
   d. Anyone who has a disagreement or is upset with anyone else has the responsibility of telling that person directly.
4. John
   a. John will be with us every other weekend.
   b. When John is with us, he will abide by the contract, house rules, and his assigned jobs.
   c. When he is with us, we are a five person family.
   d. Bud and John need private time together and will be doing some things by themselves.
5. Mike, Danny, and Lena
   We each need private time together and will be doing some things by ourselves.
6. Bud and Lena also need private time and will be doing some things by themselves.
7. **Round Table (Feedback)**
   a. Once a month, on the third Wednesday, we will meet and discuss anything pertinent to the family from 7:30 to 9:30 p.m. Every one is to be present. Time can be changed if there is a school required event at the same time, but advance notice must be given.
   b. An agenda will be planned but there can also be spontaneous discussion.
   c. A different person each month will lead this meeting.
8. **Non Negotiatiables**
   a. There will be times John will receive things from Bud that Mike and Danny won't.
   b. There will also be times when Mike and Danny will receive things from Lena that John won't.
   c. Job chart and house rules must be abided by.

9. This contract will be re-negotiated in three months and feedback is invited at any time.

Signed:

Both of these contracts reflect basic ground rules, responsibilities, and expectations regarding the new living arrangement. There are few non-negotiables and much room for flexibility so that each party to the contracts may maneuver in his or her own personal adjustment. There are guidelines to insure discussion, communication, and problem solving. Enough specifics are clarified to avoid common frustrations without there being so many that the individuals feel rigidly hemned in or inhibited. These people are continuing the process of building together.

There are many other couples in the Testing Stage who, contrary to Bud and Lena, find that all they are building together is trouble. At this point they have invested a great deal of time and affection in each other. They are known as a couple. They are comfortable with each other. However, because of differing value systems and/or lack of compatibility, either one or both realizes in the Testing Stage that long term exclusive commitment is not a very good idea. Not wanting to lose what they have had and not wanting to face the pain of termination, such couples quite often try to coast on chemistry alone rather than becoming again involved in the shifting kaleidoscope of the anxiety-ridden Interaction Stage. These couples need to realize it is time to let go. Contracting can help by re-defining the Relationshipping and setting new goals for resource and support.

Big D. and Corrine were such a couple. For two years they tried to bridge their different preference systems because of mutual appreciation, admiration, and respect. Both goal oriented individuals, they had difficulty accepting that it simply would not work between them. Big D. finally decided that Corrine was marriage phobic, but Corrine said to me, "The big signal to me was that we never could seem to resolve issues. Once there was a sore spot between us, it stayed sore. It was always there and we just learned to avoid those and any similar issues. Being together was really nice, but underneath were all those things we couldn't say and all those things we couldn't do. We never wanted to lose each other so we developed a loving friendship to help us let go of each other and venture out to start all over again."

Transition Contract between Big D. and Corrine
Sept. 27

Purpose: To establish the terms of a friendship between two loving people:
    a) the parties recognize their mutual love.
    b) they agree it is unlikely this love will lead to marriage or an exclusive arrangement.

c) the parties mean to develop their friendship with new ideas in the Relationshipping by:
   1. broadening our horizons.
   2. finding new experiences.
   3. developing our understanding of the world and each other.
I. Friendship
   A. We are two people who want our lives to mix for our mutual benefit.
   B. It will lead to and promote an open discussion of our worlds.
   C. Each will be able to seek advice of the other.
   D. We will provide mutual assistance in solving problems for household items, illness, moral support.
II. It is agreed that we will not "date" each other. However, if desired, each can accompany the other to activities where both will be in attendance.
III. Economics
   A. Either may treat if announced in advance, but generally each is expected to meet own expenses.
   B. Either may make gifts to the other.
IV. This is a non-exclusive, non-sexual friendship.
V. Both of us agree to make every effort to maintain this relationshipping in spite of developing others.
VI. Both of us agree to make an effort to give each other time to be together.,
VII. Holidays
   A. Primarily family times.
   B. We agree to spend some time together sometime within 8 days of Christmas and birthdays.
   C. We agree to be mutually supportive and sensitive to each other at holiday times.
VIII. Our children will often be included in our activities, but not so often that we do not have private time together.
XI. Friends
   A. The person who has the friend may elect to expose the other to that friend.
   B. Each will make a special effort to be acceptable to the other's friends.
X. Ethics
   A. We will be truthful with each other about other Relationshipping.
   B. We will not surprise each other with dates when we are both going to the same event.
   C. When we meet at such events we will be pleasant to each other and to the other person's date.
XI. Term
   A. One year, but evergreen.
   B. First review and re-negotiation in June, regular review each June thereafter.
   C. Feedback each January and June unless a crisis arises, then immediate feedback.
XII. Termination
   A. This contract does not look to termination during the mutual lives of Big D. and Corrine.
   B. It can be and will be modified to fit the parties' circumstances.
   C. Both parties agree to find viability somehow!

(You wouldn't throw out a Rembrandt if your new spouse didn't like it.)

Big D. and Corrine were able to adjust to the new guidelines of their Relationshipping gradually over time due to their strong affection and motivation. Each also realized that the balance of their romance was too delicate to survive the Negotiating Stage. Rather than lose each other completely, they were able to make the transition.

Similarly incompatible couples should either not renew their contracts or should follow Big D. and Corrine's example of redefining the Relationshipping. The Testing Stage provides more information regarding happiness potential than any other stage. Comfortable couples who are not really compatible are challenged to recognize the information available.

Compatible couples who combine Relationshipping theory and contract communication to accomplish their Testing Stage developmental tasks are ready for long term commitment. They have successfully completed the foundation and can continue to move along the Relationshipping continuum with strength and confidence.

CHAPTER IX

The Negotiating Stage

The Interaction Stage is a time of discovery; the Testing Stage is a time of exploration and blending; the Negotiation Stage is a time of change. It begins at the point of long term commitment and is the longest stage on the Relationshipping continuum. It includes most of a long term couple's life together. They key issue in the Negotiation Stage is maintaining the warmth and emotional intimacy of the couple's bonding in the midst of chronic changes in family, friends, and circumstances.

Most partners have little difficulty maintaining their warmth and couple bonding as long as there are only the two of them. Job changes, major moves, deaths of relatives, and other life changes require adjustment, and partners tend to be supportive of each other. Partners are primarily concerned with each other and with themselves. There is no one else to worry about and no one else to hide behind. There is an automatic focus on the couple because they are the only two who are there.

The lengthy Negotiation Stage, however, usually features the arrival of (1-?) children, (more) bills, (more) responsibility, and (increasing) coordination in terms of activities and events. The focus is no longer on the couple; it is on the *family*. Partners become parents; the couplehood begins to blur in the midst of additional involvement and additional responsibility.

Heidi and Matt met on a blind date. Her best friend Poppy dated Matt's best friend Louis, and it had seemed like a good idea to double date. Most of their early dates were a foursome because Louis was the only one who had a car. Heidi still lived at home and was going to school to be a dental hygienist. Matt had just landed a new job at the foundry. They had much in common: similar backgrounds, similar interests, and similar dreams for the future. They married two years later and proudly moved into a tiny apartment which the landlord allowed them to redecorate. They were in their early twenties. They had a car, a little savings, and they both had good jobs. They continued to see their best friends Poppy and Louis (who had married the year before), and they also developed other friends and activities. Heidi calls these first four years "the best years" because it seemed like there were no problems that she and Matt could not solve. They continued to be very close even after Dean was born around their fourth anniversary. Matt was considerate, shared child care, and even got up with Dean in the middle of the night. Lottie came soon after (a little too soon), and she was a real handful. She was a fussy baby and seemed to be sick all the time. Heidi quit work because she worried too much about being gone with Lottie sick. Besides, having two children was very different from having one child. It was a full time job all by itself. The medical bills piled up, and for awhile Matt worked two jobs. They outgrew their apartment, but were lucky to find a house they could rent with an option to buy. They fell into a division of labor habit. Heidi took care of the children, their doctor's and dentist's appointments, nursery school and related activities as well as cooking, cleaning, and homemaking activities. Matt brought home the paycheck, maintained the yard and household repairs. They, like their neighbors, were a typical family oriented young married couple.

Ten years later, Lottie is no longer sickly. She and her brother Dean (a superior hockey player) are involved in many activities. Matt still works at the foundry and makes a good living, but it isn't quite enough for the family's needs and wants. Heidi went back to work three years ago. She and Matt go out together once in awhile, but mainly their activities revolve around getting the children where they are supposed to be, going to Dean's sports events, and figuring how they can stretch the paychecks a little further. Lately, Heidi is a little depressed. She confided to Poppy that she wants more from Matt, but she doesn't know exactly just what she wants. She feels comfortable but not close to him, and she wonders if she still loves him. Their fifteenth anniversary will be here soon, and it doesn't seem like a very big event to either of them. In the middle of being mother and father, provider and homemaker, economist and chauffeur, the real business of being wife and husband has been lost in the shuffle.

Matt and Heidi have become two individuals who are married to each other rather than a couplehood with its own rich and special bond. They have their children, their assets, and their struggles in common but no emotional intimacy, no feeling of being in love. They are not miserable, but they are not happy either, and though they are careful not to talk about it, both Heidi and Matt know it.

Heidi and Matt have fallen into typical Negotiation Stage preoccupation which few couples escape. Couples become preoccupied with details outside of the couplehood in their efforts to live comfortably and to manage the various aspects of their lives. They neglect crucial developmental tasks and find themselves feeling distant and emotionally unfulfilled. It is not a matter of money. Couples who have more money do not have less Negotiation Stage risks.

Once there was a couple named James-and-Olivia. He was a little shy and a serious worker. She was out-going and a little frivolous with her energy, and always had two or three projects in process while actively participating in at least four organizations. James was easy going and had trouble expressing his feelings. Olivia was periodically moody and expressed more feelings than most people knew what to do with. They had the same values, however, and similar systems of dealing with everyday life. They became the perfect couple with James acting as stabilizer and emotional anchorman for Olivia while Olivia lightened his serious vein, opening social channels for him. From the beginning, they did everything right. They dated for five months before becoming involved sexually. They took trips together to continue to determine their compatibility. They took a class together, developed couple friends, and evaluated each other in the other's environment. They fought, broke up, developed ground rules, reconciled, and blended together. They became James-and-Olivia. When they married, three years after meeting and with a six month engagement, they had a strong foundation and a good couple identity. Their best characteristics were the ability to establish goals together, their ability to compromise, and their ability to work together as a team.

For example, James wanted to live on the East Coast; Olivia wanted to go back to school. They accomplished both by looking for jobs only in locations where there were colleges featuring certified programs in her field. James-and-Olivia were patient, organized, and mutual consultants to each other in all major and minor decisions.

They did not get into trouble until they had met all their predefined goals, several years into the Negotiation Stage. At that point, they departed from mutual goals to individual goals, inadvertently reversing doing everything right to doing everything wrong. At ages 30, James-and-Olivia had finished their educations; they had two children, good jobs, a lovely house, and they were established in the community. James had all he had ever wanted and his major priority gravitated toward the further development of his career. Olivia, always goal oriented in several directions at once, wanted a cottage, wanted to travel, wanted to study something else. To James, all of her "I wannas" took away from time he wanted to spend at the office. Frustrated and seeing his example, Olivia began to channel her energies into developing her own career. Instead of pulling together, they began pulling apart. They neglected to develop new mutual goals. They forgot to continue to nourish the couple bond they had so patiently and carefully developed. At ages 35 they were divorced.

James-and-Olivia unnecessarily died of neglect and starvation. Out of respect I went to the funeral, commonly called a divorce hearing. Each bright, likable, and successful, I suppose they shall live happily ever after. But not together.

Couples who have major difficulties in the Negotiation Stage usually have not successfully built their foundation in the Interaction and/or Testing stages or have not continued to develop the couple bond. In either case, the result is a loss of couple identity. The blending of the two personalities disintegrates. It is no longer "our" way but either "his" way or "her" way; the individual integrity asserts itself.

The Negotiation Stage is a time of major life changes and must also be a time of major attitude changes. The couple is constantly balancing to maintain contact and equilibrium between partners in the face of these changes.

James-and-Olivia are therefore unusual only in that they did so many things right as they progressed along the continuum. They were more prepared than most couples to withstand the upheavals of the Negotiation Stage. During their 10 years of marriage, they successfully adjusted to two major moves, three major job changes, graduate education, the birth of two children, one partner's surgery, and a dramatic illness of one partner's parent. In the process they accumulated a two story house with nice furnishings, two cars, rental property, a lot for a dream home, various stocks and bonds, a decent savings account, and all the accompanying responsibilities and stress of such assets. These are all usual and expected changes in a couple's life together.

However, job changes, moves, children, and finances are only the beginning. For most couples, not only is providing a satisfactory life style a continuing burden but in addition the couplehood is assaulted by differing personal preferences and goals. The balancing act begins.

The time frame of the Negotiation Stage is forever or until termination, whichever comes first. If an emotional graph of this period on the continuum could be drawn, it would resemble the track of one of the popular gigantic roller coasters: two parallel lines depict the separate personalities; the steel supports between illustrate the couple's bonding; the ups and downs indicate the changes they must accomplish together over the course of the Negotiation Stage. The safety system undergirding the thrills and chills of this ride is knowledge of the primary feelings, characteristics, risks, and developmental tasks inherent in this particular stage of the continuum.

Primary Feelings of the Negotiation Stage

The primary feelings of the Negotiation Stage are growth, accomplishment, and contentment. There is no implication that each partner of every couple experiences these primary feelings every moment of every day. One of the attractions of a roller coaster ride is the variety of feelings experienced, including anticipation of each major curve, climb, and fall as well as relief when each portion is finished. But this is a long ride with many plateaus and mini hills between the larger challenges. Couples have time to view the past with satisfaction and the future with confidence.

Growth

Because of the amount of change encountered, there is growth on the part of each individual making up the couple and on the couplehood itself. With experience each person becomes more tolerant, more open, and more secure. The couplehood matures. There is a sense of age as attainment, becoming better, maturing like fine wine.

Accomplishment

The feeling of accomplishment is the result of achieving goals and successfully adjusting to the changes encountered. Problem solving skills, so carefully developed in the Testing Stage, provide for the smooth transition from one life phase to the other, engendering confidence in each other and in the partnership.

Contentment

The third primary feeling, that of contentment, is the emotional expression of mutual well being. It is the sense of moving jointly along the continuum with an intimacy and strength that can only be temporarily interrupted regardless of the disruptions.

Primary Characteristics of the Negotiation Stage

The primary characteristics of the Negotiation Stage are adaptation to change and preoccupation. Adjusting to differing environmental and personal circumstances becomes automatic. People tend to become preoccupied with factors that are external to the couplehood.

Adaptation to Change

Little Johnny is intensely aware of change and fascinated by it while his parents seem to take it as a matter of course. He regularly outgrows his clothes, eagerly measures his height against the door frame, and personally experiences the passing seasons with careful examination of bird's nests, colorful rompings in fall leaves, and the icy frothy taste of new snow. He progresses from tricycle to bicycle to racing bike while his parents philosophically buy his clothes, rake the leaves, shovel snow, and plan the budget to accomodate new needs and new circumstances. Adaptation becomes a habit for both Johnny and his parents. Children grow; jobs are obtained and lost; family size increases and decreases; living accomodations change. People adapt from one change to the next, sometimes easily and sometimes painfully, but these changes are an expected part of life.

Partners adapt to what is required of them. A couple equilibrium evolves in which each partner independently pursues mutually beneficial tasks while keeping the other partner informed of the schedule and progress. The traditional example is the male's earning an income for the family while the female provides for the family's care and maintenance. Both communicate to the other regarding the different spheres so that each partner is aware and involved in the other's primary endeavors. The couple equilibrium is a balance of behavior and communication between the two spheres and between the two partners. It provides for continued adaptation as change continues to occur. Whether partners conform to the traditional model or utilize a different system, they are influenced by their activities and by their experiences. Most people grow and develop over time although the process may be quite subtle. It is especially subtle when both partners, through emotional intimacy and communication, grow and change together. When this happy process occurs, the partners are rarely aware of changes because change has been mutual. People are continually adapting, both to the external world and to each other.

Preoccupation

Preoccupation, the second primary characteristic of the Negotiation Stage, is a matter of focusing on external events rather than on the couplehood. A mattress company has the clever ad stating that the rest of one's days depends on the rest of one's nights. This ad could equally apply to the couplehood. In the Negotiation Stage, however, couples are generally preoccupied with budgets, schedules, activities, upcoming events, and on-going tasks. Most communication involves exchange of information and project planning. Rare moments of emotional intimacy are saved for vacations ("when we can relax!") or occasional getaway weekends. There are many partners who do not seem to notice each other until they find themselves in bed together at night. This preoccupation is not a sign of lack of loving; it is a focus on immediate events. Loving becomes the background while day to day events and activities occupy more attention and energy.

Negotiation Stage Primary Risks

Perceived personal threat, depression, premature withdrawal, and parallel lives are the four primary risks of the Negotiation Stage. They are a result of reversion to penguinhood, either through refusal to adapt or through poor adaptation systems.

Perceived Personal Threat

People tend to expect changes in their lifestyle and in their environment, but they do not expect changes in their partner. During the Negotiation Stage, one partner often dramatically changes in attitude or behavior, upsetting the couple equilibrium and requiring adaptation on the part of the other partner.

Edith is an example of such a dramatic change in behavior and attitudes. She and Erwin have been married 17 years and she has always been the perfect wife and mother. That is, until recently. She began working in July and met a group of working women, some divorced. Now she's out running with them two to three nights a week. She doesn't seem to care if the house is clean, and the family hasn't had a home baked cake in months. Erwin doesn't mind her working, and he doesn't mind her going out from time to time with the girls. However, he feels as if suddenly he isn't important to her, and he's worried about where all this will lead. She doesn't seem like his shy and housewifey Edith anymore. She's just not the same person.

Lee, a prominent corporate attorney in the prime of his career, changed too. He broke down after his 25th high school reunion and told his wife Irene that he wanted to quit his job, sell their assets, and join the Peace Corps. He had just come face to face with his youthful ideals. Once ignored but obviously not completely abandoned, the urge was strong enough for him to want to jettison everything for which the couple had worked so hard. At first Irene was sympathetic and understanding but unyielding. She viewed this atypical emotionalism as a temporary reaction to the reunion. However, Lee persisted in this new goal and a year later was still resentfully going to work while regarding his wife as the thwart to his ideals.

Jeannie and Dirk have been living together quite compatibly for six years. There are just the two of them since his three children live with his former wife in California and her two daughters are grown and long gone, an advantage, Jeannie often states, of having originally married very young. One morning they received a phone call from the Sacramento Juvenile Department saying that the Judge has awarded custody of 14 year old Dirk, Jr. to Dirk because the boy's mother has said she can't control him and he needs "a father's strong hand". Overnight Jeannie sees her freewheeling devil-may-care Dirk making sounds like a responsible father. All this from a man who has had to be practically forced to send his kids Christmas presents for the last six years. As for Jeannie, the last thing she wants is to "do the mother act one more time, especially for a kid with problems."

Joel complains, "Since the birth of the baby last year, Holly is hardly fun anymore. She used to be career minded and had a thousand stories to tell about her advertising job downtown. She was the life of any party. Nowadays, all she knows are diapers, nutrition, and the current authority on children. She doesn't want to go back to work ('that rat race', she says), and it takes a crowbar to get a sitter and pry her out of the house. She isn't interesting to talk to or be with, she doesn't fix herself up, and besides all that, our sex life is practically non-existent."

Then there's Betty, who is really worried about her husband Bart. He recently was passed over for promotion for the third time and he seems to have lost interest in work and most everything else. The work part isn't so bad (it's nice to have him putting in only eight hours a day instead of ten or more), but he's developed such a negative attitude. Nothing escapes his criticism, particularly nothing Betty says or does. It's like living with a constant grouch.

All of these people are out of sync with their partners because of major attitude and/or behavioral changes to which there has as yet been no adaptation. Neither Erwin nor Joel know what to think about their wives' dramatic turn-abouts. They feel ignored and unimportant. Irene and Jeannie feel frightened. If they go along with their partners' radically new attitudes, they face tremendous changes in the lives they have known. Betty feels picked on. She realizes she is rapidly becoming Bart's scapegoat for frustration. None of these partners has yet adapted because they don't know what to do. The changes are unexpected and not within their partner's usual patterns. All five couples are at risk.

It is at times like these that penguin snouts can re-emerge on the most metamorphosed platypuses. People who have learned to communicate straightforwardly often revert to the penguin practices of "playing by ear" or dealing indirectly with unfamiliar situations. The first penguin reaction to a change in behavior is usually suspicion. Erwin is suspicious as he observes his previously housewifey Edith socializing at night without him rather than in the daytime. He has not stopped to think that because of her new working status, evening is her only time to develop friendships. Thus he perceives a personal threat that causes unnecessary anxiety.

Perceived personal threat is a hold-over from the penguin collective unconscious which believes that a change in the partner's behavior will negatively change the couple. The unchanged partner over-personalizes in terms of best self interest without considering that adaptation on his or her part could open a whole new area of couple closeness and development. Consequently, Erwin feels ignored, Irene and Jeannie fear the loss of their lifestyles, and Joel holds on to being a husband rather than adapting to the role of father. They are personalizing their partner's changes and guarding their penguin perceptions of their own best self interests.

Partners must realize that change in people, whether it be in appearance, in behavior, or in attitudes, is a natural fact of life. Guarding the status quo results in anger, resentment, and confusion. Most changes are healthy internal responses to outside stimulation and environment. Partners must adapt, as did Erwin, Irene, Jeannie, and Joel (See Contract Communication: Negotiation Stage) to maintain the couple equilibrium and to continue their mutual progress along the Relationshipping continuum.

Depression

The psychiatric condition of depression is a broad clinical category which includes symptoms of sleep disruption, appetite changes, loss of motivation, inability to concentrate, feelings of hopelessness, helplessness, and gloom. The condition varies in severity and can cripple a person's ability to function. The colloquial condition of depression, though called by the same name, is an entirely different state. This depression, which is the second primary risk of the Negotiation Stage, involves one partner's non-productive reaction to the other partner's behavior. It is a refusal to adapt and can cripple the couplehood without necessarily debilitating the depressed partner. It is a focus on the *problem* without seeking solutions to the problem. A partner begins a passive resistance to the other partner's behavior by feeling (and acting) helpless and hopeless; in short (sigh), a victim. Rather than attempting to resolve the issue, the non-adaptive partner resents the issue and enshrouds himself or herself in gloom. Betty, scapegoat of Bart's frustration, punished him with her depression as much as he punished her with his criticism. This couple required therapy to aid them in climbing out of their separate trenches of resistance to the middle ground of adaptation. Bart and Betty were able to realize that the ultimate fulfillment lies not in career, parenting, or productive work but in Relationshipping. When work is done, when children are grown, when retirement is waiting, it is the warm intimacy and investment that remains and brings the greatest satisfaction. Most depressed partners can alleviate their gloomy feelings by trying a series of adjustments to evaluate which one works best. To avoid the risk of depression, partners must keep their focus on the couplehood rather than on the individual selves that compose its parts.

Premature Withdrawal

Premature withdrawal is the third primary risk of the Negotiation Stage and is yet another manifestation of refusal to adapt. It is more prevalent in second and third marriages and with long term cohabitants than in first marriages.

This risk is not to be confused with those marital mistakes which never should have happened. Losey and Starr, for example, met in late March, moved in together in late May, and married Labor Day weekend. Their divorce was filed the week before their first anniversary. This couple, having done everything else wrong, had no choice but to withdraw from a destructive situation. They had never accomplished the developmental tasks of the Interaction Stage, much less the Testing Stage, and their progress along the continuum stopped short long before the Negotiation Stage could be glimpsed.

Premature withdrawal is the decision to opt out of *historically successful* Relationshipping rather than attempt to resolve the problems that have arisen.

Bitsy filed for divorce the day after she discovered Arnold was having an affair with his secretary. When we discussed the unpleasant reality of contemporary extra-martial liasons, she declared it was not *her* reality, and further, "I refuse to live with a man who has been unfaithful to me." Bitsy preferred to withdraw rather than to adapt to the event and examine the issues that may have led to Arnold's involvement with another woman.

Non-assertive Lydia called the lawyer and the movers the day Russ left on a week long business trip. What she saw as *their* problems had little to do with Russ. He had historically worked to resolve any issue she had presented to him. However, she had presented few issues. She (penguin-like) believed that he knew them already and was purposefully continuing his behaviors to hurt her. When Russ returned, he found his clothes in the closet and an otherwise empty house except for: one skillet (small), one mug, one plate, one fork, one glass, one chair (not his favorite), one mattress (on the floor), and one sheet, no pillow. When I talked with Lydia about anger release and fair fighting techniques, she said, "I'm through. I don't want to deal with it anymore." She was and she didn't. Lydia was mad. Rather than resolve their issues, Lydia preferred a divorce as the ultimate expression of her anger.

I believe James-and-Olivia could have survived, but James said, "It is easier to start all over with someone new than to try to resolve the problems between us." James believed their problems were caused by the particular combination and did not realize problems would crop up again regardless of with whom he was matched. He preferred to avoid the work of adaptation in the penguin belief that he wouldn't have to do it with someone else.

For those couples who have accomplished the respective developmental tasks in the Interaction and Testing Stages, there are few problems that cannot be resolved. However, contemporary society encourages individual rights rather than couple commitment and adaptation. Women's advances have made it possible to live without male support. The opportunity to withdraw for either partner has never been more attractive. Unless all alternatives have been explored, including professional help toward healthy adaptation systems, previously successful partners need to be reminded that such withdrawal may be premature.

Parallel Lives

Parallel lives is the most common maladjustment of the Negotiation Stage and it is prevalent among partnerships of more than ten years duration. It is a penguin adaptation system as it results from indirect or limited communication. Parallel lives has some merit for a couple as it allows the partners to avoid issues, to pursue his and her own separate interests, and to stay together rather than *be alone*. Having certain topics such as children and/or activities as safe topics for discussion, partners can thus maintain a life together and an image of a relatively problem-free modern couple. The cost for this arrangement is communication, mutuality, bonding, couple identity, and emotional intimacy.

"We have more of an unspoken arrangement than we have a marriage", said 46 year old Celia, an attractive woman who became involved in therapy to problem solve "private" issues she could not discuss with her husband or friends. "He tells me what he wants me to know and I tell him what I want him to know and neither of us asks questions about the rest. We are good parents to our three children; we participate as a couple in the community; and then we each have our own private lives."

Celia says their arrangement was not difficult to effect as it evolved naturally. "There was a time when Lloyd was all involved in work and I was all involved in children. I said to myself, 'Well, if you're going to be *that* way, I'll just have to find something for myself.' We were already in separate worlds. As the children required less, I began to follow my own interests during the day, and Lloyd went to his clubs at night. It was around then I took my first lover. I was surprised at how easy it was to keep things from Lloyd. We don't really have very much in common any more, but we've always liked each other and we live together very easily."

Without careful attention to maintaining bonding, the division of labor and traditional sex roles foster the development of parallel lives. When one partner works in one location while the other partner either stays at home or works in another location, it naturally follows that each develops a different set of friends and interests. If a couple does not actively work to blend those friendships and interests, each easily embarks on a separate and private life. It is dependent on each partner to involve the other. The urge to grow and expand exists with or without a partner's cooperation. If one partner does not seek mutual growth, the other may well choose individual growth. The different locations and schedules provide the means and opportunity.

Celia remarked with surprise at how easily she had concealed events from her husband. This is an indication of their lack of communication and their lack of emotional intimacy. She also remarked on how little they now have in common, an indication of their failure to involve each other in individual interests and friendships. Concealment would have been impossible with partners who had nourished the couple bond and who therefore felt that they had each other in common regardless of the differing interests or occupational pursuits. Whatever one partner feels or experiences is of particular interest to the other because they are a couplehood. Maintaining that couplehood, however, requires effort. Those couples who do not want to exert themselves need not be surprised to find they have slid comfortably into the alliance of parallel lives.

Negotiation Stage Developmental Tasks

Because of its lengthy duration and the many changes which beset a couple both internally and externally, the Negotiation Stage is a particularly vulnerable time. Partners fall into roles of provider, homemaker, parent and worker to which they invest a good deal of effort, expecting the Relationshipping to slide into place as time and energy allow. Too often it is the couple who slides — either off the continuum itself or into the alliance of parallel lives. Attention to Negotiation Stage developmental tasks prevents breakdown of the couple bond and allows partners to continue their joint and mutual progress. These developmental tasks are: nourish the couple bond; adjust jointly to change; develop new couple goals and interests; provide room for the partner's growth; achieve non-defensive negotiation.

Nourish the Couple Bond

There is a man in Midland, Michigan, who, at the beginning of each year, sits down and randomly scrawls across various days the following notations in his appointments calendar: give Winnie a call; send Winnie a flower; check if Winnie would like to meet for lunch; arrange an afternoon off with Winnie, etc. Friends of the couple say Winnie is no great beauty who must be pampered lest she be lured away by another man's attentions. Neither is she a whining insecure woman who demands such behaviors. Her husband, T.E., confided that he uses these reminders because he knows he often becomes preoccupied at work and he does not want to lose sight of the most important aspect of his life: his Relationshipping with his wife. No one has told him to do this. I don't think Winnie knows about it. T.E. is a closet platypus.

Other T.E. priorities include going away alone with Winnie for long weekends four times a year, insuring that they have at least one hour's private conversation each day, and being attentive (even staying home from work) on those rare occasions when Winnie is ill. T.E. is nourishing the couple bond. Somewhere along their 22 years together, he has realized that it does not matter how much one partner loves the other if that affection is not demonstrated on a regular basis. He could love Winnie more than his life, but if he does not show it by his behavior and his words, it is the same as if that love were not there as far as Winnie knows. T.E. has made his marriage an *active* priority. His active efforts are what make him successful in all areas of his life, work as well as his Relationshipping.

Other behaviors that nourish the couple bond are participation in marriage enrichment classes and marriage encounter weekends. These programs concentrate exclusively on communication and emotional intimacy between partners. They are reminders of successes experienced together in the past and of successes yet to come. They renew couple commitment.

Partners who are interested in less formal forms of nourishing can be creative with personal attention and consideration. Cards and short personal letters mailed to the partner take little time and are often saved and treasured. Remembering special couple occasions in addition to the wedding anniversary is fun and enriches the couple bond. There is a couple who annually remembers the night they got pregnant, another couple who commemorates the anniversary of one partner's sobriety, and a third couple who celebrates the date when one partner walked again after recovering from a serious automobile accident. Remembering and celebrating together renews closeness. Remembering events needs to be more than a token expression, however, to have the enriching effect. A partner who offers a check or a gift certificate or who takes a partner out to dinner but has nothing to say during the meal will still be appreciated, but will have done nothing to enhance feelings of closeness or bonding.

The greatest form of nourishment is personal time and positive personal attention. It does not matter whether partners are creative or traditional in their techniques or whether they choose formal or unstructured situations as mediums to provide that time and attention. When the time and attention occur on a regular and consistent basis, the couple bonding is strengthened to withstand the greatest Negotiation Stage changes.

Adjust Jointly to Change

Although different people adjust to change at different rates and different levels, it is important that partner's attitudes end up in the same general ballpark at the end of the adjustment process. Otherwise, more non-negotiables are manufactured and the integrity of the couple is severely threatened. In order for the couple to adapt successfully, each partner must be aware of the necessity for *joint* adjustments; each partner must be willing to move from his or her own position toward the middle ground. (See following chapter for efforts made by Lee and Irene, Jeannie and Dirk, Joel and Holly.) Sometimes it is necessary to seek outside help from a therapist, marriage counselor, or minister to aid one partner in moving from a position that is untenable for the other partner.

After living in Metropolis for five years, Garrett was promoted and transferred with his wife and children to Bucolic City. The wife and kids were enthralled with grass, back yards, safety, and low tension atmosphere. Garrett became a snob and continued to regard his staff as country bumpkins while his wife became the happiest coffee klatcher in town. Pretty soon, Garrett had begun to regard his wife as a bumpkin, too.

Hawkins "temporarily" works the factory night shift while Flo is a day shift nurses aid. Hawk says night shift pay buys campers, vacations, and Home Box Office TV. After three years of opposite schedules, Flo retorts that it can also pay for a lawyer and alimony.

Lamont and Rena suffered the tragic loss of their 10 year old daughter in a boating accident five years ago. Nowadays they are almost strangers to each other. Rena will approach neither boat nor beach and does not want to take vacations, saying she doesn't want time to think. She declines lovemaking with her husband, and devotes herself to their remaining child and her own bookkeeping job. Lamont participates in community events, has a light affair every now and then, and wishes life were different.

Eileen has kept 12 pounds after each pregnancy, and her husband has taken to calling her "Gunboat", a not-so-affectionate nickname which increases her appetite which, in turn, increases his irritation. Their five children are healthy and happy, but the parents don't spend much time together. In fact, they bought twin beds as a joint gift to celebrate their anniversary.

Sometimes a person can become so preoccupied with his or her feelings of ambition, resentment, tragedy, or irritation that the partnership is forgotten. Because of what one person feels or wants so intensely, the feelings and desires of the other person seem irrelevant. Each of the couples above has been through an adjustment process and each partner has adjusted differently. The Relationshipping has broken down in each situation, and there is no attempt on the part of either partner to reach a middle ground for the couple. Unless there is outside help to negotiate a more tenable position between partners, these couples cannot happily and healthily survive together.

It is the process of constant negotiation from which this stage takes its name. In the face of change, partners must continually be willing to maneuver to a compromise choice in order to maintain the partnership. Each partner must accept a responsibility toward joint adjustment.

Develop New Couple Goals

The third developmental task of the Negotiation Stage is to develop new couple goals as old goals are accomplished. This task does not seem particularly important until it is realized that the Negotiation Stage encompasses the time span from couple commitment to couple ending. Both circumstances and priorities change over the course of this time period. The Negotiation Stage may include a time of security when most required education is completed, children require less attention, houses have been purchased, jobs are as stable as they can be, and groceries are assured. There is opportunity for personal enrichment which also enriches the couple. However, there must be a sense of direction for the couple itself as well as a sense of joint effort and participation. New interests and goals revitalize a couple, continue partners' growth and development together, and generally prevent boredom and stagnation.

Goals may be long term or short term, and they should include a variety of practical and fun related projects. For example, one couple established a goal of going to Europe in three years. They also established practical short term goals to make the trip possible and more enjoyable. These short term goals included opening a separate vacation fund savings account, having a meatless meal once a week, taking classes together in French, and taking a photography class offered by the local YMCA. They planned to backpack through France in spite of the fact they had no backpacking experience. They therefore joined a community backpacking club to gain experience and meet people who had successfully made such trips. Some couples work toward obtaining citizenship, earning their G.E.D., or being the first in the family to send a child to college. Other couples buy, build, or remodel cottages with a future eye to retirement. Some develop skills together to go into business at a later time. Whether it is trips, education, retirement, a business venture, or other joint efforts, a couple needs to have the sense of direction and purpose provided by establishing and working on goals. A couple also needs on-going short term participation in new projects, new interest areas, and new people to provide stimulation and couple enjoyment.

Provide Room for the Other's Growth

As people adapt and mature throughout the Negotiation Stage, they often feel urges toward interests and self expression that were unappealing or unavailable to them at earlier stages of their development. Sometimes circumstances prevent the inclusion of the partner. Sometimes the partner's presence is not wanted. Self expression is a quirky feeling that often fears teasing or ridicule. Sometimes a person feels it's a good idea to keep the partner in the dark just in case it doesn't work out.

In their mid-30's, three unrelated women (Katrina, Ada, and Toby) all took classes unknown to their husbands because they feared they would be thought silly and childish. Katrina began ballet; Ada took up watercolor; Toby (all 206 pounds of her) enrolled in belly dancing. Although each has funny stories to tell regarding near-miss discoveries, Toby's attempts to avoid her husband's derision resulted in his certainty that she was having an affair. Her account of Stan, dressed in his version of a Mickey Spillane trench coat, breaking through the door in a rage to confront her and her supposed lover, where instead he found twenty-five scantily clad women gyrating in half light to Syrian music, has been the favorite story of many a cocktail party.

Men are not exempt from being shy about trying something new. Lumpy Ralph began working out at a local gym on his lunch hour. Flint, the father of five daughters, became a secret Big Brother. Watson wanted to write short stories and would wait until after his wife went to bed (and to sleep) before working on his literary skills. Watson's wife thought he had become impotent and was avoiding bedtime.

Not everyone has had Toby's or Watson's experiences, but nearly every partner, when proposing a new solo experience, has heard one or more of the following responses:

"Why do want to do a silly thing like that?"

"Oh yeah? And who's going to take care of the kids?"

"Why is it you never want to stay home anymore?"

"Don't you think you should spend a little more time with the family?"

"That's a waste of money."

"Next you'll be wanting to jet to Hawaii every weekend."

"After you learn it, what can you do with it?"

Not everyone responds like Spence did to Isabelle when she announced she wanted to attend a week long women's health and exercise experience, locally known as "Fat Camp". Isabelle, already perfectly lovely, needed to go to Fat Camp like Fred Astaire needed dancing lessons. Spence, however, reacted by saying it sounded like just what she wanted and asked if he could do anything to help her get ready. He then set about thinking about creative ways to give her a supportive welcome home. When Isabelle returned, she could see her initial greeting while still standing at the curb. A life size drawing of her in a swim suit emblazoned "Welcome Home, Skinny!" covered the front door. Inside, on the kitchen table stood a borrowed three foot tall advertising cut-out of a beautiful woman in a swim suit. Attached to the out-stretched cardboard hand was a florist's box containing a single long stemmed rose. At the base of the display figure lay a mushy card with an enclosed gift certificate to a nice ladies shoppe. Isabelle not only felt supported, she also felt as if she had just been crowned queen.

Isabelle's reception took time and planning, but Spence went further. He listened to Isabelle's Fat Camp stories. He met the friends she developed there and was willing to socialize with them and their partners. His message to Isabelle is clear: "What you are doing is worthwhile. The people you chose are likable. I support you. We are a team even when we're not together." He is actively making room for her to grow.

Because of underlying penguin suspicion and perceived threat, it is difficult for many partners to encourage each other toward self growth. New endeavors are seen as disruptive, and the partner who stays at home often feels abandoned and deprived.

Russell definitely did not like the idea of Imogene going back to school. He disliked the idea so much that he began to engage in little acts of sabotage. At first he only hid her textbooks or saw that she "misplaced" assigned papers or reports. Undiscouraged, Imogene merely sat down and rewrote her papers with books borrowed from her classmates. Russell advanced to big acts of sabotage. He siphoned gas from the tank an hour before she was about to drive to class. Once he went to the college parking lot and let the air out of the left rear tire. Imogene coped with all these "accidents" until she caught him one night in the act of removing the distributor cap. At that point, in tears and frustration, Russell confessed his fears: if she kept going to college, she would think she was smarter than he was and not respect him any more; she would want to take classes every night instead of just one night; she would meet some other man in her class and get involved; they weren't going to have anything in common any more. Imogene was so relieved that she wasn't going crazy that she forgot to become angry for Russell's interference. She listened to his fears and they then planned weekly quality time together. Russell had no more problems with her taking night classes.

Mavis had a similar reaction to Porter's newfound interest in the company's all men's basketball leagues. On practice and game nights, dinner was always late. Mavis was often not feeling very well. Sometimes, she felt too sick to be left alone. If Porter went to the game, it meant that he didn't love her. Porter eventually gave up basketball, and Mavis eventually got better. Without his physical outlet, Porter felt trapped and restless. He also felt resentful although he tried to keep it under control.

Partners like Mavis usually don't realize they are wet blankets to their mate's enthusiasm and are unaware of the resentment and feelings of suffocation they engender. They become less restrictive, however, when more attention is paid to the developmental tasks of nourishing the couple bond. Porter began conscientiously supplying Mavis with quality time and personal attention. He continued his attentive ways and was pleased to reap a smiling instead of sickly wife who waved him off to a new interest in golf when the summer came.

In most people there is an innate urge to grow, to participate, and to be a part of a larger group. Today's environment creates a yearning for self fulfillment, stimulation, and new experiences. A partner who restricts the other in these areas is perceived as stifling and constricting. Resentment can, and does, grow. On the other hand, a partner who provides room for the other's growth is more lusted after than Robert Redford or Raquel Welch.

February, 1981. Dawn. Cold. Seventy two excited women, mostly housewives, board a bus in an otherwise deserted shopping center parking lot. Their destination: Toronto and four days of shopping, attending plays and the ballet, generally having fun together and, most especially, for getting away from kids and husbands. Over the hubub comes the cry, "Honey, you forgot something!" Then, "Pass this to Connie". Hand over hand, over the heads and down the aisles, a good sized package is passed to the back of the bus where Connie sits, watching its progress and declaring that she has not forgotten anything. Someone notices the package is labeled "Toronto Survival Kit". All eyes on her, Connie opens the package and then opens the individually wrapped contents. A note flutters to the floor. The box contains two bottles of wine (one red, one white), a Playgirl magazine, a jar of nuts, packages of her favorite snacks, and two lapel buttons — one depicting a haloed angel and one presenting a mischievous devil. (The bus lurches; luggage doors have been slammed and locked.) The fallen note is retrieved, read, passed along, read, again passed along in progress to Connie. The note says: "I love you, honey, Hope these goodies will add to a good time. Love, Rodney". The bus begins to move and so do half its occupants. They want to look out the opposite window. They want to look at Rodney. For a few minutes, 72 women lust after Rodney and wish they were in Connie's shoes. That was February, 1981. They still talk about that trip, and they still talk about Rodney.

Achieve Non-Defensive Negotiation

The last developmental task of the Negotiation Stage is to achieve non-defensive negotiation. Those couples who learned to resolve anger together in the Testing Stage are best prepared to accomplish this delicate task. They have learned to address the issue regardless of internal anger. They have learned that their partner may have a legitimate point regardless of their own internal reactions. The major characteristic of non-defensive negotiation is open-ness. The major tool to achieve it is listening.

There is a couple who developed a serious-discussion-in-three-parts system. It has been so successful that many of their friends have followed their model. This is the process:

Part I may begin in one of two ways. One partner may approach the other saying, "Let's have a serious discussion" or a topic may appear spontaneously and receive a sharp reaction, at which point one partner says, "This sounds like a serious discussion". The words "serious discussion" act as a cue for listening and for beginning their procedure for non-defensive negotiation. Once the issue is pinpointed as a serious discussion, one partner may then present all his or her feelings and opinions on that issue (and that issue only) without being interrupted. No other discussion is held for a minimum of an hour to give the other partner an opportunity to think about what has been said. If the issue has spontaneously arisen and it is not covenient for one reason or another to begin talking at that time, a time and date is agreed upon. This is the framework for Part I.

Part II is partner's response time. After carefully considering the opinions presented and identifying one's reaction to those opinions, the responding partner proffers his or her thoughts and feelings about the issue (and that issue only) without being interrupted. There is no discussion for a minimum of an hour to give the original partner an opportunity to think about what has been said. In addition, each partner is to think about possible solutions. This is the procedure for Part II.

Part III begins with a discussion of solutions. No feelings about the issue itself are allowed until at least two, and if possible, three, solutions have been examined. The partners then relate their feelings and any new opinions they may have reached through listening and processing, and one of the previously offered solutions is picked for at least a trial effort. This is Part III.

Admittedly, this is a structured procedure. Sometimes, it is a long drawn-out procedure. When this couple was deciding whether or nor to have a third child, Parts I and II were replayed for a little over two weeks. When one partner who had learned to play the guitar wanted to take a late night job in a bar, Parts I and II tensely took more time than that. The partners have found that for heated issues it is sometimes better to wait a day or even two days instead of an hour to feel reactions and to process. It is a procedure which works for them and for the other couples who have taken it for a model.

Regardless of whether partners use a structured procedure or discuss issues spontaneously, they must be carefully aware of three indispensable requisites to achieve nondefensive negotiation. They must listen to each other; they must address only that particular issue; and, as quickly as possible, they must move past their feeling responses to solutions. I particularly like the structured procedure of Part III because possible solutions are offered before feelings are discussed. Feelings are then used as guidelines to select which solution is optimum. The important task is to be able to be open with each other and to agree on a subsequent path to follow. Once that has been accomplished, non-defensive negotiation has been achieved.

Negotiation Stage Questions

The Negotiation Stage is a lengthy period accompanied by great and small changes. It is a time when partners often lose touch with each other in the midst of adjustment to these changes. Partners may better keep their fingers on the couple pulse by asking themselves the following questions when they encounter difficulties along this stage of the Relationshipping continuum:

1. *Do I arrange to have a minimum of two hours a week quality personal time with my partner?*
2. *Are my partner and I growing together or growing apart?*
3. *What compromises are possible?*
4. *What are our new couple goals?*

Negotiation Stage Summary

The Negotiation Stage is the longest stage on the Relationshipping continuum. It begins at the point of serious couple commitment and most of a couple's life together involves the feelings, characteristics, and risks encountered in this stage. Partners are constantly confronted with change, both internal change as a result of maturation and self growth, and external change in circumstances and environment. It is the time when partners tend to be preoccupied with issues other than the couplehood, and previously successful long term Relationshipping often breaks down. Couples who would survive together happily must devote time and effort to accomplishing the developmental tasks of this stage. These developmental tasks focus on nourishing the couple bond, adjusting jointly to change, and providing open avenues for couple growth. This focus does not automatically exist. It requires effort on the part of both partners. Those couples who combine the knowledge of this difficult stage with a contractual framework for communication are best able to maintain equilibrium in their joint progress along the continuum.

CHAPTER X

Contract Communication: Negotiation Stage

Many people who religiously promote simple initial, interim, and term contracts are lackadaisical regarding Negotiation Stage contracting. This inconsistent attitude is symptomatic of the penguin philosophy which places all importance on "finding a relationship" but expends little energy on keeping it going. This emphasis is unfortunate because Negotiation Stage contracts, called renewal contracts, are the most salient agreements of the entire Relationshipping process. Simple initial and interim contracts minimize anxiety and provide for understanding of what is required for a successful match. They supply a framework for evaluation of data, and they also immediately institute open healthy communication patterns instead of the usual indirect penguin system. Term contracts aid couples in working and blending together and insure that resolvable conflicts are indeed resolved. Renewal contracts, however, are the glue that keeps it all together. Without Negotiation Stage contracting, all the prior effort, evaluation, and investment are worthless. The magical feelings of emotional intimacy and love can, like all things magic, simply disappear. Renewal contracts stimulate continued closeness. They prevent platypuses from reverting to penguinism.

Renewal contracts uniquely express each individual couple experience. They are in effect for a period of one year, and the annual review date is most effective when combined with either the couple anniversary date or with new Year's Eve/New Year's Day celebrations. These occasions are traditionally times of introspection and evaluation. They are thus ideal dates for partners to discuss and renew their Relationshipping in the contractual framework. Renewal contracts contain the following clauses: definition of purpose, couple quotient, unfinished goals (both joint and individual), new goals (both joint and individual), problem identification with solutions, and intended renewal date plans. Proper names for the partners are always used in writing the contract to maintain an air of objectivity. One partner acts as recorder for the couple. Because of the one year term, renewal contracts should be written to prevent strain on memory. In addition to avoiding misunderstanding of what agreements were reached and what problems were identified, these written documents create an especially beautiful and poignant journal of a couple's life together.

Definition of Purpose

As with preceding contracts, the definition of purpose in renewal contracts makes a statement of the partners' emotional intentions toward each other. It explains what they are doing together. During the Negotiation Stage it is basically a statement of commitment.

Couple Quotient

The couple quotient can be compared to the President's annual State of the Union address. Like that speech, the couple quotient is a status report. Focusing on the couple instead of the country, the couple quotient summarizes the emotional condition of the couple, their economic status, and all major factors between them that may have changed or may be causing stress. As previously mentioned, it is best to use proper names and third person pronouns so that the couple quotient will not have a one sided effect. For example, it is better to write "John and Mary moved into the new house" rather than "John and I moved into the new house". Otherwise, the contract phraseology, beginning with the couple quotient, tends to have a favored slant toward the person recording it.

In examining themselves to find their couple quotient, partners often realize concerns that are present but unexpressed by non-contracting couples. By offering an opportunity and a framework for discussion, the couple quotient thus becomes an early warning system for recognizing issues that are building and which would become more highly charged and problematic at a later time. The couple quotient is a device to maintain awareness and emotional closeness between partners.

Unfinished Goals

Couples must refer to the previous contract to evaluate their progress regarding last year's joint and individual goals. This clause promotes unity and reminds partners of the process nature of the Relationshipping continuum. Any unaccomplished goals should be noted along with the reasons those goals were not obtained. Also, a notation should be made as to whether or not those unfinished goals are still desired and whether or not they will remain a focus of effort. Partners consequently receive explanations for any contradictions between stated intentions and follow through in these areas, and they also become aware of changes in partners' interests and priorities.

New Goals

This clause is closely allied with the developmental tasks of the Negotiation Stage. Goals should be specified for joint couple efforts and for individual efforts. Joint goals should focus toward nourishing the couple bond, developing new couple projects and interests, and helping each other to adjust to change. Individual goals should be oriented toward personal growth and stimulation. Both joint and individual goals may include efforts to remedy potential problems discovered as a result of determining the couple quotient. This clause promotes mutuality and joint couple growth.

Problem Identification with Solutions

Identifying problem areas and working together to resolve such issues are the key efforts which result in maintenance of the couple unit. There are some problems which offer no solutions, and couples must add these rare issues to their list of non-negotiable items. However, most supposedly unresolvable problems are really only areas in which one or the other partner refuses to adapt or in which one or the other partner has reached a maladjustment instead of an adjustment. There are few problems which motivated partners cannot resolve once they attempt to adapt and move toward compromise. This clause aids a couple move beyond the problem itself to focus on joint efforts toward resolution. It provides a framework for negotiation. It also provides a built-in alarm system to alert partners to serious breakdown in the Relationshipping. Couples who have extreme difficulty with this clause should seek outside help. However, couples be warned: any minister, marriage counselor, or therapist, regardless of credentials earned, who advises whether one partner is right or the other partner wrong is an outside agent who cannot be of help. The right or wrong of an opinion is irrelevant. The important task is to reach a position, usually by trial and error, that is acceptable for both partners. The outside agent's job is to motivate the couple to attempt alternate avenues to resolve issues. In this way, each partner becomes better able to fit the definition of an incurable optimist: a person who is willing to try anything that works. Partners can resolve any issue once they have reached this level of openness to each other.

Renewal Date

The renewal date usually occurs in one year and is best planned for either the couple's anniversary date or on New Year's Eve or New

Year's Day. These occasions already exist culturally as couple holidays, and contracting is a natural extention of the thoughts and emotions experienced at these times. Many couples arrange to take a weekend away to have uninterrupted privacy to reflect on their Relationshipping. Others take advantage of special New Year's or weekend rates at local hotels to spend one night and the better part of two days to focus particularly on their progress along the continuum. These retreats can be enriching and they can be disturbing. Couples emerge knowing their strengths and their weaknesses together. The contractual framework provides data people need. Those partners who are not pleased with the information obtained know what steps must be taken to attempt remedy. These partners usually prefer an earlier renewal date in order to review the success of solutions which have been proposed. Although couples who have successfully progressed to Negotiating Stage contracting generally are able to take long strides in overcoming problematic issues, it is a fact of this stage that some adaptations require shorter step by step procedures. The renewal date is thus a flexible tool which depends on the issues encountered.

The combination of these topics into a working format is the common denominator of Negotiation Stage contracts. The content of the documents is as varied and unique as the personality combinations composing each couple. The two contracts below are examples of differing life situations and differing issues which can be encountered in the same stage. LaVerne and Roy as well as Angelina and Elliott pinpoint issues pertinent to progress along the Relationshipping continuum.

LaVerne and Roy's Renewal Contract

Purpose: To work together to make our eleventh year and our first year in our "new" house the best year it can possibly be.

Couple Quotient: We have been married 10 years. Teddy is one year old. We are still basically adjusting to him. We have just bought a house. Finances are tight until we pay off the second loan we took for the down payment. Otherwise, everything is good between us.

Unfinished Goals:

Joint: We dropped out of the square dance club because we didn't know anyone and because we felt silly. We should have joined something else in its place. All our other joint goals were met.

LaVerne: I did not get to take that sewing class and I still want to take it. I also wanted to take that exercise course at the 'Y' to get my figure back and didn't. I still want to exercise regularly. The reason I didn't take these classes is that I have to take care of Teddy all the time and Roy wouldn't help so I could go out and do some of these things.

Roy: All of my personal goals were met, but apparently at some expense to LaVerne because of child care with Ted. I hadn't realized this.

Goals for this Year:

Joint:

Projects:
1. Paint the different rooms in the house. We will take a long weekend and paint the kitchen, living room, dining room, bathroom and hall within the next six months. We will schedule Teddy's room, our room, and the guest room for paint later in the year.
2. Plant two apple trees in the back yard.
3. Join a parents' reciprocal child care club and keep other people's kids overnight occasionally in return for their keeping Teddy.
4. Start visiting churches and join the one we like best so Teddy will have a religious background.

Fun:
1. We will investigate inexpensive fun activities and plan to go out together once a week. We will renew our interests in roller skating, ice skating, bicycling, hiking, and just plain walking. Emphasis will be also on picnics, free concerts, and $1.00 matinee movies. Dinners out will be at *McDonald's only* except for birthdays and anniversary.
2. We will get to know the neighbors and see if there are any we might like to develop as friends and have over for hot dogs, etc.

Roys:
1. I want a night out each week to get away from both work and family, maybe swim regularly with Jeff at the 'Y'.
2. I want to pay off that second loan as fast as we can.
3. I want more time with LaVerne, just us.

LaVerne's:
1. I want to take that sewing course so I can make more of Teddy's and my clothes.
2. I'll develop my own daily exercise routine at home.
3. I want a night out too. It can be the sewing class at first, but after it's over I want to visit friends or go shopping.
4. I want to develop women friends who have children around Teddy's age.

Problems and Solutions:

Roy feels like LaVerne is always involved with Teddy and has little time for Roy. Especially at bedtime. LaVerne feels Roy doesn't share enough child care responsibility, and that's why she's so tired at night most of the time. LaVerne says Roy has hardly changed a diaper. He comes home from work, flops down to read the newspaper and relaxes while she's trying to fix dinner and keep Teddy occupied. Then after dinner clean up, it's bath and bedtime for Teddy, and then she has to pick up the house. No wonder Roy (all relaxed!) is full of energy, and she's so tired when it comes time to go to bed.

1. Except for Wednesday and his night out, Roy agrees to take over with Teddy (after a 30 minute break) when he gets home from work. Instead of reading the paper, Roy agrees to occupy Teddy while LaVerne is fixing dinner, and he also agrees to help with bath time and settling Teddy down for bed.
2. Every Wednesday LaVerne agrees to skip Teddy's afternoon nap, feed him early, and put him to bed early. Wednesday will be *our* night. Nothing else will be planned on Wednesdays.
3. LaVerne agrees to take a nap each afternoon while Teddy is sleeping (except Wed) and not worry so much about a super clean house.

Finances are a problem and will be a problem until we pay off this second loan.
1. We agree not to make any major purchases (like new furniture) this year.
2. We agree to give up going to plays, expensive restaurants, and joining organizations where there is a continuing fee.
3. We agree to focus on family and friends this year, casual entertainment and simple outings around public facilities.
4. Roy agrees to brown bag. LaVerne agrees to pack his lunch.
5. LaVerne does not want to find a job and that is agreed. She does not have to provide money for this houshold — she's working hard enough with Teddy!

Renewal Date: We will review this contract next year on April 23rd, our eleventh anniversary.

LaVerne and Roy are an example of a couple whose renewal contract discussion revealed resentful undercurrents that were affecting the Relationshipping between them. Roy, feeling a loss of attention and otherwise preoccupied with the money situation, had never connected LaVerne's lack of sexual interest with her over burden of child care responsibilities. Perhaps LaVerne had not cognitively made the connection either. However, a disruption had begun, and it was their routine renewal discussion that made it possible to address the issue openly and take positive steps toward remedy.

Elliott, on the other hand, was fully aware of the effect on the marriage of his wife's continuing preoccupation with pregnancy. He used the renewal discussion as an opportunity to begin working past the problem to a point where solution or adjustment was possible. In addition, both compromised on a family issue that had become a push-pull between them.

Angelina and Elliott's Renewal Contract

Purpose: To keep on growing and communicating together.

Couple Quotient: This is our sixth anniversary. We still don't have any children. We work at the same companies as we did last year. Elliott received a merit raise and might be supervising some people this year. Angelina likes her job but there's no future there. Both of us have friends and individual interests and lots of quality time together.

Unfinished Goals: We met all our joint and individual goals last year except for getting pregnant (which wasn't our fault). We still want to have a baby.

New Goals:

Joint:
1. Get pregnant.
2. Continue building up the savings account to save for a house.
3. Join a Little Theatre goup to investigate new people and new interests.
4. Do all our Christmas shopping for Angelina's family by Thanksgiving.

Elliott:
1. Since my boss recommended it, I want to start my MBA. I'll just take one class per semester.
2. I would also like to take a course in CPR.

Angelina:
1. I'm going to work on the family history and see how far back I can trace both Elliott's and my families.
2. I want to start yoga and learn to feel more relaxed inside. Maybe that will help to get pregnant.
3. I want to spend more time with my little sister still living at home and get to know her better.

Problems and Solutions:

We might as well face the fact that we might not be able to have children. We've been trying for five years and nothing's happened yet. Angelina seems depressed about it, and talks about it all the time. We've always assumed we'd have children. If we're not, we'd better get adjusted to it and stop planning for there to be five or six of us eventually. Angelina is 30 years old and it may not be safe for her. We both agree we probably don't want to adopt.

1. We agree, as soon as possible, to get a referral to a fertility specialist and have complete tests and exams for both of us. Elliott will make the appointment and the initial contact.

2. We agree to make future plans after we hear what the doctor has to say and not worry about it until then.
3. We agree to become involved with other things (like Little Theater) and talk about other things so we're not constantly wondering what's wrong with us.

Angelina has noticed that Elliott is less and less interested in visiting her parents. We used to go for every holiday and most Sunday afternoons. Lately, he only wants to go on major holidays like Christmas and Easter. Elliott feels her parents are too nosey and give too much advice. He says they want their fingers in all our pies. Angelina feels they're not nosey; they're just interested.

1. We agree to visit less often than every Sunday and every holiday, but more often than we have visited lately. We'll start out trying every six weeks.
2. Angelina will have a private talk with her mother about some things being our private business. This would include the baby status, the financial status, and personal talks about how we're getting along. Also, Elliott is not going to go into business with Angelina's father, and her parents need to stop hinting and talking about it. Hopefully, this talk will take off some of the pressure.
3. While visiting, we'll organize some kind of game like cards or softball or croquet or outdoor cooking with Angelina's five brothers and sisters and their husbands and wives. With everybody more active instead of just sitting around and talking, these extra-personal talks are less likely.

Renewal: We will amend and add to this contract after we talk with the doctor. Otherwise, we will renew as usual on New Year's Eve.

Elliott used the renewal discussion to work through current Negotiation Stage issues. Some couples, however, must do make-up work during the Negotiation Stage. Partners who, in spite of best intentions, did not actually accomplish the crucial developmental tasks of preceeding stages, must re-apply their efforts to this old business. Partners who, out of ignorance, were unaware of pre-requisite groundwork, must backtrack somewhat. People who have not properly built a foundation together inevitably encounter major problems for which they are unprepared and for which they have no skills to resolve. In these instances, concerns that were a feature of earlier stage focus make their appearance in Negotiating Stage contracts.

Maxine and Smitty did not begin contracting until they were exposed to this concept in their marriage counseling sessions. Married 14 years, they nonetheless had never developed a feedback system, an Interaction Stage developmental task. Neither had they achieved the Testing Stage task of learning to resolve anger together. Their communication had predictably broken down, and they had no framework to organize their thoughts, emotions, or efforts. Their renewal contract offered them those guidelines, and featured the appearance of earlier stage concerns in addition to the typical Negotiation Stage contract items.

Maxine and Smitty's Renewal Contract

Purpose: To get back in touch with each other, to maintain this marriage, and to be able to have confidence in each other again.

Couple Quotient: We have been married for 14 years. Our children are ages 10 and 12. Our economic status is secure. Smitty was promoted again last year. We have everything we want, but Smitty just discovered Maxine is having an affair with our dentist. Neither of us wants to divorce, but both of us are very angry at each other. We are going to try to put it all back together.

Unfinished Goals: This is our first contract. We didn't have any goals last year. Besides, we are starting all over. Nothing in the past counts.

New Goals:

Joint:
1. To communicate with a feedback system, beginning with the exercises we learned in counseling.
2. To learn to fight fairly by using the fair fighting rules.
3. To spend more time together as a family.
4. To spend more time together as a couple.
5. To stop trying to put blame for what has happened and to start improving for the future instead.

Maxine:
1. To start expressing my feelings with words instead of acting them out with my behavior.
2. To terminate my outside relationship.
3. To get a job so I can feel good about myself in other areas besides just being Smitty's wife.

Smitty:
1. To be a better friend and lover to Maxine by listening better, being more supportive, sensitive, and considerate when she tries to talk to me about her life and her concerns.
2. To keep this turmoil from affecting my work.
3. To spend more time with my wife and family.

Problem Identification and Solutions:

In trying to be a good provider and good worker, Smitty has neglected wife and family. Maxine has not directly tried to tell him of her loneliness and unhappiness. This resulted in an affair.

1. Smitty agrees to leave work each night no later than six o'clock, *no matter what* is happening.
2. Smitty agrees to make a priority of attending children's activities: school open houses, recitals, sports events, etc.
3. The affair has been discussed enough: we both agree not to bring it up again.
4. Maxine agrees to have no further contact with him.
5. We agree to continue to have a minimum of one hour each night private talk time. This will be at 10:00 p.m.
6. We agree to tell each other if we have a difference of opinion or are irritated with each other. This includes discussing any violation of this contract.
7. If we get into a fight, we will stop and get the fair fighting rules to keep us from using dirty fight techniques, and also to help us make sure we resolve issues.
8. We agree to do a family activity and a separate couple activity at least once a week.
9. We agree to continue with marriage counseling, both joint and individual sessions.
10. The hardest thing is to look ahead instead of backwards, but with each other's help, we are going to do it.
11. We agree to find a new family dentist.

Renewal: We will review this contract in two months on New Year's Eve to evaluate our progress, and will renew in 14 months on the following New Year's.

Maxine and Smitty had more than the usual amount of work to do during their contract. They were simultaneously focusing on Interaction, Testing, and Negotiation stage developmental tasks. Most renewal contracts, however, are primarily concerned with the business of compromise and adaptation. The following two contracts were written by couples who were grappling with the spectre of major changes in their life situations.

Lee and Irene's "You-want-to-go-*where*?" Renewal Contract

Purpose: To keep our closeness and our marriage together as we consider a dramatic change in our lives.

Couple Quotient: We are in a crisis. After 23 years together working toward the top, Lee wants to go back down again: quit his job, sell everything, and join the Peace Corps. Irene wants to continue our present lifestyle, enjoying the pleasures and luxuries that are the result of all our work and plans together. However, she does not want to enjoy these things without Lee. Irene did not realize how strongly Lee felt or how bitter he was about her refusal to consider it until this renewal discussion.

Unfinished Goals: Irene broke her leg last year and we did not go on the British walking tour vacation which is irrelevant now. All other personal and joint goals were met.

New Goals: We are focusing completely on compromising to this issue.

Joint Goals:
1. We will apply to the Peace Corps to see if we are accepted.
2. Lee will investigate to see if the Peace Corps qualifies for the company's one year leave of absence public service program.
3. If we are not accepted by the Peace Corps, we will develop a new contract right away.
4. If we are accepted but the Peace Corps does not qualify for the leave of absence program, Lee will resign from the company.
5. We will not sell anything. We will give our friend and family attorney our power of attorney, and he will manage our interests in our proposed absence.
6. We will store the furniture and rent the house.
7. The real estate company will manage rentals for the condominium and the cottage.
8. If we are accepted, Irene will, for one year, participate to the best of her ability with no unusual grousing and will be enthusiastic. At the end of that year, both will return home if she does not want to continue.
9. If we are not accepted, this will be the end of the Peace Corps idea and any self dedication will be done on the local level. We will explore alternatives if and when the need arises.
10. In the meantime, we will both participate in a physical fitness program to increase our stamina and toughen our bodies.

Renewal: We will review this contract on our next anniversary or when acceptance/rejection is received from the Peace Corps.

Lee and Irene did not exactly follow the format for renewal contracts. They were in a crisis and knew it. All of their attention and energy focused to find a middle ground tolerable to both. Jeannie and Dirk had similar attitudes when negotiating to keep their couplehood while dealing with an unexpected addition to their living situation.

Jeannie and Dirk's "Three's A Crowd" Renewal Contract

Purpose: To decide whether or not we want to keep living together under new circumstances.

Couple Quotient: We've been living together for six terrific years. Jeannie still does not want to get married, but Dirk has had a change of mind. The court has given him custody of Dirk, Jr., who will be arriving as soon as arrangements are complete. Dirk, Jr., has lots of problems. Things are going to be very different around here if we continue together.

Unfinished Goals: We accomplished all of last year's goals. We've had the perfect combination of separate things and together things. It couldn't have been better.

New Goals:

Joint:
1. To function together as a family as well as a couple.
2. To keep our close relationshipping with the addition of a new person.
3. To have nights out together once a week after Dirk, Jr. is stabilized.
4. To do more at home projects like finishing the basement.

Dirk:
1. To be a good father for Dirk, Jr. and help him through his problems.
2. To continue to be a good roommate and lover to Jeannie.
3. To get involved with Dirk, Jr. in activities like baseball, soccer, etc.
4. To cut down on my other outside activities.

Jeannie:
1. To continue with my usual outside activities.
2. To help Dirk, Jr. when necessary.
3. To join the National Organization for Women (NOW).

Problems and Solutions:

Jeannie feels things can't possibly be as good after Dirk, Jr. arrives. He's going to need lots of time and attention. Our whole life will change. Jeannie does not want the responsibility of a teenager. She does not want to give up the freedom we have. Dirk says we have no choice. We've either got to do this together or we're going to be blown right apart. He cannot abandon the boy, and he admits he's been a lousy father. He wants to make it up to Dirk, Jr. In four years, Dirk, Jr. will be out on his own anyway. He believes we can be as close and enjoy ourselves as much as in the past, only in different ways. He says he will make a special effort to consider Jeannie and talk things over with her.

1. We agree to try this new family status for one year.
2. We agree to seek family counseling at Family Service and work together toward a good adjustment. Dirk will make the appointment.
3. We agree to develop a contract with Dirk, Jr. so that he will know our expectations of him and we will know his expectations of us.
4. We agree that Jeannie may attend any outside event or activity she wants, but Dirk requests that she not do it to avoid him and Dirk, Jr.
5. We agree that Dirk and Dirk, Jr. will help with the cooking and household chores. Dirk will reinforce this.
6. We agree to discuss together any problem that arises with Dirk, Jr. and we will be unified in dealing with him.
7. If one of us disagrees with the way the other handles a situation, we will discuss it privately between ourselves and find a compromise.
8. We agree to give Dirk, Jr. a welcome and to act as if we really want him rather than were forced to take him by the Court.

Renewal and Review Dates: We will review this contract on the first Sunday night of each quarter and will check these dates and put them on the calendar so we won't miss them. We can add and subtract items at these quarterly reviews according to how things are going. We will evaluate the year's progress on January first and decide if we want to continue living together or not.

Less dramatic but no less important to the people involved, the next two contracts illustrate two couples' struggles with more typical Negotiation Stage life changes. The partners' attempts to adjust jointly to altered conditions and to reach a middle ground toward problem resolution are evident.

Edith and Erwin

Purpose: To adjust to each other at this new point in our lives.

Couple Quotient: Things are not good. Things are not bad, but they are not good either. We've been married 17 years. The children are 15 and 11 and doing well in school. Edith started working four months ago and now is gone most nights. Erwin in not happy with the changes. We argue more frequently. The atmosphere in the house is tense.

Unfinished Goals:

Joint: The three week family camping trip out West was wonderful, but it cost more than we thought. That's why we didn't get the new dining room suite. We did not take the class in investments together. We dropped off in going out together and have gotten into the habit of going out for special occasions — about once a month instead of once a week. We didn't go on the fall foliage tour we'd planned. We didn't take golf lessons together.

Erwin:
1. I didn't build the shelves for the pantry because I couldn't seem to get our son interested in helping me: this was supposed to be a father-son project.
2. I didn't continue with the weekly poker game. Since Fred moved, I haven't had much interest in it.
3. I didn't join the men's club to make new friends. They meet at lunch and it's just too hard to get away from the office at that time.

Edith: I met all my personal goals, including getting a job. Also when Erwin backed out of the golf lessons, I went ahead without him.

New Goals:

Joint:
1. To have more time together. We will schedule one special time together each week.
2. To make that time quality time by planning ahead.
3. To start following through on plans for the economic situation at retirement.
4. To follow through on making investments to provide for the children't college education.
5. To pay more attention to each other and our differing rates of adjustment.
6. To take a class in ballroom dancing together.

Erwin:
1. I have got to push myself into getting involved.
2. I want to follow through on both joint and personal goals and need encouragement from Edith.
3. I will join the men's club.
4. I will build the pantry shelves, with or without help.
5. I will get back into the poker game or find a substitute activity involved with people.

Edith:
1. I realize I've gotten carried away with going out and getting involved and have pretty much left Erwin to fend for himself. I will be more considerate in this area and cut down of my outside interests. After all, Erwin is right: I don't *have* to go to every shower and going-away party that is held. Or if I go, I don't have to stay so long.
2. I want to set priorities regarding my available social time.
3. I will practice saying 'no' and become more comfortable with turning people down.
4. I will be more encouraging of Erwin's getting involved.
5. I will take time out to make special couple dinners for us.

Problems and Solutions:

It looks like we're getting into parallel lives. Erwin is holding back and Edith is charging ahead without him. Erwin doesn't like to go it alone. He's still adjusting to Fred's move and doesn't have a best friend anymore. He lets things ride if there's no one to do it with. Edith makes friends quickly and participates easily. Because of this, we're losing touch with each other.

1. Edith agrees to talk more about her new interests and include Erwin in the activities if possible.
2. Erwin agrees to act interested instead of hurt when Edith talks about people at work.
3. We will invite people at work to dinner or go out with them so Erwin can meet and get to know them.
4. We will each work on our new joint and personal goals to enrich our lives and our time together.

Renewal: We will review this contract and our progress in three months and every three months afterwards until our anniversary when we will officially renew. We need this frequent review to stimulate our motivation.

Edith and Erwin's problems were typical Negotiation Stage issues after many years of marriage; Joel and Holly's problems were typical Negotiation Stage issues of early marriage.

Joel and Holly

Purpose: To re-establish contact with each other and help us adjust to being a family instead of just a couple.

Couple Quotient: We've been married four years. The baby is eight months old. Holly isn't working and doesn't want to go back to work when her leave of absence expires. Our lives are completely different and everything, even our personal relationshipping, revolves around the baby.

Unfinished Goals: All our last year's goals (mainly getting ready for the baby) were accomplished. We took the classes, fixed up the nursery, and bought the layette. We realize now that all our personal goals were wrapped up in the baby.

New Goals:

Joint:
1. Find a way to spend more time together, just us.
2. Go away for a weekend from time to time and let Joel's mother keep the baby for us.
3. Meet other couples with young children.
4. Develop additional interests besides the baby, like cards and photography.
5. Develop a list of trustworthy babysitters.

Holly:
1. Get rid of this fear that something terrible will happen if I leave the baby.
2. Meet other mothers with young children.
3. Learn crewel embroidery.
4. Get more organized betweeen child care and housework.

Joel:
1. Get involved with interdepartmental athletics at work.
2. To start being more of an active father.

Problems and Solutions:

Joel feels there's too much emphasis on the baby and not enough emphasis on the Relationshipping between Joel and Holly. In fact, he's afraid he and Holly are rapidly going downhill. She's always tired, doing baby things or housework when we're together, and he doesn't feel close to her anymore. Holly says this is all true, but it's because she has to do it all herself. Joel hardly helps at all, and Holly is terribly afraid she is going to make a mistake. She doesn't feel Joel listens when she talks about her worries. He says they're silly. She admits she feels closer to the baby than to Joel. To her, he doesn't seem that interested in being a father.

1. Joel agrees to be more supportive of Holly in the future, and to be more responsive when she's talking about her fears and concerns.
2. Joel agrees to learn how to bathe the baby and if Holly will change from breast feeding to the bottle, Joel will take over the night feeding.
3. We agree to hire a cleaning lady.
4. Joel agrees to become more involved with child care and Holly agrees to make known to him what is to be done.

5. Holly agrees to ask Joel for help instead of trying to do it all by herself.
6. Holly agrees to stop her work and her projects after the baby is down for the night and spend that time as quality time with Joel.
7. We agree to join a child study club and go to the monthly meetings together.
8. We agree to join that new card club. We will offer our apartment for a meeting place.

Renewal: We will review and renew this contract on our fifth anniversary.

Renewal contracts are helpful whether a couple is dealing with a new house, a new baby, an extra-marital affair or a projected move to West Ngumbaland. They are designed to aid couples negotiate together in the midst of the most dramatic or everyday changes. These agreements are not always easily reached. People are often caught unaware when they discover a partner unhappy about an attitude or event which had passed unnoticed until renewal. Renewals are full of conflict as often as they smoothly dovetail. Perhaps the most important renewals are those in which partners find themselves in opposition. The opportunity to address directly the existing but unrecognized issues enables a couple to avoid potentially debilitating covert contracts. Following the format for renewals forces the individuals to move past their own opinions to a middle ground – to create compromise. Negotiating differences gives birth to strength and confidence. The annual renewal contracts become a focal point of a couple's life and depict the process by which partners grow and progress together.

CHAPTER XI

The Termination Stage

Termination is not limited to the Termination Stage; it can occur at any point along the Relationshipping continuum. Endings are difficult for penguins and platypuses alike. All terminations contain some element of pain; it is only the degree which varies. Appropriate pain is dependent upon the amount of investment in the Relationshipping combined with the distance traversed together along the continuum. Sometimes, penguin-like, a person invests more in what *might be* than in what is. On these occasions, the pain of termination is inappropriately high.

Marjean went out with Davis only three times but had had great hopes regarding Relationshipping together. As far as she was concerned, they would have been the perfect match. First, he had asked her to a movie. Two weeks later, he had asked her to dinner. Their last date had been at her invitation to her office party. She still saw him occasionally, and he was friendly, but he didn't ask her out again. Marjean went into a fit of depression when she finally accepted that Davis probably wasn't going to call.

Marjean's situation, and others similar to it, do not really qualify as terminations. They fit better in that highly populated category of interactions that never develop to Relationshipping. Endings like Marjean's have appropriate pain at the "ouch" level. Anything more is unnecessary and unhealthy. Marjean did not interact with Davis long enough to know whether or not he fulfilled her fantasy of the perfect match. Her depression was a result of the loss of what *might have been* (her hopeful fantasy) rather than the loss of Davis. People who react like Marjean must learn not to live these initial interactions as if they were the first moments of the rest of their lives. Unnecessary depression and pain can be avoided by properly orienting themselves as not yet being on the continuum and limiting emotional investment to what *is* rather than what it *might* become.

Unlike Marjean and Davis, Georges and Gigi did begin a continuum together. They met on their respective winter vacations in a tropical resort and were surprised to find they resided only four hours apart. French Canadians, they shared six rich and warmly emotional months before coming to an unexplainable end. Gigi noticed it first and raised the issue with Georges by telephone. The truth is that Georges had too many unresolved past issues and Gigi was too preoccupied with current issues for either of them to relationship successfully, but neither had this insight. They only recognized that their time together was done. Georges compared it to a fire of straw: "It burst into flame, burned brightly for a while, and then was completely gone." Once recognized, the two of them were wise enough not to question and not to hold on. Though tempting, they also did not give in to pretending they would "be friends" to avoid finalizing their parting. They reviewed their time together and felt good when both determined what each would have done differently. They said their thank-you's:

"Thank you for the warmth you gave me."
"Thank you for bringing light into my life."
"Thank you for all our good times together."
"Thank you for sharing your family with me."
"Thank you for teaching me about myself."
"Thank you for teaching me about giving."

They both cried. They both agreed not to write, call nor see each other again. Each was richer for knowing the other, and each would remember. They both sensed that future time together would be less than the past, and they therefore terminated.

When asked why she was only sad instead of miserable, Gigi replied, "Because all our times together were good times . . . because we had no regrets . . . because we did not spend time planning a future together . . . because we were always honest and direct with each other . . . because we kept our own friends and activities due to the distance between us . . . because I learned from him, and he from me . . . because we could go no further . . ."

Gigi and Georges appropriately experienced pain at the sadness level. There was no fantasy future to mourn, and each realistically diverged into their separate paths.

Catherine and Charmin' Charles were also fated for separate paths, but only one of them felt sad at termination. The other felt confused. Catherine and C.C. worked for the same organization and saw each other on a daily basis. They ate at the same time in the company cafeteria and shared the same coffee break in the same employees lounge. They were both out going Beautiful People: a natural match. However, after one and one half years of dating Charmin' Charles and riding back and forth with him to various events, Catherine realized she was still as anxious and off-balance as if they had just begun dating. There were no feelings of couplehood, no security and comfort, and when she really needed him emotionally, no Charmin' Charles either. They had established a cycle: they saw each other a few times and felt very close; C.C. became late or forgot dates altogether; Catherine kept her distance for a few weeks during which time C.C. would ardently pursue her. The whole cycle would then begin again. For her own sanity, Catherine decided to terminate. The push-pull was wreaking havoc with her emotions and her self esteem. In addition, she found she was not psychologically available to anyone else if she were even peripherally involved with Charmin' Charles.

Catherine's pain was at the anger-frustration level. Unaccustomed to puzzles without answers, she had invested 18 months attempting to relationship with a Magician who turned his magic on and off. She had invested much time but had achieved very little distance along the continuum. Catherine was angry at the situation, angry at her gullibility, and angry at his cycle of tricks.

She was more angry than she needed to be. Charmin' Charles could not help himself. Magicians are incapable of sustaining in-depth Relationshipping and must use their tricks when they perceive a situation as threatening. Catherine's anger was helpful in extricating herself from the involvement. Beyond the termination, however, her anger was inappropriate and she suffered more than necessary.

Anger was only one of the emotions felt by Blaine and Kelly when they terminated after fifteen months of Relationshipping. Moody and incredibly lonely for each other, each felt inadequate in resolving their differences. Each was miserable and depressed. They had broken up before, but there would be no getting back together this time. Blaine and Kelly had progressed into the Testing Stage on the Relationshipping continuum. Their appropriate pain level was the experience of the Termination Stage.

All couples who have progressed along the Relationshipping continuum well into the Testing Stage experience the Termination Stage. The feelings of closeness, mutuality, and security which have evolved are not easily jettisoned. These partners have developed habit patterns of being together and have focused their lives each on the other to form the couplehood. Termination requires a splitting of all prior integration. The pain of the splitting can be extraordinary. The emotions cling; the psyche rebels; anxiety and panic emerge. No matter how often the two people have disagreed or how practical it is to terminate, very few partners who have traveled such a distance together want to break it up.

The emotional barometer of the Termination Stage measures the pain and ambivalence in a frantic up and down gyrated line. The Termination Stage rivals the Interaction Stage in the intensity of feelings experienced. A couple begins with the height of euphoria; a couple ends with the depth of misery.

Primary Feelings of the Termination Stage

Although there may also be some subsidiary feelings of relief, freedom, and joy, the primary feelings of the Termination Stage are anger, inadequacy, guilt, loneliness, misery and depression. As previously described, the depth and range of the emotions felt by each partner depend upon the amount of each person's investment in the partnership and upon the distance traveled together along the continuum. It further depends upon which person has made the decision to terminate. One person nearly always *appears* to suffer more than the other. In cases where one partner has consistently given less than the other, the appearance is not deceiving. Low level investment partners who have been generally inconsiderate and/or uncompromising tend to emerge relatively unscathed from the termination process. The more giving partner tends to grieve longer and harder. However, regardless of the giving ratio, the person who makes the decision to terminate appears to suffer less. This phenomenon occurs irrelevant of the Relationshipping category. Whether it is friendshipping, romantic Relationshipping, work-related Relationshipping, or attempts to sever family ties, it is the person who is helpless to alter the decision who manifests more turmoil. The decision-maker does not necessarily hurt less, but has hurt earlier, in advance of announcing the decision. Also, the fact that this person is in cognitive control helps to balance the pain. All invested partners experience the Termination Stage primary feelings although each person may experience them at different times, at different depths, and for different durations.

Anger

Anger, one of the first emotional responses to termination, is not only a strong emotion but also can be a helpful emotion in the termination process. It is manifested toward the partner with a tendency to blame that partner completely while one's own role assumes angelic martyr-like dimensions. Anger is also directed toward the situation. Partners become preoccupied with the irrelevant issue of fairness and the conviction that they don't deserve such treatment. They become angry with themselves for being unable to solve the problems. The degree of anger can be augmented or diminished according to how directly and how considerately the termination is handled.

Roland, for example, approached Inge following their thirty-second fight in five weeks. He told her he believed the two of them were too different to be able to get along compatibly. He did not like himself when he responded to her as he had in the past month, and he didn't believe things between them were going to change. Attempts to compromise had not worked out. He would honor any future concrete commitments they had made, but otherwise he wanted to terminate. Inge did not like what she heard, but she recognized the truth of it. On a scale of one to ten, she experienced her anger about the four level. She appreciated his direct discussion.

Sol, on the other hand, indirectly informed Sadie of his desire to terminate by taking a new date to a favorite spot patronized by Sadie and her friends. Thus assuring himself that Sadie would be informed, Sol rehearsed claiming "only friends" with the new woman and then breaking up with Sadie because of her "extreme jealousy". Sadie felt manipulated, embarrassed, and humiliated. She experienced her anger at the ten level.

Occasionally, the natural upsurge of anger is directed punitively at a terminating partner regardless of how well termination is approached. The impulse is to retaliate, usually with literally below the belt acid comments. Dixie told Preston that he was a lousy lover and that she had been faking orgasm since their beginning. Rich told Cleo he was becoming "bored with a board in bed". Poisonous remarks insinuating sexual inadequacy extend to position preferences ("Only perverts like it that way") and body condition ("You've gotten so fat that sex with you is disgusting"). Additionally, hurtful remarks can include outside references such as, "You can't even hold a decent job" or "My friends (or family) never liked you". Since the purpose of the pot shots is to punish the partner for leaving (rejection!), truth is often sacrificed for the sake of hurt potential. People who have relationshipped at least well into the Testing Stage know their partners' soft spots. Punitive anger recalls the armour chinks and discards truth in favor of causing the most pain. Although anger is a natural response to termination, ventilating it in this manner is vicious and unhealthy. It is a poison retrospectively tainting the good times earlier shared. It indeed gives the partner something to remember one by, and the memory becomes distinctly unpleasant.

Partners who have been long term, while avoiding non-productive chink-in-the-armour attacks, must allow their anger to flow freely as an aid in separating from the couplehood. As with teenagers preparing to leave home, certain differences must be emphasized and realistic conflicts accentuated in order to withdraw from all the warmth and comfort which is also available. Anger thus helps in disconnecting from the couple unit, and provides a distinctly individual focus. It is totally appropriate to be angry at the various mis-steps that created dysfunction and led to termination. Such anger is also productive in identifying pertinent issues that require work and resolution to prevent future Relationshipping from duplicating the same mistakes.

Anger is a normal response to the loss of love and companionship. If the termination is properly handled (See Chapter XII, Contract Communication: Terminations), the anger can be channeled to help a person move beyond the pain toward acceptance and self-growth. An angry person is a motivated person, and a properly motivated person learns from the experience.

Inadequacy

Every person feels inadequate in the face of parting. Each feels inadequate to articulate the inner turmoil, inadequate to solve the problems, and inadequate to make the other person understand. Partners also feel inadequate as people. Soul searching reveals such thoughts as:

"I just wasn't man (or woman) enough to keep her (or him)."
"Am I wrong about how I relate to people?"
"Maybe I wasn't meant to be married."
"I wonder if I'm capable of Relationshipping with anyone."

Worries about surviving alone in the future contribute to already existing feelings of inadequacy. Tasks and activities previously performed by two people are neither easily nor enthusiastically assumed by one person. Self confidence is shaken and new risks which provide opportunities to regain self-assurance are avoided. The same opportunities, reasons the psyche, might bring more rejection and further prove the inadequacy already felt.

Feelings of inadquacy are born of a sense of failure. Partners are aware of earlier goals, hopes, and dreams which have rapidly dissipated along with the partnership. The failure of a marriage or of a long term couplehood is perceived as a failure for the person. For partners who were not well matched in terms of chemistry, compatibility, and similar value systems, the idea of failure is inappropriate. No couple can survive without the vital characteristics being present. Partners who were properly matched, however, have indeed failed. Usually through ignorance but nonetheless with stubborn perserverance, such partners have botched their opportunities for continued happiness together by failure to feedback, failure to resolve anger, and failure to negotiate toward the middle ground. Both persons have participated in the covert but certain agreement toward eventual dissolution of intimacy. Both persons have failed. Termination is therefore an humbling experience. However, the only failure that is significant and long term is the failure to learn from errors. The inadequacy felt by each person is a signal for self evaluation and needed change.

Annalee was a woman who had been married three times and who had wanted each husband all to herself. She had been unwilling to share her respective spouses with grown offspring, in-laws, outside activities, or close male friends. Her consistent starvation techniques led to the men's eventual exits. Although the pattern had repeated itself in three marriages, she nevertheless had no appreciation of her persistent efforts to abort her marriages. She instead cried and wrung her hands because of the disloyalty and fickleness of men while actively seeking another male who would make it all up to her. Her former husbands who had each erred by not resisting her extreme possessiveness had, in the meantime, been more assertive with successive partners and had each established more mutual Relationshipping. They had turned failure into success while Annalee was turning failure into a career. She had refused to look at her own inadequacies and had missed the signal for growth and change.

Guilt

Guilt is associated with termination because every partner could have done *something* better. Each has contributed to the breakdown and each shares the fault. Each accordingly also feel guilty, and feels it in proportion to the designated causes. For example, if Jack drinks too much and Jill designates the drinking as the reason she is leaving, Jack feels more guilty about drinking than Jill feels about leaving. In addition, there is another guilt that is felt particularly by the person who has made the decision to terminate. It involves feelings of having abandoned the Relationshipping and the concomitant responsibilities. It involves watching the partner hurting and knowing that oneself is the cause. It is the guilt of purposefully causing disruption and pain regardless of the infinite number of reasons which validate the decision. Some level of guilt is felt by all invested long term partners.

Loneliness

The loneliness of the Termination Stage is not to be confused with the generalized loneliness of an unpartnered person who wishes for a companion. As yet unmatched people yearn for a vague someone with a composite of positive characteristics with whom they can share their feelings and their lives. Termination Stage loneliness is intense longing that focuses on the one particular and absent partner. It is a hunger for the specific person with all the characteristics, both positive and negative, that have blended into the couplehood. It is a feeling of emptiness and of being incomplete. One man said, "It's like being unable to play the game because half the team isn't here." Termination Stage loneliness is the emotional equivalent of withdrawal trauma due to addiction.

The longer partners have been together, the more interdependent they have become. They have developed daily thought and behavior patterns that are intricately involved with each other. As they have blended and traversed the continuum together, each has become a habit to the other. The daily coordinated actions and thoughts have filled time and provided comfort and security. Termination tears the blended couple into two separate and partially complete individuals who must rebuild themselves into the gaps created by the loss of the partner. Termination Stage loneliness is the manifestation of splitting the whole into its separate parts. It continues in a greater or lessor extent until the developmental tasks of the Termination Stage have been accomplished.

Misery and Depression

Misery and depression are the major feelings which have contributed to the expression "going through" a divorce. They are typically present following the loss of any long term in-depth Relationshipping, but they are particularly apparent in the loss of romantic love. Misery and depression are the combined whole of the other Termination Stage feelings of anger, inadequacy, guilt, and loneliness. Misery and depression are manifested through loss of appetite, lack of motivation, poor self esteem, sleeplessness, and inability to concentrate on tasks at hand. Terminating long term relationshippers lose an average of 17 pounds and six months before regaining their emotional and physical equilibrium. The time frame for complete adjustment averages one year if appropriate attention is given to Termination Stage primary risks and developmental tasks. Although it is a difficult and vulnerable time, the people who successfully work through the misery and depression have a particular sense of their own strength and of their ability to survive.

Primary Characteristics of the Termination Stage

The primary feelings of anger, inadequacy, guilt, loneliness, misery and depression give birth to behaviors which are the primary characteristics of the Termination Stage. The mourning process, the need for support, and trial and error behavior are observable characteristics which are typical of this time of adjustment.

Mourning Process

Mourning the death of the couplehood is distinguished from mourning the death of a person by its lack of social rituals. There is no black clothing, no funeral home, and no graveside ceremony unless the partners were married. If the partners were married, a "graveside ceremony" is held in the courtroom. Another distinction is the continued and regular contact with the dearly departed if there were children of the couplehood. In compensation for the lack of clear cut rites, social custom allows terminating partners to go a little bit crazy.

The mourning process includes weeping, fault finding, and reviewing the Relationshipping. In between these three activities, terminating partners also have impulses toward abnormal behavior which they act out in varying degrees. A favorite behavior is to make a noisy and early morning appearance at the former partner's house or apartment following an evening of excessive drinking. The police are rarely called and disturbed neighbors are understanding once they are aware of the circumstances. There are also suicide threats and some actual suicide gestures. Another common irrational act is much less flamboyant but much more habitual. It is the frequent and inconvenient passing of the former partner's domicile or workplace "on the way" to and from another destination. Sometimes there is no pretense and a former partner may drive by in order to occupy a sleepless night or to relieve a particularly lonely day. Being able to see the former partner's car or dwelling is somehow comforting. The sight of a strange car and the realization that the former partner has already begun another Relationshipping continuum is debilitating knowledge. Tearful scenes in person or by telephone ensue.

Krystal's two a.m. drive-by assumed dramatic proportions when she spotted her best friend's car parked in the driveway of the former marital home. Observing that all the lights were extinguished, Krystal deduced that not only was the best friend still in her house, but was also probably in her bed. Her reactive impulse, which she immediately followed, was to drive over the curb, over the lawn, and into the master bedroom of the aluminum sided house. There, by the light of glaring headlamps, she confirmed her supicions. The circumstances were apparent when the police arrived: Krystal hysterical amidst cascading tears and two other very embarrassed people, one of them obviously in a place she wasn't supposed to be. Appraising the situation, instead of taking Krystal to jail, the police took her to the local hospital where she voluntarily admitted herself to the psychiatric unit. At the subsequent trial, even the prosecuting attorney pled extenuating circumstances. Although the case was not dismissed, the penalty for Krystal's behavior was one year's probation, no fine, and continued involvement in psychotherapy.

Krystal's case is an extreme example of the social leeway allowed for erratic behavior of terminating partners. General forebearance is seen in everyday life. Employers lower their expectations of employees during the terminating process. Families and mothers have another chance to nurture. Friends are long suffering and available if the process doesn't go on too long. Ordinarily unusual acts in the community are tolerated. Women have been known to leave full carts standing at the check-out counter upon spotting a former partner in the grocery store. Usually conservative men become regularly drunk and maudlin at public bars. Both men and women bolt from restaurants, forgetting to pay, to avoid confrontations.

All of these activities, from weeping to running, play a part in the mourning process. People need to realize that the more extravagant behaviors and impulses are counterproductive and retrospectively embarrassing, usually causing more pain and complications than one would ordinarily experience. However, by giving a somewhat free rein (within reasonable limits) to their emotions and impulses, many people gradually give up the partnership and reassert themselves as individuals. There is a certain amount of social approval to the process and very little penalty if no major laws are broken.

Need for Support

Throughout the Termination Stage there is a tremendous need for support. Couples who have severed friendshipping ties by centering now face isolation and alienation. Close friends and family are the most important resources of the Termination Stage. Through them a person receives empathy and validation as well as a listening ear and relief from being alone. Support does not necessarily involve agreeing with the distressed person. It is mainly a matter of being available and of being patient. It is actively including the mourner in activities and keeping a sensitive eye on moods and behavior. Friends and family protect against a little too much craziness and also provide rescue when cars break down or one of the children becomes ill. They can take over when there's too much misery in the day. By having the need for support satisfied, a separated partner feels validated, worthwhile, and relieved of the burden. The transition from separated partner to separate person is shared and more easily accomplished.

If friends and family are not available, the need for support is so strong that a person in the Termination Stage will often talk to anyone who will listen: fellow employees, hairdressers, bartenders, gas station attendants, waitresses, ministers, librarians, mental health and social service agency counselors. Of the people listed, ministers and professional counselors provide the best resources if neither friends nor family members are available. However, one should utilize one major outlet consistently. There is little relief or benefit derived from indiscriminate mourning with a variety of strangers.

Women are increasingly forming support groups to aid them during the Termination Stage. Men's groups are also forming. The value of such groups is tremendous. People with parallel needs who are experiencing comparable situations struggle together within their common bond. They are able to validate and be validated while developing each other as resources for the tasks that lie ahead.

Trial and Error Behavior

All beginnings are hard. They are especially difficult when one must begin again in the face of loss. Recently terminated partners are not accustomed to doing things alone. Habituated to interdependence, they are unsure of independent action. They are uncertain of which new activities to pursue and feel insecure regarding how to act and what might happen. They enter a system of trial and error behavior to help determine what works best as each person changes from a joint path to an individual path.

Making mistakes is natural when one proceeds with the trial and error system. Yet it is precisely the fear of making mistakes that for a time prevents a person from venturing out into the new world. Eventually, however, one realizes the destructive effects of withdrawing, and emerges with tentative steps to determine the rules applicable to an unpartnered person in a coupled world. People who advanced to less than the Negotiating Stage have less catch up work to do. However, persons who advanced far beyond often discover that social customs and circumstances have vastly changed. Trial and error behavior then becomes a way of life for awhile.

Different people try different behaviors and different resources. Reggie bought a monster motorcycle during his separation period. For eight months he vroom-vroomed everywhere, including (in his sedate coat and tie) to his job as a teller in the bank. As he stabilized, he began to feel a little silly and exposed. He later traded the cycle for a camper. Wendy panicked at her front door. After spending the entire evening trying for her first pick-up, she suddenly didn't want to go through with it. She had images of being covered with Herpes II and suddenly remembered that her mother had recently begun dropping by for weekend breakfasts together. Remembering her comforting High Episcopal childhood and wanting to develop new friends, Hallie accepted an invitation to go to church. She ended up at a Born Again tent meeting and was converted six times before she made her escape. Sometimes, ideas do not keep their appeal and sometimes they turn out differently than expected. However, it is important to keep trying.

It is also important to realize that one's attitude vastly effects one's success rate when attempting new behaviors. If one views the endeavor as a challenge or an adventure, great success and much fun can be obtained as a result of the experimental actions. If, however, a person regards each new attempt as a threat or a chore, the outcome is usually as unpleasant as anticipated.

The mourning process, need for support, and trial and error behavior are all primary characteristics of the Termination Stage. They typify the process of letting go and beginning again. They also uniquely place the participant in an emotionally and behaviorally vulnerable position.

Primary Risks of the Termination Stage

The Termination Stage is a time of emotional exhaustion and readjustment. The anguished traveler on the Relationshipping continuum must complete an emotional termination with the partner as well as a physical termination before this particular continuum is ended and before total readjustment is achieved. Because of the terrible drain on both inner and outer resources, the relationshipper is singularly susceptible to the risks of this stage. These risks, fixation, overfear, and The New Puppy syndrome, effectively inhibit the successful accomplishment of this stage. These risks also significantly reduce the chances of positive progress in future Relationshipping.

Fixation

Fixation is a matter of becoming emotionally fixed on an event or a person to the extent that it continues actively in the throughts or emotions long after the event is past or the person is gone. The feeling may be anger or love, but the strength of it provides a continuing emotional bond. All subsequent attempts at Relationshipping are filtered through thoughts and feelings which remain preoccupied with the long gone person or long past event.

Maggie had been widowed seven years and still lived in the same huge house which she and her husband had occupied. Only 42 years old, she nevertheless acted if she were 62 and as if she had a husband for 40 years who had only recently met his demise. In reality, Maggie had been a second wife and had beeen married 11 years. She had mothered her husband's children from a former marriage, and they were grown before her husband's death. Nevertheless, her husband and his children, their interests and their accomplishments, were the focus of Maggie's conversation. Her husband's clothes still hung in the closet, and his personal items remained where they had lain at the time of his death. In her thoughts and behavior, Maggie continued to be married to a man who had died seven years ago. Sometime during the initial course of the Termination Stage, Maggie had decided not to go on. The continuum was still intact for her, and there was no room for any other Relationshipping because of the amount of her fixated investment.

Bebe says that she certainly hadn't had that trouble when her husband died: "In fact", she emphatically relates, "when my sonafabitchin' second husband was hit by that car, I was trying to decide which lawyer to see. He was bad enough, but you should have seen my first husband. For 16 years he knocked the you-know-what out of me on a daily basis, and I still thought the man was God himself. Of course, I was only 17 when I married him, and it took me a long time to get out from under, especially with three babies. But even now, if a man wants to touch me, I'm ready for anything."

Whenever Bebe is in a social grouping, it somehow happens that her experiences with both her first and second husbands appear in the conversation. Unless her age at the original marriage is mentioned, most people think her experiences were comparatively recent events. However, though she doesn't look her age, Bebe is 52 years old. Her first divorce was 19 years ago. She was widowed ten years ago. In spite of the passing of the years in between then and now, Bebe remains fixated on those events and on those husbands with a strong emotional investment. Not surprisingly, Bebe has had no successful Relationshipping experiences with men. These two are constantly in the undercurrents of her mind, and that is why they always surface in conversation. There is no room in her thoughts nor energy remaining for her to invest whole-heartedly in anyone else. Bebe has never emotionally terminated with these men.

To avoid fixation the relationshipper must let go of the former partner in thoughts and feelings as well as in physical presence. It gives no benefit to wonder what he or she is doing or to recall past pleasant or painful events. Several months following divorce or (in the case of unmarried partners) following the termination talk, people should have very few thoughts or passionate feelings regarding their former companions. If preoccupation continues, the relationshipper must actively work to substitute other thoughts and neutral feelings in order to bring the continuum to a complete ending. When a thought or a mental picture spontaneously occurs, it is helpful to think instead, "That was nice, but it was a long time ago. I have other things to think about now" and then actually to think about more current but also pleasant events. Sometimes it is a negative thought about the past that is ongoing and intrusive. A person must mentally respond, "That's all behind me now. I don't have to worry about that anymore. Things are better now" and then must actively think about the improved circumstances or future goals that will provide yet more improvement. Many people have an urge to recycle the old events and old loves. This must be strongly resisted. The risk of fixation is damaging to personal growth and adjustment as well as to future happiness.

Overfear

Overfear, the second primary risk of the Termination Stage, is a sort of phobic reaction to Relationshipping. A person is filled with an overwhelming fear (and sometimes a certainty) of being hurt again. Overfear is manifested in two completely different scenarios. Stretch is an example of the first.

"Sure, I like women", Stretch meditated aloud. "And people at the office are always trying to fix me up with somebody. But you didn't know my wife. She was the sweetest woman you'd ever want to know and if we didn't have a happy marriage, I sure didn't know it. She ran off with a fellow out at the college, said it was just something she had to do. Well, I don't know if she had to do it or not, but I do know that I can't go through that kind of thing again. And you just can't tell who is going to do it to you. Being a sweet wonderful person doesn't make any difference. So I just do my own thing. Sure, I'm lonely sometimes, but I'm happy enough."

Stretch's attitude, quite overtly, is, "I've been burned. I don't know how to keep from being burned again, so I'm not getting involved." it is an active cognitive decision on his part, and he is aware and accepting of the consequences. The second variety of overfear, illustrated by Rafe and by Yolanda, is not so clear cut.

Rafe dates women who are interesting and attractive, and, unlike Stretch, wants feminine companionship instead of a time consuming hobby. He tends to date one woman steadily until reaching the Testing Stage when he begins to feel anxious instead of comfortable and secure. He becomes reluctant to plan far in advance and finds himself wondering about and interested in other women. He becomes more and more uncomfortable with his current steady until she eventually notices. They gradually see each other less often due to Rafe's discomfort. Any attempt at analysis is short lived since Rafe is usually attracted to a new woman before giving himself a chance to figure out why he's no longer attracted to the last one. This process is a fairly frequent and predictable occurance for Rafe.

Yolanda also enjoys dating, but experiences no discomfort upon reaching the Testing Stage. When it comes to marriage, however, the timing is never right for Yolanda. First, she couldn't think about remarriage until she had established herself with a good job. Then she wanted to wait until after she had her next promotion. Then it was a matter of going back to school for further training, and currently, she thinks she should wait until the children are grown and leave home. Yolanda has sequentially outlasted three patient men who have proposed matrimony. She will probably outlast as many more because the timing is never going to be right for Yolanda.

Stretch, Rafe, and Yolanda have all succumbed to the risk of overfear. Stretch has mentally processed his experience and has come to a cognitive decision over which he has conscious control. He may at some later date realize that he is not so terribly fragile and that, after all, there are different ways of relating and communicating that reduce the chances of heartbreak. Because Stretch made a conscious decision, he can also consciously change his mind. Rafe and Yolanda, however, are working at an underground level and have no awareness regarding their difficulties with commitment.

The first variety of overfear is easily identified and fairly easily changed when the individual decides to venture again. The second form of overfear is identified by tracing the pattern of past and present Relationshipping. A decision made at the unconscious level can be better discovered by behavior than by discussion. People who have a history of a major loss followed by a history of stopping at a particular point on the continuum are probably suffering from overfear. Similarly, a person who has had a major loss followed by other priorities which prevent commitment also is overfearful. Unconscious defenses are acting. He or she is thus being protected against what is wanted. A professional counselor is needed to help unravel conscious desires from unconscious defenses.

The New Puppy Syndrome

The New Puppy Syndrome is the third and last primary risk of the Termination Stage. It receives its name from that school of thought which says: if the children's dog unexpectedly dies, one should quickly obtain a new puppy so the children will not be upset and have to deal with death. The same philosophy applied to the Termination Stage says: if one loses a romantic partner, one should quickly obtain a new love so that one doesn't have to feel the pain and deal with the death of the couplehood.

The New Puppy Syndrome is seen by many people as the solution to the pain of lost love. For suffering relationshippers, it seems logical enough, especially since one feels so inadequate and so much in need of sympathetic support. If someone else were to love one, it would prove that the person really was acceptable, lovable, and okay: all those qualities that one was beginning to doubt because of the turmoil of termination from the original partner. The belief is that by quickly obtaining a new partner, the agony of losing the other will be over.

Many people's last months (and often years) with partners are cold and/or argumentative with little positive attention or closeness. They therefore view the warmth of initial attraction with a new partner as a reversal of the negative characteristics of the former partner. They have instead usually found the warmth, attention, and affection of The New Puppy Syndrome. It is a false start rather than a true beginning. A terminating partner seeks a positive substitute for the past partner rather than mutual Relationshipping. The person is avoiding rather than investing.

People tend to forget that Relationshipping ends for reasons. A new partner, like a new puppy, may be warm and reassuring, but the reasons for the failure of the old Relationshipping remain. The continuums begun with new partners at this point are hardly ever successful. Since people are seeking warmth, attention, and affection instead of chemistry, compatibility, and similar value systems, the first major Relationshipping following a termination is almost always a poor match. Unless people take time to resolve and remedy those issues which were their contributions to the demise of the couplehood, those same issues will reoccur to be resolved on another continuum. Newly parted people involved in The New Puppy Syndrome have neither the interest nor the stamina to weather more turmoil so soon. They are primarily interested in being provided with warmth, affection, and reassurance. They are involved in the difficult business of repair work. It is a rare new partner who could fit into the ragged edges from which the old partner was torn. It is better to wait until the person has completed himself or herself before attempting to relationship again. People relate better to people than to jagged holes, and it is new partners instead of new puppies that form the long term continuum.

Developmental Tasks of the Termination Stage

Relationshippers who focus on the developmental tasks of the Termination Stage rather than on the loss of the partner tend to work through termination agony fairly risk free. The developmental tasks are geared for grief, acceptance, and growth. Knowledge of them provides the needed guidelines for personal rebuilding and allows the individual to emerge as a healthy complete person from the ending of the continuum. The developmental tasks require the terminating partners to grieve the couplehood, to accept the realistic personal statement, to utilize the crisis situation for personal growth, and to develop a continuing support or resource group.

Grieve the Couplehood

The first developmental task which aids in avoiding Termination Stage risks is to grieve the couplehood. Grieving is both a joint and an individual process. It should be the couple's last act together as united partners, and each person's first act toward becoming a separate and whole individual again.

Positive grieving requires awareness and control when participating in the joint aspects of termination. Partners who refuse to listen and refuse to channel their anger into more appropriate areas will increase their vulnerability toward the primary risks. In the midst of all the anger, inadequacy, guilt, loneliness, misery and depression that are typical of this stage, two partners sit down together to evaluate their missteps and to determine where it all went awry. The procedure is the joint review of the Relationshipping, and it is a method of saying good-bye.

The joint review of the Relationshipping is both a gift and an act of respect. The gift is feedback, still the most valuable commodity one person can give another. Each partner gives one's positive and negative opinions regarding the course of the continuum for each to evaluate later. Each partner also gives tribute to the virtues and rewards resulting from the partnership. The joint review is not a fault finding expedition. Rather, it is a summation of the life of the couplehood, from glory to pain. As partners pursue the joint review, they are aware of admiration at what they have accomplished together, and they are seized with sadness because of the realization of what might have been. The joint review integrates the then and the now and respectfully lays the couplehood to rest. (See the following chapter for the framework for the joint review.)

Partners leave the joint review with specific data which aids them in continuing the individual grieving process. As they individually grieve the loss of the partner, they are also aware of areas to focus their energies for rebuilding. In evaluating the data, they are able to substitute future goals in place of each aspect of the couplehood that is left behind. The cognitive process in the midst of the turmoil of emotions and impulsive behavior is the first step toward becoming a separate and whole person. It is the individual aspect of grieving the couplehood.

Accept the Realistic Personal Statement

In order to accept the realistic personal statement, one must acknowledge having been wrong, having made mistakes. The temptation is to look only at recent problematic behavior which offers the convenient opportunity to blame the partner as much as possible. To accomplish the developmental task of accepting the realistic personal statement, one must acknowledge one's own contributions to the deterioration of the partnership.

Tamara, for example felt unnoticed and unfulfilled at home. She began to double her energies at her job, staying late hours and bringing home work which preoccupied her in the evenings. Her husband Wright, unknown to her but also feeling unnoticed and unfulfilled, developed an affair with a sweet young thing while involved on a community service board. After a surreptitious year, Wright decided to file for divorce.

On the surface, the marital breakdown is totally the fault of Wright and his involvement with Sweet Young Thing. However, in order to accept the realistic personal statement, Tamara must realize and admit that there were other opportunities open to her beyond immersing herself in her work. She could have channeled her energies into nourishing the couple bond. Difficult to admit and more difficult to accept, Tamara actively contributed to her husband's defection.

Because people do not always understand *why* they are doing *what* they are doing *when* they are doing it, accepting the realistic personal statement is doubly important. The mental backtracking process reveals alternatives unconsidered in the past. Errors in judgment are more obvious when seen retrospectively, and errors are always present. Mentally healthy couples well matched in chemistry, compatibility, and value systems do not fall apart without reasonable contribution on the part of both partners. The realization of personal contribution is prerequisite in the adjustment process. Awareness not only aids in avoiding the primary risks of fixation and overfear, but also provides a base for personal development.

Utilize the Crisis Situation for Personal Growth

People are most vulnerable to maladjustment in times of crisis. They are also most motivated toward change. The emotional turmoil of the Termination Stage combined with the often drastic changes in daily life routine and responsibilities create an environment equally conducive to personal growth as to psychological damage. Although the Termination Stage is the worst possible time to begin a new romantic continuum, it is the ideal time to cultivate personal development and to pursue individual goals.

Former partner's complaints are often useful in determining personal growth goals. In spite of a reluctance to injure feelings, people are usually straightforward with each other and honestly express their opinions during the joint review. The problem is that their sincere evaluations are, of course, possibly distorted by their own misperceptions. Also, the most pertinent issues may not have been addressed. Data obtained from a former partner must therefore be appraised as to validity.

Luwanda was sure she would never survive when she and Dr. Darby separated. Although she had put him through medical school 14 years before, she had not worked since he had begun practice. She had, in fact, strongly resisted his encouragement to develop a career of her own. In the joint review, Darby told Luwanda that he found her uninteresting, and he felt they no longer had anything in common. Luwanda realized that she not only was boring to her husband but also equally boring to her friends. Darby's imput had been valid. In accepting her realistic personal statement, Luwanda also realized that she had resisted growth and change with a passionate dedication. She then set about utilizing the crisis for her own growth and development. Luwanda's ensuing self growth program began with volunteering in community action organizations to find an interest area and ended with her specializing in work with handicapped children.

Glenda told Harv that he was selfish and inconsiderate because they never went on nice vacations and he always told her "no" when she wanted to buy something nice for herself. Harv did not accept her opinions as valid. His own evaluation and realistic personal statement indicated he had allowed Glenda to spend twice as much money as he earned. His self growth program included learning to be more assertive and to communicate more directly.

By taking the data obtained from a partner during the joint review and sifting it through the appraisal of one's own realistic personal statement, a person is able to target areas for personal growth. The couple crisis can become a great springboard to mobilize toward personal development.

Develop Resource Group

The ending of a romantic continuum unfortunately often brings about the ending of inter-related friendshipping continuums. Set adrift from couple friends and associations, terminating partners must develop new resources as replacements. Hopefully, centering has not occured, and neither partner is completely isolated. Personal friends who were maintained throughout the couplehood remain important and prominent resources. However, terminating partners must also forge ahead to develop additional resource groups. The resource group may be an actual group of people such as a club, organization, or existing friendship group, or it may be several unassociated persons who are each individual resources. These people must be *developed* and development takes time. Interaction Stage feelings, characteristics, risks, and developmental tasks apply in beginning all new continuums. In the meantime, one's old friends act as prime resources until the dependency can be reduced by time and investment in the new associations. Eventually the new associations not only aid the terminating partner but also enrich the old friendshipping.

New resources are important for replacement value, for a sense of belonging, and for validation. They also give encouragement and focus for new endeavors. Though it takes time to become comfortable, a resource group of new friends and interests provides needed assurance and helps fill the void created by the loss of former habits and former companions. People as resources can be developed through work, clubs, community interest groups, and civic activities. Through the resource group, one may be accepted, be validated, and be encouraged.

A person continues emotionally in the Termination Stage, regardless of new continuums begun, until the developmental tasks are accomplished. The tasks are geared for grief, acceptance, and growth. Through grieving the couplehood, accepting the realistic personal statement, utilizing the crisis for personal growth, and developing a continuing resource group, the person emerges from the end of the continuum healthy, whole, and healed for future Relationshipping.

Termination Stage Questions

The following questions are helpful to terminating partners in checking their progress toward the completion of the Termination Stage. Unless one can answer all questions fully, one still has ties to the old continuum and has not successfully completed the developmental tasks.

1. *Have I, either with my partner, or by myself, completed the review of the Relationshipping?*
2. *What have I learned from my former partner's complaints?*
3. *What personal goals have I established and begun?*
4. *Which people have I developed as new friends?*

Termination Stage Summary

Terminations are not limited to the Termination Stage, but all couples who have relationshipped together at least a significant distance into the Testing Stage experience the Termination Stage to some degree. Because they have blended together, the ending requires a tearing apart. The amount of pain suffered by the tearing depends on the amount of emotional investment of each partner and the distance traversed together beyond the Testing Stage. The Termination Stage is a time of emotional crisis and grief. It also provides an opportunity for great personal growth. In the transition from couplehood to whole individual, a person concentrates on developmental tasks to avoid susceptibility to the primary risks of fixation, overfear, and The New Puppy Syndrome. It is not until the developmental tasks are accomplished that the Termination Stage may be considered completed.

CHAPTER XII

Contract Communication: Termination Stage

Terminations are the most poorly handled of human interactions. Because of a fear of hurting others and a stronger fear of being hurt themselves, people avoid official endings with each other as if evasion could nullify the accompanying pain. Like other penguin behaviors and beliefs, this one exists because of simple ignorance. People have not known how to terminate gracefully, and they have never been taught that endings are as important as beginnings. Like beginnings, all endings are hard. All the emotional investment and shared dreams must be abandoned. Though painful, it is part of the natural cycle. All beginnings inevitably end. All endings result in new beginnings. Unless the cycle is abused, each person learns from each experience and develops progressively to richer and more rewarding Relationshipping. Children learn from relating to parents and siblings, applying the benefit of experience which allows them to relate well to teachers and peers. Adolescent interactions continue to refine skills, and young adults end their time at home to begin their own independent lives. They develop long term partnerships which, with skill and attention, will continue until the death of one or the other partner. However, if ending occurs at an earlier time, people must rejoin the cycle. They must learn from the experience and begin again. In order to benefit from the experience, they first must learn to terminate properly.

Endings should always be formalized. Assuming two people have had a beginning together (five or more interactions), they should also have an ending. Formal endings provide feedback and avoid ties to old continuums. They also avoid confusion and negative self images. The structure, content, and dynamics of graceful exits (termination agreements) are discussed in Chapter VI.

Couples who successfully blended together in the Testing Stage and progressed along the continuum into the Negotiation Stage are less easily separated. They must endure the pain of the Termination Stage. Contract communication is immensely helpful in resolving the emotional crisis. It provides a structure for the work each has to do.

The format for Termination Stage contracts is simple. It contains three major topics for discussion: (1) Problem Identification (2) Review of the Relationshipping, and (3) Future Behavior. As partners engage in communication, they experience a warm intimacy that is reminiscent of their earlier times together. It is the catharsis of resolution.

The emphasis in Termination Stage contracting is communication and information, but, unlike contracts associated with other stages, there are few agreement clauses. Although there is a format, Termination Stage contracts are rarely written. The contract format provides structure for couples to deal productively with pertinent issues in order to prevent repetitive, destructive, and extraneous discussion. Such guidelines are especially important to separating and emotionally agitated partners. However, attempting to record the contract interrupts the free flow of communication and gets in the way of issues the couple must address. People who want a record of pertinent points should make notations following the discussion for their own use after the former partner has gone.

Problem Identification

For proper problem identification, partners must list and describe their complaints regarding the other person's attitudes and behaviors. Defense of one's actions and beliefs is not required and is not a good idea. The problem identification clause is feedback regarding how one partner perceives the other partner, and one who is defending cannot listen with full attention. It must be realized that the behaviors and attitudes described are symptoms of a much larger issue which are to be discussed in the following clause. In addition, problem identification gives each partner a clear idea of possible personal missteps that may need to be corrected for future personal growth.

The Review of the Relationshipping

The review of the Relationshipping first requires partners to view themselves as joint travelers along the Relationshipping continuum rather than two separate individuals. Regardless of complaints listed in clause one, no couple with well matched chemistry, compatibility, and value systems deteriorates due to Matilda's having gone to work, Percival's stinginess, or a variety of other perceived individual sins. The couplehood fails because appropriate developmental tasks were not accomplished. Partners were unsuccessful in resolving anger together, failed to nourish the couple bond, refused to develop new goals and interests, resisted adaptation, or otherwise disregarded crucial developmental tasks. Because of a lack of attention to the joint enterprise, many partners succeed admirably as people, but fail miserably within the couplehood. The review of the Relationshipping requires each partner to locate missteps along the continuum. The knowledge of error in process provides partners with true understanding as to why they have arrived at the point of termination. There are several cases of couples reconciling after realizing that process errors were mutual while perceived unacceptable behaviors and attitudes were only contributory. Whether partners decide to try again or proceed to the second part of the review, there is a recognition that self-actualization notwithstanding, partners work in tandem. Whatever one partner does or feels has a direct effect upon the other partner and thus on the couplehood. Understanding the core couple interplay helps produce a resolution of the Relationshipping.

The second part of the review of the Relationshipping involves recalling particular experiences together which are of special import to one or the other partner. It is an opportunity for each person to say 'thank you' for a partner's appreciated characteristics and behaviors or for memorable events. Partners also recall not so happy occasions and remark on what could have been done differently with perhaps a different result. Commonly called "thank-you's and regrets", the second part of the review completes the resolution of the Relationshipping.

Future Behavior

Partners must set some guidelines as to their future responses to each other. Sometimes written, these guidelines are the only agreement clauses in Termination Stage contracting. There are some former partners who regularly have lunch together, remember each other on birthdays and Christmas, and generally act as friends and resources to each other. They have renegotiated their romance to a friendshipping contract. People who can sincerely achieve this transition, especially after one or both have new partners, are creatures more rare than platypuses. Most old lovers do not adjust well to friendshipping, and most new partners of old lovers do not like it if they do. It is best to agree to the clean crisp cut (no future interactions) following the review of the Relationshipping. Otherwise, the healing process is retarded. Further interactions disrupt the feelings of resolution, and cause new cuts on old wounds.

Danny and Sugar

Danny and Sugar relationshipped for almost six years, and were terminating during the last 22 months. Their termination contract occurred after four years together. During the review of the Relationshipping, they identified couplehood issues of being unable to compromise or to resolve conflict. In addition, Danny wanted traditional exclusive couple centered goals while Sugar wanted more open outward centered goals. They had been unable to develop joint goals. Realizing they would not be able to accomplish developmental tasks they regretted being unable to see each other's viewpoint. They recalled their wonderful trips together, and they thanked each other for particular instances of spontaneous giving and creative thoughtfulness. Each had never before known such a considerate partner. They agreed to be friendly when accidentally encountering each other, and they agreed to be available to help each other in a pinch. They also agreed not to plan regular or continuing contact.

Danny and Sugar each felt the calm of resolution until experiencing the Termination Stage torment of loneliness. They then impulsively and "accidentally" sought each other by frequenting favorite couple haunts and dropping in on favorite couple friends. Though supposedly terminated, neither Danny nor Sugar developed new friends or interests and thus chronically encountered each other on almost a daily basis. They would have coffee together from time to time which led to fixing Sugar's drippy kitchen faucett which led to taking a trip together. They learned that what had not worked in the past continued not to work, but it took them 22 months to learn it. In addition to the back and forth agony they had just ended, they still had to face the entire length of the Termination Stage.

As with most terminating couples, Danny and Sugar would have spared themselves time and turmoil if they had utilized the clean, crisp cut. However, when children are involved or when the community is not large enough to provide distance and anonymity, the clean, crisp cut is not possible. Terminating partners must then establish some criteria so that they will know what to expect and how to behave in otherwise awkward social situations. Most Termination Stage contracts feature agreement to greet each other upon accidental encounters and to be pleasant to each other's companions. There are also usually agreements concerning behavior when children are present. The clear guidelines prevent many future misunderstandings and provide for confidence in social situations as well as in arranging for visitation with children.

James-and-Olivia

James-and-Olivia managed to accomplish all the developmental tasks of the Termination Stage and also to produce a workable "operating manual" regarding the children's activities and events. In their review of the Relationshipping, James saw Olivia as selfish, overly independent, and defensive. His perceptions were quite right. Olivia had quit giving, was more oriented to her own career than to the couplehood, and resisted any suggestions on his part to slow down her outside interests. Olivia saw James as chronically neglectful of her, oriented to the job rather than to home or family, and unwilling to set new goals. She, like James, had seen the behavior clearly. James was from the old school which traditionally assumes that wife and family revolve around what the man wants and what the man does. It had not occurred to him to apply the same energy at home as he applied at work. James, who at the same time his wife was pregnant, knew the circumference in centimeters of every pipe and valve to be used in building a pilot plant a year in advance, did not know the way to the hospital when his wife's pains were three minutes apart.

James-and-Olivia had done much right, but they had left much undone. In the review of the Relationshipping they realized they had neglected to nourish the couple bond, had adjusted individually rather than jointly to change, and had failed to develop new couple goals. The push-pull behaviors between them were symptomatic of soundly flunking the Negotiation Stage developmental tasks. They said their regrets:

"I wish I hadn't left you so much on your own".

"I wish I could have told you my feelings instead of going outside to achieve".

"I wish you could have gotten along better with my parents".

"That was my fault. I felt angry with them when I was really angry at you".

"I wish I had shown you more appreciation".

"I wish I had found a way to tell you I needed it without sounding demanding".

"I'm sorry I wasn't there all those times you needed me".

"I'm sorry I became so independent".

They said their thank-you's:

"Thank you for the really special presents you gave me: like the fancy phone, the cameo, and the statue that took time and thought to pick out".

"Thank you for being willing to move to a completely different part of the country".

"Thank you for helping me grow up. I'm not a dependent little girl any more".

"Thank you for giving me another viewpoint of life. Remember that night we were caught in the snowstorm? I though we had had it, but you kept us going".

"Thank you for all the good years we had".

"I'm sorry they're over".

"Me, too".

In written form, they agreed for the future:

1. To close personal friends, we will confide any aspect of our marriage or our divorce that we want, but to people we don't know very well, we will only say, "Things just didn't work out".
2. We will never criticize or otherwise badmouth each other to the children or in front of the children. If we are angry with each other, the irritated party is responsible for calling the other party to work the issue out or schedule a time to meet when the issue can be worked out.
3. We will always speak when we run into each other. The one who sees the other first has the responsibility to speak first.
4. If we get seriously involved with anyone, we will tell each other right away so the other doesn't get surprised by reading it in the paper.
5. An operating manual regarding arrangements with the children:
    a) The general plan for visits with the children will be every other weekend, but this is flexible and can be changed by either parent depending on trips and other activities. Weekend visits begin at 5:30 pm on Fridays and last until 5:30 pm on Sundays.
    b) The children may call their dad at work or at home at any time.
    c) James may call the children at any time and may visit during the week if nothing else is scheduled and homework is done. He must call in advance and check with Olivia before asking the children.*
    d) Olivia agrees not to say no unless something is really scheduled. James agrees to give as much notice as possible.
    e) James will have some time with the children on each holiday, to be arranged according to circumstances.
    f) James will have at least a week with the children during the summer. He will tell Olivia which week(s) he wants by May first. Otherwise, he takes pot luck.
    g) James will be informed regarding report cards, parent-teacher reports, school programs, recitals, pageants, and other events in which the children are involved.
    h) Birthday and Christmas wish lists will be discussed at least two weeks prior to those occasions to prevent duplication of gifts.
    i) James prefers to pay directly for special items such as summer camp, bicycles, special clothing, skiis, etc. rather than have child support increased in future years. Olivia agrees there will be no increase as long as he continues that practice.
    j) James will be informed of any major illnesses contracted by the children.
    k) Either James or Olivia may contact each other at any time involving legitimate issues regarding the children.

Both the review and the operating manual were effective. In use four years with James remarrying after two years, the Relationshipping was successfully resolved and arrangements surrounding the children remain uncomplicated and cordial.

Without benefit of the review of the Relationshipping, unfinished business remains between partners. Without the review, the Relationshipping remains essentially unresolved. A mental and emotional bond exists in spite of a lack of contact. Marjorie says, "There was another man once and I really loved him, but it was hard for me to believe he loved me. We went together for four years in college, and we had talked about getting married one day."

"How did you terminate?"

"Well, I never did. I graduated from college and came here and got involved with Jack. It was a whirlwind courtship, and we were married in December. I sent Marty a Christmas card telling him I was married, and, of course, I've never heard from him again. I think of him from time to time, and wonder how he's doing, and how things turned out for him. I haven't terminated from him yet and that was 15 years ago."

Marjorie is not unusual. Most people carry their unresolved Relationshipping experiences locked away in inner emotional safety deposit boxes. The accumulative effect produces attitudes of defensive guardedness, poor self esteem, and reluctance toward compromise. It is difficult to conduct new business in Relationshipping when one is internally tied with the loose ends of unresolved old business. The object is to tie up as many of the loose ends as possible.

In cases in which the review did not occur at the appropriate time, my patients and students have had great success in approaching former partners for the review after a significant interval of time has passed since the last contact. The passing of time allows for settling of the emotions, and most former partners, even Magicians, have been responsive.

If the former partner is unavailable to participate in a joint review, it is recommended that one perform a unilateral review and then send it to the former partner in letter form. Violet's letter to Wally is an example of the unilateral review.

"*Dear Wally,*

We hardly ever see each other and when we do, it seems like we are so polite and trite and neither one of us knows what to say. I want you to know that I've gotten over my anger, and even with all our troubles, the four years we had together were the best years I had had in a very long time. Looking back, I think it was just too soon for both of us. We were each other's first Great Love after our divorces. Jacinth says the first real biggy hardly ever works out. I guess I'm beginning to see why. Somehow I expected you to make it up to me for everything that had gone before, and I think you expected a little of the same from me. Maybe I was to be the fantasy woman who could understand you completely, as no one had ever done before. I wish I were, but I'm really not magic. I think that's where we went wrong. We based our Relationshipping on expectations and magic — sand castles — instead of compatibility and values which we assumed would be there, but weren't. Then we

> held on and on because we were holding on to dreams and didn't want to let go.
>
> Thank you for your tenderness when my father died. Thank you for the trip to Europe. It was the high point of my life. Thank you for the beautiful pearls. Thank you for being there until I got on my feet. Thank you for introducing me to Jay and Jean. They are treasures and are still my friends.
>
> I learned from you. Looking back, I think I handled things badly. Please forgive me. I am not asking for us to start again. It's been a year since things were really over. I am writing this to put us to rest so that we may both be comfortable in going on in whatever directions life takes for us. But I will never see "Casablanca" or hear its music without thinking of you.
>
> Please acknowledge in some way that you have received this letter. We certainly don't have to discuss it if you don't want, but I do need to know that you've gotten my message. I wish you all the good things.
>
> Love,
Violet"

The disadvantages of performing a unilateral review are that there is only one person's input and that there may not be a response. A unilateral review, however, is better than no review, and there have been few instances of no response. Some former partners return a letter with their own analyses. Others drop a card in the mail with a scribbled note. One memorable man sent "roses for remembrance" and another called from Alaska after the original letter had been forwarded three times. None of my patients or students have experienced attempts to rejuvenate the Relationshipping from the unilateral review.

The unilateral review is beneficial even if the former partner has died or if his or her whereabouts are unknown and a letter cannot be sent. Although one sided, a person may achieve resolution for oneself by studying the course of the Relationshipping and forming hypotheses regarding missteps, thank you's, and regrets. Being careful to keep a joint focus, a person is often able to see oneself through the former partner's eyes. Though the former partner is unable to share, resolution for oneself is achieved.

The review is a prerequisite for resolving the Relationshipping. It allows partners to accept their experience together as a whole rather than reacting to specific negative behaviors which led to termination.

It reconciles the ending with the beginning and forms a completion. Following the review there must be an emotional and mental severing as well as a physical separation to enable the partners to heal and begin to build their individual lives.

Though inescapably painful, terminations can be rich in warmth and intimacy if they are properly handled rather than avoided. Partners who have had more than five interactions together need to terminate officially to avoid feelings of unfinished business. People who progress well into the Testing Stage together should invest their energies in a full Termination Stage contract including problem identification, review of the Relationshipping, and future behavior clauses. The final contract provides catharsis and a resulting peace. Partners have a sense of completion and satisfaction which enables them to view the joint experience as warm, worthwhile, and a part of the natural cycle of life.

CHAPTER XIII

Complicated Relationshipping

Every self respecting penguin knows one has to work at Relationshipping. In the past, before Relationshift, the difficulty has been in identifying exactly what work needed to be done and how to go about it. Now that Relationshift has correlated developmental tasks and continuum time, one would think the process of happiness inevitable if one followed the concepts of Relationshift and the practice of Relationshipping. This is true if one is dealing with pure dynamics; *no one else, either currently or from the past, is preoccupying the mental and emotional energies of either partner*. With a more open society, it is becoming increasingly more difficult to discover pure dynamics. With divorce and cohabitation more the norm than the exception, the culture has become sequentially polygamous. Defensive scar tissue forms early. The work that has to be done becomes a little more Complicated.

Complicated Relationshipping refers only to the romantic category. There are no injunctions against people having simultaneous continuums in work, friend, and family Relationshipping, but there is more of an exclusive orientation surrounding romantic love. Many people's past Relationshipping is unresolved to the extent that the former partner, though physically absent, remains an active part of the mental and emotional process. Past unresolved experiences taint the current Relationshipping and skew the dynamics. The effect is magnified if there are children from the past couplehood. Former partners who continue as parents are constant reminders of unresolved issues. Though unresolved issues also exist in work, friend, and family Relationshipping, the looser structure of the categories allows selection from more alternatives to deal with the discomfort. It is only in romantic love that overt simultaneous continuums and unresolved prior Relationshipping have a daily dysfunctional effect.

Complicated Relationshipping basically applies to simultaneous continuums on either the overt or the covert level. Relationshipping is Complicated because the factors one partner perceives are not the only factors that exist. Data is more difficult to analyze, and time and investment on the continuum do not run true to form.

The most obvious example of overt simultaneous continuums is the extra-marital affair. Whether it is a single person romantically involved with a married person (two continuums) or two married people not married to each other (three continuums), the Relationshipping is by its nature Complicated. Although individual situations vary, secret lovers do not live in the real world. Time together must be planned and limited. Anticipation lends excitement. The ever present possibility of discovery maintains a tension level and creates a sense of couple bonding. People seek in their lover that which is missing in their mate. Whether or not the lover also has the mate's positive attributes is not a focus of attention. There is little opportunity to see a lover in action as a partner on a day to day basis. Although intimates may talk about what they would do in a given situation, there is little data which proves whether words and actions would be consistent. It is impossible to evaluate compatibility and complete value systems in an affair. Because the marital continuum has a higher priority, it is also difficult to evaluate trust. Although the primary feelings, characteristics, and risks of the Interaction Stage exist, it is hopeless to attempt the developmental tasks.

Philip and Erin spent three turbulent years discovering the differences between normal and Complicated Relationshipping continuums.

Philip and Erin

Philip had been married for twelve years to an attractive self-contained homemaker when he fell in love with someone else across a conference table. She was beautiful, bright, and vibrant. An assertive career woman, she had been divorced five years and had no children. Her age, education, interests, and skills paralleled Philip's exactly. They worked together on a project day and night for six weeks before she returned to the parent company. By the time she left, they were both physically and emotionally involved. Philip was keenly aware of certain differences between Erin and his wife Faye. Erin was enthusiastic, knowledgeable, and smartly dressed. She was a delightful imp in bed. To her, life was one vast beach where she could play in the challenge of the waves. Faye was interested in Philip's work but primarily concerned with home and family. Their two young children kept her busy and tired at night. Lovemaking was more dutiful than responsive, and when she talked in bed, she was likely to say, "Don't spend a lot of time, Honey. Just get it over with. I've had a long day." Faye was conservative, deferred most decisions to Philip, and was reluctant to try most new experiences. Philip thought about Erin a great deal, and he decided that there was nothing really wrong with Faye but being with Erin enriched his life. He decided to continue the affair.

Philip and Erin continued long distance Relationshipping over the next year. It was like being nineteen again with all the typical Interaction Stage feelings and characteristics. Get-away weekends together were easily accomplished because Philip was a backpacker and had a long history of periodic weekend trips. They got to know each other better and felt comfortable with each other, but a level of excitement was always maintained because of their anticipation of being together. Both were always at their best.

Erin succeeded in obtaining a transfer to Philip's subsidiary company their second year. They saw each other daily at work but actually had less private time together in spite of increased proximity. They were able to be together more often but for less time. Instead of weekends, there were lunch-time quickies, and they developed a lifestyle complementary to Philip's marriage. They knew the same people but not as a couple. They often participated in the same activities but separately instead of as partners. Their second year was as exciting and stimulating as the first. Always ready to listen and to support each other, they began to think about life together on a permanent and legal basis.

During their third year Philip separated from his wife, virtually moving in with Erin except for maintaining a separate apartment for his children's weekend visits. After the first few months, he noticed several characteristics which had not been relevant under earlier circumstances. First, Erin did not tend to pick up after him. Although delighted to cook, she expected him to help with clean-up afterwards. She also expected him to do his share of laundry and other apartment chores. Second, she had no understanding of his desire to go backpacking alone. She anticipated joint leisure time and was hurt and upset if he wanted to spend available time separate from her. Third, she had no sympathy for Faye's pain nor for his concurrent guilt. She approached the situation from precise logic: he had wanted Erin more than Faye; he had gone after what he wanted; too bad for Faye; and, he should be happy because he had obtained what he wanted. In addition, Erin had had little experience with children. She talked baby talk to Jeff and Meggy and was impatient with their dependency. Sometimes she competed with them for his attention. In retrospect, Faye seemed a better match for him. Moderate Faye was less demanding, gave him more freedom, and was a natural mother. Exciting Erin was much more concerned with her own needs and wants, and she expected Philip to be concerned with them, too.

Three years into Relationshipping with Erin and four months separated from his wife, Philip realized he and Erin were probably not compatible on a day to day basis. Their value systems were generally different and they had built no foundation of trust. Although they had significant time and investment on the continuum, the circumstances had not been normal. The secret nature of their Relationshipping had prevented them from being able to evaluate data properly. They had not progressed beyond base line Interaction Stage dynamics. Not being able to view each other in the usual framework of life distorted their perceptions and distorted their Relationshipping.

Most people who have affairs but do not leave their spouses for their lovers realize at least at a preconscious level the probabilities of distortion. Characteristics that are missing in the mate and provided by the lover are balanced by the reverse. There is a sense that the exciting lover is more demanding than the mate: the nuturing lover more controlling, and the giving lover more dependent. Most affairs begin as a sort of personal enrichment rather than a serious consideration to change a life partner. However, as people become emotionally involved, they experience Interaction Stage anxiety combined with Testing Stage urges "to do something" with the Relationshipping. The married lover can only be called at certain times, can only be seen in certain places. The unmarried lover may be dating someone else. Inaccessibility does not build trust. The desire for reassurance and security can be satisfied only under normal conditions. Consequently, lovers begin to think of marriage though they only know parts of each other's personalities and only know those parts under artificial conditions. According to the amount of pressure applied, basically satisfied married people tend to terminate the affair because of the inner sense of caution. Less satisfied or more daring people follow their anxieties and often later discover that they had confused the distorted conditions of secret involvement with the criteria necessary for long term loving.

Another example of overt simultaneous continuums is the attempt to Relationship with a person in the Termination Stage of another continuum. Though not *officially* unavailable, a terminating partner is *psychologically* unavailable for healthy Relationshipping. It is quite Complicated to attempt to end one romantic continuum while at the same time beginning another. The developmental tasks are opposite and mutually exclusive. Termination requires the individual to give up, to grieve, and to mourn. Concommittant feelings of anger, guilt, and depression accompany the mourning process while beginning interactions feature giving, investment, and euphoria. Although a new romance often feels a balm to Termination Stage feelings of loneliness and inadequacy, the combination of the dynamics of the two stages confuses both the beginning of one continuum and the ending of the other.

Dynamics are not pure on either continuum. A terminating partner who has begun a continuum with another person is distracted from Termination Stage developmental tasks and more susceptible to Termination Stage risks. There is a tendency to view the former partner as the cause of all unhappiness. Because of the anesthesizing effect of Interaction Stage euphoria on Termination Stage self doubts and depression, there is a corresponding belief that a new partner will remedy all prior difficulties. A further skewing effect exists if there is another terminating partner who immediately focuses on the new Relationshipping as *the* problem. The former mate's betrayal becomes the issue rather than the mutual contributory aspects on the original couple's own continuum. This change in focus occurs regardless of whether the new Relationshipping existed first as an extra-marital affair to springboard the Termination Stage or whether it actually began following a couple's separation. The net result of combining the Termination Stage with new Relationshipping is distorted perception of relevent couple issues by both terminating partners. Neither person has the opportunity to deal with the pure dynamics of separation and termination.

Interaction Stage dynamics are similarly impure. The new Relationshipper enters the play in the third act pre-cast as White Knight or emotional Lady Bountiful regardless of the lines in his or her personal script. It is a Dr. Jeckyl/Mr. Hyde role since it also involves being automatic villain for the off stage terminating partner. The dual role does not at first seem difficult. The new arrival is quick to believe the potential partner's perceptions (distorted) and equally quick to champion his or her cause. Thus proving his White Knighthood or her Lady Bountifulness, the new Relationshipper reinforces the already perverse perspective.

The new continuum begins at a troubled time with unrealistic expectations. One potential partner is in a state of emotional upheaval and does not feel or react as he or she would feel and react under normal conditions and under normal emotional equilibrium. The need for support, understanding, and encouragement is primary. Emotional dependence is heightened. Feelings of anger, inadequacy, and guilt are free floating. A new Relationshipper who can fill these needs and, in addition, provide input that the sufferer is worthwhile and wonderful is indeed a welcome companion. Issues of compatibility and similar value systems are eagerly forgotten and often sacrificed — for awhile — in order to escape the pain of termination. With one potential partner in a weakened state and the other endowed with unrealistic saviour-like characteristics, the new continuum begins with covert contracts of dependency for one and emotional responsibility for the other. Overt or covert contracts which assume responsibility for another's happiness bode ill for any continuum, but they are especially problematic in Complicated Relationshipping. The covert contract remains after the upheaval has settled. Relationshippers often find themselves in inappropriate roles and with inappropriate expectations of each other. Upon reaching a state of equilibrium, the factors of compatibility and similar value systems now assume their proper importance. Previously viewed as perfect together, potential partners now seem an obvious mismatch. The new continuum comes to an abrupt halt.

The process just described occurs so frequently that to many it has become known as "transition Relationshipping." "On the rebound" is the common phrase. It once implied marriage or at least engagement to the new person. Currently, "on the rebound" or "transition Relationshipping" continues to describe premature emotional reinvestment after a termination. However, the term also now carries the implication that the partnership has not been, or will not be, successful.

Campbell and Trish

Campbell and Trish began dating about two weeks after he and his wife had separated. Eaten by loneliness and the desire to talk, Camp had been spending most of his evenings at a singles bar not far from his new apartment. He recognized Trish as a somewhat familiar face and realized they both worked in different stores of the same shopping mall. Trish seemed the complete opposite of his passive and overly dependent wife. While Madge was wishy-washy, whiney, and unorganized, Trish was direct, spunky, and competent in all her day to day activities. They began seeing each other regularly in spite of the fact that Madge hired detectives to follow them and accused Camp of having been involved with Trish all along.

Madge did not take separation easily. Neither did Camp, but he showed it less obviously. Madge made hungry and desperate phone calls, drove by Camp's and Trish's apartments, and made terrible scenes when she found them together. Most of their old friends disapproved of Camp and gave much sympathy to Madge. Camp stoically and guiltily made arrangements to buy his freedom. He offered Madge a settlement which included their house and its funishings, the existing balance in the checking and savings account, and continuing alimony for three years. They had never had children because Camp had questioned Madge's maturity and ability to be a good mother, but he thought she had a good mind and could hold a job if she had training. Offering her nearly all their assets as well as continuing financial support eased his own reactions to her emotional turmoil. His feelings of inadequacy and guilt alternated with absolute joy at being able to find so quickly a woman as wonderful as Trish. He fervently thanked his lucky stars because Trish was everything he had wanted in a woman. If Madge had only been like Trish, they would have had no problems.

Camp did not realize it, but Madge and Trish had much in common psychologically. Their personalities and situations were different, and therefore their similar needs were manifested differently. Trish had been divorced for six years and had been handling her own financial affairs long before her divorce. She had had no one to take care of her and make decisions for her and had therefore learned to do both quite competently. However, Trish did all these things secondary to one primary goal: to find a man who would love her and make her happy. She belonged to no clubs or organizations. She had no hobbies. She was uninterested in any activity other than the search. Her second home was the singles bar in which she and Camp had encountered each other, and her friends were similar habitués who were involved in the same search. Trish quickly settled in with Camp, assuming *forever* but wildly fearful that this human pot of gold at the end of the rainbow would disappear out of her grasp. Out of habit, he treated her much as he had treated Madge. He was concerned about her sleeping and eating habits, gave her advice, and bought her clothes and presents. Throughout his terminating turmoil with Madge, he spent every available moment with Trish and Trish was as happy as a little clam.

Madge too found a new lover. The divorce was finalized. Camp developed new friends — other single men who wanted him to play golf, watch football games, play poker, occasionally drink and carouse together. He no longer wanted Trish as constant and only companion. After six perfect months, they began averaging two to three arguments a week, all in one way or another concerning whether or not they were going to be together and if not, why not. Trish could not understand the change in Camp. Their covert contract, now behaviorally well established for six months, declared they would spend all their non-working time together and he would take care of all her non-fiscal needs. Camp was also confused. He could not comprehend why this sweet and capable woman who had understood all his difficulties with Madge could not also understand his need and desires to do other activities with other people. He felt hemmed in. He felt controlled. He felt responsible for making her feel badly. He felt guilty for wanting to be somewhere else with someone else. He felt just as he had felt with Madge.

Both Trish and Madge were dependent women. Camp had basically duplicated his dynamics with Madge when he and Trish became involved. Even though Trish was able to live independently, all the signs of emotional dependency were present. Camp, blinded by the pain of termination and his own needs for companionship and support, had selectively perceived only those characteristics which were different. Being on two simultaneous continuums had clouded his judgment and interfered with his ability to evaluate the situation as a whole.

Both extra-marital affairs and beginning new Relationshipping while in the process of terminating with an old partner are obvious examples of Complicated Relationshipping. In both instances the existence of other on-going partners is a felt presence. The simultaneous continuums are virtually visible. However, there is another variety of Complicated Relationshipping which is much more difficult to discern. The not-so-obvious simultaneous continuum is a result of unresolved prior Relationshipping, sometimes collective, and exists on a covert level.

Tough-on-Trudi

Trudi is a sweet emotional woman who has a tremendous capacity to give. However, within her she has a tangled mass of loose strings still hanging from unresolved prior Relationshipping, and she therefore also has a tremendous capacity to take. Surrounding Trudi is a general atmosphere of unfinished business. She has a breath of feisty defensiveness because she has been *wronged* in the past and does not intend for it to happen again. Trudi has been a victim (at least, in her own eyes) and a running catalog of sins against her are ever ready to pop into her conscious mind. She expects her current partner to make it up to her for past partners' crimes. She often over-reacts to a current partner's innocent behavior because it is reminiscent of past unresolved partnerships. Trudi has frequent backaches, neckaches, and headaches. Her pains are usually in the tension zones and can unexplainably disappear after solicitous personal attention from a partner. She usually rationalizes her current behavior in terms of past events. Extracts from daily life with Tough-on-Trudi:

"Oh, Why didn't you order anything for me?"

"Well, you were in the bathroom and I didn't know what you'd want."

"You could have ordered me something anyway. Just to be considerate. Rob was like that, too. He never was thoughtful. Now I get to sit and watch you slurp that down and I don't have anything."

"Here. Take mine. I'll get something else when the waitress comes."

"No, I don't want yours. I want mine. I know you think I'm making a big deal out of nothing, but you can't imagine the number of times Rob used to do this to me . . ."

"I just can't understand why you're so eager to take the children every time she wants to go out of town for a fling."

"It's not like that, Trudi. This is my regular weekend to have the kids. She's just taking the opportunity to get away, that's all."

"No, that's not all. Just because you don't mind babysitting while

she lives it up every weekend doesn't mean I don't. Rob never takes the kids so we can get away together. Why should we do it for her? Besides, my back is hurting and taking care of four children is a lot different from taking care of two. She's the most selfish person I ever heard of."

"Who was that you were talking to?"
"One of the fellows at work and his wife."
"Well, why didn't you introduce me? I just stood there like a lump. You don't understand how uncomfortable that is for a woman. Rob used to do that all the time, and I was humiliated."

Everything is so tough on Trudi.

Although Trudi is alert to any attitude or event which might possibly bring a repeat of past experiences, it is not current events or attitudes with which she is concerned. She is actually involved in constant re-hashing of the past, and current or anticipated future situations act only as stimulus to verbalize the running undercurrents of her mind.

The male equivalent of Tough-on-Trudi is Rough-on-Rudi. He, too, instead of learning from experience, has learned only the experiences themselves. If Rudi was married and pays either alimony or child support, he resents continuing to pay for what he no longer has. He feels uncomfortable in the presence of his new partner's old companions. He, too, feels victimized. Past hurts season current events and conversations. He, too, is much more in touch with what has gone before than what is happening now.

Trudi and Rudi (and their numerous counterparts) are easily offended and not inclined to trust. These characteristics show through as a certain vulnerability which is attractive to potential partners who have residual guilt about their own prior Relationshipping. The sense is that they can compensate for both pasts and build a hopeful future together. Such partners do not realize they are on the wrong side of the time warp. The past must be resolved by Trudi or Rudi themselves. Neither can truly connect with another partner while emotionally preoccupied with the old business of the past. Current partners find themselves constantly soothing ruffled feathers and constantly attempting to prove themselves different from Trudi's (or Rudi's) former partners.

Trudi and Rudi should be avoided as potential partners until they have successfully laid their past Relationshipping to rest. In terms of identifying them, it must be noted that not everyone who remembers negatives falls into the Trudi or Rudi category. In order to grow and change, a person must objectively remember what did not work in the past. In addition, many people have some residual irritation that never quite leaves, but the overall tone of successful resolution is a fairly neutral stance. People are able to look backward and see the good times as well as the bad. Former partners are viewed retrospectively with *both* their positive and negative characteristics. Mutual missteps can be identified. In spite of a few residual sore spots, people have closed the door on the past and are able to start fresh with new partners. There is a realization that every experience with someone who was once attractive is in some way enriching. Not so with Trudi and Rudi. They see nothing enriching about past Relationshipping. They are fixated. They see no positives in their former partners nor in anyone else's former partners. They have never really terminated.

To identify Trudi and Rudi (and thus to avoid them), Relationshippers need only to be aware of over reactions and continuing active anger associated with the past. An additional major clue is the potential partner's inability to have proper perspective on past experiences: being unable to identify positives *and* negatives and to pull the benefit forward for present and future use. Although Trudi and Rudi may have many individual desirable attributes, they are too heavily invested in the past to pay close attention to a new continuum. Their chronic anger bonds them to the old couplehood as strongly as any loving feelings they once felt. Their unresolved and therefore recurring old business distorts their perceptions.

EXCEPTION: Trudi and Rudi are not *always* negative and angry. There are cases of positive preoccupation with past continuums, usually involving a former partner who has died. In these instances, the earlier continuums assume a halo effect. Instead of having to make up to Trudi or Rudi for past crimes against them, current partners must compete with an image of perfection. Daily dialogue implies a constant (and losing) comparison.

"*I wish you were more handy around the house, Crockett could have rewired that lamp in a minute.*"

"*Why don't you just get a new one? That lamp is pretty old, you know.*"

"*I hate to spend the money when it's so easy to fix it. That man could fix anything. And right away too. We never had anything broken in our house for more than five minutes. I'm just not used to broken lamps and drippy faucets and squeaky doors.*"

"*I don't think I could ever love anyone as much as I loved Peggy. Oh, don't get me wrong. I really love you. But it was different with Peggy. She was so sensitive to me. We never fought. She always knew just what to say or do. I guess you run into someone like Peggy maybe once in a lifetime."*

"This is a really nice place to come for the weekend."
"I hoped you'd like it. I found out about it from one of the guys at work."
"It reminds me of the place Giles and I went on our honeymoon. That was the most beautiful place in the world. But this place is nice too."

The positive variation of Trudi and Rudi also features the imbalance in viewing past Relationshipping. They see only positives. Instead of being preoccupied with unresolved complaints, they are chronically concerned with past virtues. In order to invest completely in the current continuum, they too need to lay the past Relationshipping to rest.

Whether overt simultaneous continuums like Philip and Erin or covert simultaneous continuums of the Trudi/Rudi varieties, Complicated Relationshipping involves more factors than the individuals see and believe to exist. Energy cannot be successfully simultaneously invested on more than one continuum without a keen awareness of the underlying and concurrent dynamics. Data is more difficult to analyze, and time and investment on the continuum do not run true to form. Complicated Relationshipping should be avoided.

Partners already involved in Complicated Relationshipping find contract communication an invaluable aid. Contracts keep the focus on the current continuum and provide for a separation between past and current events.

CHAPTER XIV

Contract Communication: Complicated Relationshipping

People who begin their continuums with full application of Relationshift concepts and who consistently practice contract communication rarely become involved in Complicated Relationshipping. They are able to avoid mismatches in chemistry, compatibility, and value systems as well as those possible partners who are incapable of successful long term Relationshipping. Additionally, because of the rich intimacy and communication shared with partners, there is no desire for the outside satisfaction of the extramarital affair. These people have no need of this chapter.

There are other people who are already involved in Complicated Relationshipping. They co-exist with impure dynamics because they are committed to partners whose emotions and attitudes are fixated or to partners who are legally committed to someone else. Such partnerships are often permeated with seemingly unresolvable anxiety, tension, frustration, and relationshit. Although the odds are strongly against these couples achieving the quality of communication, closeness, and mutuality that would otherwise be available, contract communication can prevent the extraordinary perplexity. There is no method which can completely smooth the course of Complicated Relationshipping; it is by nature difficult. However, because of the clear guidelines established, contract communication helps prevent many of the impulsive behaviors which can cause irrevocable damage. Contract communication significantly reduces tension and relationshit and alleviates anxiety and frustration. People already involved find that contract communication prevents the Relationshipping from being more Complicated than it has to be. It is for these people that this chapter is written.

Complicated Relationshipping applies only to the romantic category and exists when people are attempting to relationship on simultaneous continuums. The simultaneous continuums may be covert due to unresolved past Relationshipping or they may be overt due to concurrent romances. (See Chapter XIII) The image portion of the brain (the seat of emotions and impulses) cannot differentiate between these two continuums. The logic portion of the brain must constantly apply and interpret Relationshift theory to the emotions and impulses, separating the continuums and allowing the person to deal effectively with his or her feelings. Contracting is essential in Complicated Relationshipping. Relationshift provides the logic portion of the brain with knowledge of what can be expected at different stages of the Relationshipping process. Agreements provide additional information regarding individual expectations and behaviors. The logic portion of the brain requires both *process* information and *specifics of the individual partnership* in order to analyze properly and to keep the respective continuums in perspective.

Developing successful Relationshipping with simultaneous continuums is PhD level Relationshipping. It requires a great deal of study, practice, and effort to obtain the necessary skills to become effective. The rewards are manifested through less confusion and less tendency to destroy the Relationshipping with impulsive and inappropriate behavior.

Contracting with Covert Simultaneous Continuums

Contract format is flexible when covert simultaneous continuums exist. Partners use the form for interim, term, or renewal contracts according to their progress along the continuum. The issue of the unresolved Relationshipping is addressed along with other significant topics. It should not be relegated to the list of non-negotiable items. Partners must discuss various options for laying the past Relationshipping to rest.

Fixated partners usually do not realize their own preoccupation with past people and events. Considerate but direct feedback often spurs recognition and inspires motivation to resolve the prior Relationshipping. A fixated partner who realizes the problem should be encouraged to complete the joint or the unilateral review. (See Chapter XII) When confrontation brings denial, fixated partners should be encouraged to seek professional counseling to become more aware of their unconscious processes. In either case, contract clauses should include various agreements regarding specific behaviors that are indicative of the covert continuum. The following portion of Bernadette and Karl's term contract illustrates such clauses:

Contract between Bernadette and Karl
Jan. 15

Purpose: To resolve our differences in a better way, to work together better as a team, and to become more acquainted with each other's family and friends.

    1. Previous contract agreements about frequency of time together, punctuality, finances, and sex still apply.

2. Resolving differences:
   a. We agree to tell the other person directly within 24 hours (instead of not talking, crying, looking hurt, pouting, or walking off) when something happens that makes us angry or hurts our feelings.
   b. Bernadette realizes that Karl is not Patrick and probably won't do the things Patrick used to do. Because what Patrick used to do can cause arguments between us, we understand and agree to the following:
      1) Bernadette will remind herself that Karl is being friendly and sociable when he talks and dances with other women at parties. He has no intention of making passes and picking them up like Patrick did.
      2) When Karl goes to the bar with the bowling league, it is to enjoy himself with his teammates. Bernadette will quit cross examining him every Tuesday night after bowling.
      3) Karl's sex drive equals about once a week. That is normal for him. It does NOT mean he does not love Bernadette and is going to leave her.
      4) Both Bernadette and Karl will keep count of the number of times she compares Karl to Patrick (both mentally and out loud.) If it really is more than three times a day or five times a week, Bernadette will call the mental health center to get some help in getting over Patrick.

Bernadette and Karl are in the Testing Stage and are experiencing the usual periodic conflicts of blending. (See Chapter VIII.) The blending process itself, however, is being inhibited by Bernadette's anxiety and her increasingly obvious comparison of Karl to Patrick, her previous partner. Although Bernadette last saw Patrick three years ago, she is so preoccupied with his behavior that she does not view Karl as a separate person. She wants Karl to avoid any Patrick-like behaviors in the hope that she can avoid Patrick-like disappearances. Patrick's spectre accompanies their Relationshipping; they are three on the continuum. If Karl were to acquiesce, the two partners would be blending into Bernadette's fears rather than into a couplehood. As the contract indicates, Karl has appropriately refused to change his habits on her irrational assumption that he would behave the same as Patrick under the same circumstances. If he yields to her fears, Bernadette will continue to mistrust him as well as Patrick. Instead, Karl works to help her realize her fixation.

Exorcising the covert simultaneous continuum requires the non-preoccupied partner to be patient and firm. People with unresolved past Relationshipping view themselves as victims. They are usually overly sensitive, defensive, and easily threatened regarding their irrational attitudes. Their partners must consistently persevere to provide reality factors regarding the difference between past and present partners and past and present continuums. This information enables the logic portion of the brain to differentiate between the two continuums. It allows the fixated partner to realize the problem and to work toward resolution.

Contracting With Overt Simultaneous Continuums

There are two groupings of overt simultaneous continuums: (1) Termination mixed with Interaction and (2) Concurrent Romances. The first grouping involves people in transition. A new continuum is begun before the existing continuum is fully completed. The second grouping involves maintenance of a secondary continuum due to a lack of fulfillment on the primary continuum. Both groupings have their particular problems which contracting helps to minimize.

Termination Mixed With Interaction

The key issue in beginning one romantic continuum while terminating another is keeping separate the feelings, characteristics, risks, and developmental tasks of each stage of each continuum. It is Complicated Relationshipping and not an easy task. The uninformed have little hope of being successful. Most first major Relationshipping attempts begun during termination from another continuum do not work out. Relationshippers must have a firm grip on Relationshift theory and a firm contract to define issues and expectations. Agreements should include anticipation of the mourning process, separate time for the development of the new continuum, and recognition that behavioral contracts currently established will probably be subject to major change after stabilization. These additional items are incorporated into simple initial, interim, and term contracts until the Termination Stage is completed.

Steve and Patsy are a rare couple who survived the turmoil of opposite feelings and opposite developmental tasks. They began Relationshipping in the midst of Patsy's separation from her husband of six years. Their success is credited to Steve's knowledge of Relationshift theory, his insistence on the performance of both Interaction Stage and Termination Stage developmental tasks, and his introduction of a series of contracts to guide their Relationshipping.

Simple Initial Contract between Patsy and Steve
May 17

Purpose: Realizing that Patsy is recently separated and this is a bad time to begin a new romance, we agree to see if we can develop a supportive friendship at this time with an eye toward evaluating a dating Relationshipping later.

- We agree to see each other four times in the next six weeks with a variety of activities. Patsy will suggest two activities and Steve will suggest two. The first activity will be a movie on May 20. The next time together will be planned at the end of each activity. After each activity, we will feed back both positive and negative impressions about each other and about the activity.
- Steve will assume financial responsibility for activities.

- If either has to cancel because of an emergency, a raincheck will be scheduled at the time.
- Each may have phone privileges at any time, conversations not to exceed one hour.
- If 50% or more of any activity consists of "divorce talk", we will have an extra activity with no "divorce talk" at all.
- There will be no sex, no necking, no petting, no extended kissing, etc. during the course of this contract.
- This is not an exclusive Relationshipping but we will not discuss other dates with each other.
- Patsy agrees to develop one new female friend during the course of this contract.
- On July fourth this contract will terminate. We will have a picnic and discuss how this contract has worked for us and where we go from here.

Signed:

Interim Contract between Patsy and Steve
July 4

Purpose: To continue our supportive friendshipping with an eye to evaluating compatibility and value systems later. (We already know we have the chemistry!)

- We agree to see each other twice a week for the next two months, one a "divorce talk" activity and one activity for "us" with no divorce talk. One of our activities will be a double date with Patsy's new friend Julie and her boyfriend. We'll have feedback after each activity.
- Same financial responsibility, same phone privileges, and same cancellation procedures as last contract.
- Still not exclusive and still no sex.
- Steve agrees to help Patsy move when her lease expires Aug. 30.
- Steve agrees to teach Patsy how to do the review of the Relationshipping during one of our "divorce talk" activities.
- We will investigate taking different community education classes in the fall. We can ride together if the classes are at the same time.
- We will review this contract at termination on Labor Day, give overall feedback, and decide where we go from there.

Signed:

These two contracts, extracted from a series of six, are indicative of Patsy and Steve's slow and patient progress along the continuum. Their agreements defined their Relationshipping as "supportive friends" for over a year before they began dating to evaluate the possibilities of romance. Along the way, Patsy grieved the prior Relationshipping, accomplished the joint review, developed a resource group, and established personal goals for her own growth. Steve was a regular and consistent partner who encouraged her without being pushy and who also was involved in his own growth goals and activities. Over time they developed trust and confidence in each other as well as feedback and a strong foundation for future Relationshipping. They were able to avoid the risks of both the Termination and the Interaction stages. Their slow pace, their differentiation between "their" time and "divorce talk" time, their attention to necessary developmental tasks, and their flexibility regarding behavioral contracts (evidenced in later agreements) were vital focal points in their ability to survive the impure dynamics of two simultaneous continuums.

Concurrent Romances

The second grouping of overt simultaneous continuums is concurrent romances. One Night Stands do not qualify. Concurrent romances are affairs: secret on-going emotional investment with one partner while legally and/or emotionally committed to another partner. A state of outside commitment exists whether it involves marriage or cohabitation. One or both partners in the affair may have an outside commitment.

People involved in concurrent romances deal with similar issues as people involved in covert simultaneous continuums. The fixated are unaware of their emotional dilemma; people involved in affairs enter into them voluntarily and by choice.

Affairs exist. They exist in every socioeconomic group, every age group, and every occupation.[5] They exist in staggering numbers. In his book *More Than Just A Friend*, Dr. Tom McGinnis quotes Dr. Paul Gebhard (successor to Dr. Alfred Kinsey at the Institute for Sex Research at Indiana University) as "guesstimating" extramarital affairs to be about sixty percent for males and thirty-five to forty percent for females.[6] These statistics do not reflect promiscuity as much as they reflect the general failure of the penguin system to establish and maintain emotional intimacy and quality long term partnerships. Dr. McGinnis states that not only do affairs exist, but "...they are going to continue because people want satisfying qualitative couple relationships, and if they don't find them in their marriages, they'll look for them elsewhere. Some people prize their affair as the only meaningful human relationship they have ever had."[7]

Because of ignorance of the facts of Relationshipping, many people are mismatched with their legal partners. Other committed couples have fallen prey to risks which prevent them from productive problem solving. Either predicament results in emotional distance and dissatisfaction. Although many people are reluctant to abandon their commitments (i.e. divorce), they also refuse to be emotionally stagnant. In many instances, affairs are alternatives to divorce. Because a primary partner is a poor match, refuses or is incapable of in-depth communication, people seek intimacy and fulfillment on a secondary continuum.

In one respect, affairs are contrary to the philosophy of Relationshift. Since primary partners are unaware of the involvement with a secondary partner, affairs contradict the goals of open-ness, honesty, and mutuality. Affairs contribute to, and maintain, emotional distance between partners on the primary continuum. The secondary continuum (the affair) distracts emotional energy and investment from its proper perspective.

On the other hand, Relationshift is defined as "the knowledge, mental attitudes, and thought processes involved in the successful developing of a long term partnership." The definition features no distinctions as to marital status. Typical feelings, characteristics, and risks manifest themselves along each stage of the continuum regardless of other commitments. If the partners to an affair apply Relationshift knowledge, attitudes, and thought processes openly and directly through the use of a contract or agreement, they too are Relationshipping.

Partners to an affair have particular problems in Relationshipping. The first is a lack of *normal* time and contact. Because this element is missing, there is a chronic Interaction Stage flavor regardless of distance traveled on the continuum. Lovers have an artificial stimulant ("stolen" hours) and an artificial bond (*their* affair) which day to day socially sanctioned couples do not have. Without normal time and contact, lovers cannot objectively evaluate the full range of chemistry, compatibility, and value systems. Lack of normal time and contact further makes it impossible to perform the developmental tasks. Although lovers may be able to determine whether or not they are discreet enough, mature enough, and responsible enough to cope with an affair, the lack of normal time and contact makes them uniquely unable to evaluate their suitability as marital partners.

Another problem is misinterpretation of data. Since lovers knowingly enter into an affair, there is not as much blurring of continuums as exists with simultaneous covert continuums. There remains a tendency, however, for the logic portion of the brain to compare the two partners and the two continuums. Since the partners (one a spouse, the other a lover) have different roles, and the continuums are at different stages (one at Testing or Negotiation, the other at Interaction), the resulting conclusions are faulty. The role of a spouse includes much more than relating only to a partner while the role of a lover is totally partner centered. Faulty logic often concludes that the spouse is insensitive and uncaring while the lover is *the ideal*. There is little realization that the lover would probably relate in a very similar manner were he or she in the spouse's role. The different continuum stages also result in unfavorable comparison. For example, a Negotiation Stage spouse may be preoccupied and may also be leery of a mate's adjustment to change. At the same time, an Interaction Stage lover may be performing special behaviors and totally accepting of the partner's behavior and attitudes. Misinterpretation of data results in increased dissatisfaction with the marriage and idealization of the lover.

A third problem is *marriage is implicit as a goal between* lovers. If the affair reaches the Testing Stage with the characteristic urge "to do something" with the Relationshipping, a married partner to an affair may jettison family and economic status for a match that he or she does not yet have the data to know is appropriate. Lovers instinctively aim toward marriage. If one of the partners is immature, dependent, or demanding, the implicit goals and the urge "to do something" combine to an intolerable level. Lovers then fall prey to the risk of permanize or terminize.

The problems can best be avoided through the use of a contract. By making clear definitions and agreements, lovers benefit from the special nature of their Relationshipping rather than misinterpreting data, magnifying dissatisfaction, or making inappropriate decisions. The contract gives specific guidelines to the logic portion of the brain which is then able to keep this concurrent continuum isolated and in perspective. Lovers discover whether or not each other is discreet, mature, and responsible enough to cope as a complementary partner. They also discover whether or not the affair is worth the contradiction of open-ness, honesty, and mutuality to the primary commitment or marriage.

Extramarital contracts pay particular attention to definition of purpose, privileges clauses, ground rules, and short term goals. They also specify frequency of contact, emergency procedures for contacting each other, and conditions for termination of the affair. Wording should be as specific as possible to leave little room for doubt or confusion. The written contract is preferred. Lovers who are leery of putting anything in writing are more at ease with unidentifiable pet names in typed agreements. The following contract between "Hon" and "Kazoo" is a good example of clear definitions and understandings between two people on a concurrent continuum.

Contract between Hon and Kazoo
Nov. 1

Purpose: Although we did not intentionally seek romantic involvement, we have decided to continue as loving partners to enrich each other's lives through communication, sexuality, and emotional closeness. To prevent covert contracts and covert expectations, we clearly state and agree to the following:

We have no marriage goals. Kazoo's marriage and family are his priority. He seeks in our special Relationshipping the communication, emotional expression, and sexual satisfaction that are missing in his marriage.

Hon is a free agent. As a single woman she may develop romantic Relation-

Contract Communication: Complicated Relationshipping 195

shipping with someone else with a marriage goal. This is not to be a topic between us unless and until we need to change from lovers to friends.

1. **Frequency of Contact and Privileges**
   A. We shall try to be together an average of once a month. Sex is not required on these occasions, but talk time is a priority. If time is so limited that we can either talk or make love, we shall talk.
   B. We shall aim for telephone contact once a week. Kazoo will initiate regular calls. Hon may call Kazoo at work, but not too often.
   C. As Kazoo's circumstances permit, we shall try to get away for a weekend together.
   D. Gifts and letters may be exchanged. (Gifts to Kazoo must not be identifiable as of a romantic nature. Letters to him must be sent to work.)
   E. Kazoo is responsible for financial expenditures. (Hon may offer to cook instead of eating out.)

2. **Ground Rules**
   A. Since this Relationshipping is confidential, we agree to be discreet in our behavior and in our conversation with others and not call attention to this Relationshipping.
   B. Hon will not make demands of Kazoo as to time or attention other than agreed upon in this contract except in case of genuine emergency.
   C. We will focus on the time and contact we have, day to day, rather than anticipating long term planning and events.
   D. We will not embarrass each other in any way.

3. **Goals**
   A. In-depth Communication
      We can discuss any topic not prohibited by this contract and want to develop in-depth expression of feelings and ideas. We will advise and confide in each other. We will be emotional supports. We especially agree to mention any negative impressions or opinions that would affect us, so we can resolve any problems that might come up. We will help each other to be as clear and direct in our communication as possible.
   B. Other short term joint goals as arise
      We will establish other joint goals in progress such as gathering information for household improvements, reading lists for personal growth, etc. so that we will have a feeling of unity and working together.

4. **Emergency Procedures**
   A. In case of genuine emergency, Kazoo can be contacted out of work hours through his friend Blitz.
   B. If unable to be located by phone, Hon can be contacted through her friend Inez.

5. **Conditions for Termination**
   A. If Kazoo's wife finds out, both contract and Relationshipping are immediately terminated.
   B. If Hon overinvests or has trouble coping with the limitations agreed upon, she may make a unilateral decision to terminate.
   C. Neither person will terminate without directly informing the partner and saying why.

6. **Review**
   This contract is on-going and may be amended at any time following discussion and agreement by both parties. Hon will be "keeper of the contract" and it will remain in her possession.

The above contract is clear and well defined. It leaves no doubt as to the status and priorities of the partners or of what one can expect of the other. It inhibits marriage as an implicit goal by overtly proscribing it and by focusing on other short term goals. It directly states the priority of the primary continuum. It inhibits immature, dependent, and demanding behavior by the unmarried partner. It provides for emergency contact and for conditions of termination. This and similar contracts help prevent impulsive behaviors and mental blurring particular to a concurrent romance.

Contracts in Complicated Relationshipping do not alter the complex nature of the endeavor. The contract between "Hon" and "Kazoo" is not easy to follow. Emotions and impulses consistently rise to war with logic. Kazoo is accessible only at certain times, not necessarily when Hon wants or needs a loving partner. Kazoo, in spite of his intellectual priorities, has an ever present tantalizing image personifying all that he desires in a partner. Regardless of a contract, his dissatisfaction increases if his spouse refuses, or is unable, to work to resolve their problems. The frustration and anxiety behind Bernadette and Karl's contract is almost overwhelming. Their agreement helps them to work to resolve those feelings, but does not change Bernadette's terror at parties or on Tuesday nights as Karl leaves for bowling. Karl's frustration at his partner's irrational thinking and her attempts to control his behavior are made tolerable only because he is now hopeful it will not last forever. Patsy and Steve's contract required grim and persistent patience since Patsy had been a dependent woman, sometimes seductive. She would have clutched at Steve as a Warm Puppy rather than develop the capability of healthy Relationshipping. Contracts do not make it easy. They do not make Complicated Relationshipping less complex; they merely prevent the Relationshipping from becoming *more* complicated than it inherently is.

Complicated Relationshipping requires advanced study, practice, and effort and is most successful when attempted by accomplished platypuses. Penguins who find themselves involved in simultaneous continuums would benefit from the guidance of a professional counselor who is trained in Relationshift.

CHAPTER XV

On Becoming a Platypus

Although Relationshift may seem dramatically different to those who have not practiced its concepts, it is much less complicated than the penguin patterns which are in such wide use. Both methods are simply a matter of habit systems. One method involves habit patterns of guesswork, covert contracts, manipulation, and indirect communication. The other method involves infinitely preferable habits of openness, direct communication, and mutuality. Because Relationshift is different does not mean it is complicated.

There is always an awkward period when a person begins new endeavors. Great pianists once practiced scales one handed. They practiced them over and over again. The most fluent linguists once conjugated verbs. They learned their vocabulary a word at a time. Each began with unfamiliar basic steps. In developing new skills attention is paid to step by step procedure, and concentration is on each of the steps rather than on the overall process. The new endeavor at first feels jerky; it feels uncoordinated; it feels wrong.

It is the same with Relationshipping. The concepts require active cognitive attention. Well-thumbed copies of *Relationshift* are stashed in purses and glove compartments for quick reference. Peoples' perspective begins shifting from expectations of instant intimacy and perceived rejection to the time line of evaluation regarding chemistry, compatibility, and value systems. (They are learning their vocabulary.) Novice relationshippers awkwardly experiment with simple initial contracts. (They are playing scales one handed.) With more experience people begin to develop favorite contract clauses. Practice brings smoothness and confidence. People begin to relationship automatically. No longer awkward or mechanical, the new habit patterns become a natural aspect of peoples' behaviors.

Different people apply Relationshift in different ways. The knowledge of the theory itself is of great aid in understanding what is happening between two people. There are many people who never contract but who are keenly aware of the feelings, characteristics, risks, and developmental tasks of each stage. By mentally applying the theory to their own experiences, these people avoid much personal pain and also are better able to control their own impulsive (and self-defeating) penguin-like behavior. Although they report significant positive changes in the course of their continuums, these people reap only half the benefit. They are unilaterally applying Relationshift and have not involved their partners in the process. They have taken the time and the effort to learn the concepts, but the effect is one sided. They do not have the richness of mutuality and communication which comes with Relationshipping.

There are many other people who do relationship but only in special situations. They apply the concepts of Relationshift through contract communication when it is important to them to continue with a particular partner. They want the course of this particular continuum to go well. Otherwise, they relate in a general penguin fashion for superficial situations and save their platypus skills for in-depth involvement. They enjoy the choice of being either penguin or platypus and are discriminate in their application of Relationshift concepts. These people reap two-thirds of the benefit. In one or two on-going situations, they establish rich and rewarding continuums of mutually satisfying depth and communication. Many people do not ask more of life.

Those who do ask more use Relationshipping in all significant areas of their lives. They apply Relationshift concepts with family, friends, colleagues, and loving partners. They do not instantly contract with everyone they meet; indeed, their written contracts may be limited to romance and close friendships. However, the general flavor of their conversation is clear and permeated with feedback. There is a noticeable lack of manipulation; agreements are verbally identified. These relationshippers function smoothly through feedback and negotiation. Their long term continuums, characterized by flexibility, openness, and mutuality, create a broad spectrum of adventures in communication, caring, and closeness. These people have incorporated Relationshift concepts into their daily lives and into their habit patterns. They realize the maximum benefit.

Establishing and maintaining successful long term partnerships is not difficult; it is only a matter of time, effort, and focus. People may choose the manner and method in which they wish Relationshift to impact their lives. Benefit will result whether they choose to wade mentally and unilaterally in the theory, to practice Relationshipping discriminately, or to don full platypus suit for the most rewarding and full application. However, though not difficult, to realize the benefits people must be willing to invest time step by step on the continuum. They must be willing to use their efforts in active and continuing participation with a partner. Finally, they must be willing to focus on achievement of appropriate developmental tasks inherent in each stage. It is well worth the time, effort, and focus. With Relationshift, loneliness becomes a resolvable issue. There is no reason why anyone should be lonely any more.

INTERACTION STAGE

3-6 Months Normal Time & Contact

Emotional Graph:

Developmental Tasks
1. Decide whether a relationshipping situation is desired
   a. Compatibility
   b. Values
   c. Chemistry
2. Decide which category of relationshipping is desired
3. Develop behavioral contracts
4. Develop feedback
5. Develop trust

Primary Feelings
1. Anxiety
2. Erratic mood swings
3. Feeling of "false" intimacy

Primary Characteristics
1. Guesswork/mindreading/unanswerable questions
2. Waiting
3. Communication
4. "Special" behaviors (sometimes)

Primary Risks
1. Too much too soon
   a. Magician
   b. Clinger
2. High drop-out rate
3. Perceived rejection

Questions to be Answered
1. Is this person open to new ideas?
2. Does this person make commitments?
3. Does this person follow through on commitments?
4. Does this person communicate directly?
5. Does this person communicate honestly?
6. Is there a difference between philosophy and action?

TESTING STAGE

6 Months - 1 Year

Emotional Graph: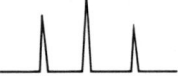

Developmental Tasks:
1. Establish ground rules
2. Determine goals
3. Identify non-negotiable issues
4. Learn to resolve anger together

Primary Feelings
1. Security/comfort
2. Urge to "do" something

Primary Characteristics
1. Routine
2. Couplehood
3. "Special" behaviors drop off

Primary Risks
1. The "Great Disappearing Act"
2. Centering
3. Assumptions-expectations
   a. Past thinking
   b. Wishful thinking
   c. Defeatist thinking
4. Permanize or terminize

Questions to be Answered
1. How does this person get along with my "significant others?"
2. Can I disagree with this person?
3. Does this person "fight" fairly?
4. What are the non-negotiable issues? How many? Can I live with them?
5. Except for the non-negotiable issues, are disagreements resolved?

NEGOTIATION

Emotional Graph:

Developmental Tasks
1. Nourish the couple bond
2. Adjust jointly to change
3. Develop couple goals, interests
4. Provide room for the other's growth
5. Achieve non-defensive negotiation

Primary Feelings
1. Growth
2. Accomplishment
3. Contentment

Primary Characteristics
1. Preoccupation
2. Adaptation to change

Primary Risks
1. Perceived personal threat
2. Depression
3. Parallel lives
4. Premature withdrawal

Questions to be Answered
1. Do I arrange to have close, private communication — minimum of two hours per week — with my partner?
2. Are my partner and I growing together or growing apart?
3. What compromises are possible?
4. What are our new goals?

TERMINATION

Emotional Graph:

Developmental Tasks
1. Grieve (give up) the couplehood
2. Accept the realistic personal statement
3. Utilize the crisis situation for personal growth
4. Develop resource group

Primary Feelings
1. Anger
2. Inadequacy
3. Loneliness
4. Guilt
5. Misery

Primary Characteristics
1. Mourning process
2. Need for support
3. Trial and error behavior

Primary Risks
1. Fixation
2. "Overfear" — Fear of being hurt again to the extent that it inhibits positive relationshipping
3. "New Puppy" syndrome

Questions to be Answered
1. Have I, either with my partner or by myself, completed the review of the relationshipping?
2. What have I learned from my former partner's complaints?
3. What personal goals have I established?
4. Which people have I developed as new friends?

Footnotes

[1] Nathaniel Brandon and Devers Brandon, *The Romantic Love Question and Answer Book* (Los Angeles: J. P. Tarcher, Inc. 1982), p. 147.

[2] Daniel Cappon, *Coupling* (New York: St. Martin's Press, 1981), p. 25.

[3] George Bach and Peter Wyden, *The Intimate Enemy* (West Caldwell, N.J.: William Morrow & Co., 1969).

[4] Jacinth Ivie Baublitz, "Transitional Treatment of Hostile Married Couples", *Social Work*, July 1978, p. 322.

[5] Tom McGinnis, *More Than Just a Friend* (Englewood Cliffs, N.J.: Prentice-Hall, Inc. 1981), p. 2.

[6] Ibid., p. 23.

[7] Ibid., p. 4.

Bibliography

Bach, George and Wyden, Peter. *The Intimate Enemy*. West Caldwell, N.J.: William & Co., 1969.

Baublitz, Jacinth Ivie. "Transitional Treatment of Hostile Married Couples". *Social Work* 23(4) (July) 1978, pp. 321-323.

Brandon, Nathaniel and Brandon, Devers. *The Romantic Love Question and Answer Book*. Los Angeles: J. P. Tarcher, Inc., 1982.

Cappon, Daniel. *Coupling*. New York: St. Martin's Press, 1981.

McGinnis, Tom. *More Than Just a Friend*. Englewood Cliffs, N.J.: Prentice-Hall, Inc., 1981.